THE SIGN OF THE RED CROSS

A Tale of Old London

EVELYN EVERETT-GREEN

1st WORLD
LIBRARY
Literary Society

The Sign Of The Red Cross

Evelyn Everett-Green

© 1st World Library, 2007
PO Box 2211
Fairfield, IA 52556
www.1stworldlibrary.com
First Edition

LCCN: 2007930783

Softcover ISBN: 978-1-4218-4821-1
Hardcover ISBN: 978-1-4218-4724-5
eBook ISBN: 978-1-4218-4918-8

Purchase *"The Sign Of The Red Cross"*
as a traditional bound book at:
www.1stWorldLibrary.com/purchase.asp?ISBN=978-1-4218-4821-1

1st World Library is a literary, educational organization
dedicated to:

- Creating a free internet library of downloadable ebooks

- Hosting writing competitions and offering book publishing
  scholarships.

Interested in more 1st World Library books? contact:
literacy@1stworldlibrary.com
Check us out at: www.1stworldlibrary.com

1ˢᵗ World Library Literary Society

Giving Back to the World

"If you want to work on the core problem, it's early school literacy."

- James Barksdale, former CEO of Netscape

"No skill is more crucial to the future of a child, or to a democratic and prosperous society, than literacy."

- Los Angeles Times

"Literacy... means far more than learning how to read and write... The aim is to transmit... knowledge and promote social participation."

- UNESCO

"Literacy is not a luxury, it is a right and a responsibility. If our world is to meet the challenges of the twenty-first century we must harness the energy and creativity of all our citizens."

- President Bill Clinton

"Parents should be encouraged to read to their children, and teachers should be equipped with all available techniques for teaching literacy, so the varying needs and capacities of individual kids can be taken into account."

- Hugh Mackay

CHAPTER I

A WARNING WHISPER

"I don't believe a word of it!" cried the Master Builder, with some heat of manner. "It is just an old scare, the like of which I have heard a hundred times ere now. Some poor wretch dies of the sweating sickness, or, at worst, of the spotted fever, and in a moment all men's mouths are full of the plague! I don't believe a word of it!"

"Heaven send you may be right, good friend," quoth Rachel Harmer, as she sat beside her spinning wheel, and spoke to the accompaniment of its pleasant hum. "And yet, methinks, the vice and profligacy of this great city, and the lewdness and wanton wickedness of the Court, are enough to draw down upon us the judgments of Almighty God. The sin and the shame of it must be rising up before Him day and night."

The Master Builder moved a little uneasily in his seat. For his own part he thought no great harm of the roistering, gaming, and gallantries of the Court dandies. He knew that the times were very good for him. Fine ladies were for ever sending for him to alter some house or some room. Gay young husbands, or those who thought of becoming husbands, were seldom content nowadays without pulling their house about their ears, and rebuilding it after some new-fangled fashion copied from France. Or if the structure were let alone, the plenishings must be totally changed; and Master Charles Mason, albeit a builder by trade, and going generally amongst his acquaintances and friends by the name of Master Builder, had of late years taken to a number of kindred avocations in the matter of house plenishings, and so forth. This had brought him no small profit, as well as intimate relations with many a fine household and with many grand folks. Money had flowed apace into his pocket of late. His wife had begun to go about so fine that it was well for her the old sumptuary laws had fallen into practical disuse. His son was an idle young dog, chiefly known to the neighbourhood as being the main leader of a notorious band of Scourers, of which more anon, and many amongst his former friends and associates shook their heads, and declared that Charles Mason was growing so puffed up by wealth that he would scarce vouchsafe a nod to an old acquaintance in the street, unless he were smart and prosperous looking.

The Master Builder had a house upon Old London Bridge. Once he had carried on his business there, but latterly he had grown too fine for that. To the disgust of his more simple-minded neighbours, he had taken some large premises in Cheapside, where he displayed many fine stuffs for upholstering and drapery, where the new-fashioned Indian carpets were displayed to view, and fine gilded furniture from France, which a little later on became the rage all through the country. His own house was now nothing more than a dwelling place for himself and his family; even his apprentices and workmen were lodged elsewhere. The neighbours, used to simpler ways, shook their heads, and prophesied that the end of so much pride would be disaster and ruin. But year after year went by, and the Master Builder grew richer and richer, and could afford to laugh at the prognostications of those about him, of which he was very well aware.

He was perhaps somewhat puffed up by his success. He was certainly proud of the position he had made. He liked to see his wife sweep along the streets in her fine robes of Indian silk, which seemed to set a great gulf between her and her neighbours. He allowed his son to copy the fopperies of the Court gallants, and even to pick up the silly French phrases which made the language at Court a mongrel mixture of bad English and vile French. All these things pleased him well, although he himself went about clad in much the same fashion as his neighbours, save that the materials of his clothing were finer, and his frills more white and crisp; and it was in his favour that his friendship with his old friend James Harmer had never waned, although he knew that this honest tradesman by no means approved his methods.

Perhaps in his heart of hearts he preferred the comfortable living room of his neighbour to the grandeur insisted upon by his wife at home. At any rate, he found his way three or four evenings in the week to Harmer's fireside, and exchanged with him the news of the day, or retailed the current gossip of the city.

Harmer was by trade a gold and silver lace maker. He carried on his business in the roomy bridge house which he occupied, which was many stories high, and contained a great number of rooms. He housed in it a large family, several apprentices, two shopmen, and his wife's sister, Dinah Morse, at such times as the latter was not out nursing the sick, which was her avocation in life.

Mason and Harmer had been boys together, had inherited these two houses on the bridge from their respective fathers, and had both prospered in the world. But Harmer was only a moderately affluent man, having many sons and daughters to provide for; whereas Mason had but one of each, and had more than one string to his bow in the matter of money getting.

In the living room of Harmer's house were assembled that February evening six persons. It was just growing dusk, but the dancing firelight gave a pleasant illumination. Harmer and Mason were seated on opposite sides of the hearth in straight-backed wooden armchairs, and both were smoking. Rachel sat at her wheel, with her sister Dinah near to her; and in the background hovered two fine-looking young men, the two eldest sons of the household—Reuben, his father's right-hand man in business matters now; and Dan, who had the air and appearance of a sailor ashore, as, indeed, was the case with him.

It was something which Dinah Morse had said that had evoked the rather fierce disclaimer from the Master Builder, with the rejoinder by Rachel as to the laxity of the times; and now it was Dinah's voice which again took up the word.

"Whether it be God's judgment upon the city, or whether it be due to the carelessness of man, I know not," answered Dinah quietly; "I only say that the Bill of Mortality just published is higher than it has been this long while, and that two in the Parish of St. Giles have died of the plague."

"Well, St. Giles' is far enough away from us," said the Master Builder. "If the Magistrates do their duty, there is no fear that it will spread our way. There were deaths over yonder of the plague last November, and it seems as though they had not yet stamped out the germs of it. But a little firmness and sense will do that. We have nothing to fear. So long as the cases are duly reported, we shall soon be rid of the pest."

Dinah pressed her lips rather closely together. She had that fine resolute cast of countenance which often characterizes those who are constantly to be found at the bedside of the sick. Her dress was very plain, and she wore a neckerchief of soft, white Indian muslin about her throat, instead of the starched yellow one which was almost universal amongst the women citizens of the day. Her hands were large and white and capable looking. Her only ornament was a chatelaine of many chains, to which were suspended the multifarious articles which a nurse has in constant requisition. In figure she was tall and stately, and in the street strangers often paused to give her a backward glance. She was greatly in request amongst the sick of the better class, though she was often to be found beside the sick poor, who could give her nothing but thanks for her skilled tendance of them.

"Ay, truly, so long as the cases are duly reported," she repeated slowly. "But do you think, sir, that that is ever done where means may be found to avoid it?"

The Master Builder looked a little startled at the question.

"Surely all good folks would wish to do what was right by their neighbours. They would not harbour a case of plague, and not make it known in the right quarter."

"You think not, perhaps. Had you seen as much of the sick as I have, you would know that men so fear and dread the distemper, as they most often call it, that they will blind their eyes to it to the very last, and do everything in their power to make it out as something other than what they fear. I have seen enough of the ways of folks with sickness to be very sure that all who have friends to protect the fearful secret, will do so if it be possible. It is when a poor stranger dies of a sudden that it becomes known that the plague has found another victim. Why are there double the number of deaths in this week's bill, if more than are set down as such be not the distemper?"

All the faces in the room looked very grave at that, for in

truth it was a most disquieting thought. The sailor came a few steps nearer the fire, and remarked:

"It has all come from those hounds of Dutchmen! Right glad am I that we are to go to war with them at last, whether the cause be righteous or not. They have gotten the plague all over their land. I saw men drop down in the streets and die of it when I was last in port there. They send it to us in their merchandise."

"My wife will die of terror if she hears but a whisper of the distemper being anigh us," remarked the Master Builder, with a sigh and a look of uneasiness. "But men are always scaring us with tales of its coming and, after all, there is but a death here and one there, such as any great city may look to have."

At that moment the door was thrown open, and a pretty young damsel, wearing a crimson cloak and hood, stepped lightly in.

"O father, mother, do but come and look!" she cried, with the air of coaxing assurance which bespoke a favoured child. "Such a strange star in the sky! Men in the streets are all looking and pointing; and some say that it is no star, but a comet, and that it predicts some dreadful thing which is coming upon this land. Do come and look at it! There is a clear sky tonight, and one can see it well. And I heard that it has been seen by some before this, when at night the rain clouds have been swept away by the wind. Do come to the window above the river and look! One can see it fine from there."

This sudden announcement, falling just upon the talk of pestilence and peril, caused a certain flutter and sensation through the room. All the persons there rose to their feet and

Evelyn Everett-Green

followed the rosy-cheeked maiden out upon the staircase, and to a window from which the great river could be seen flowing beneath. A large expanse of sky could also be commanded from here, and as the inside of the house was almost dark, it was easy to obtain an excellent view of the strange appearance which was attracting so much attention in the streets.

It certainly was no star that was glowing thus with a red and sullen-looking flame. Neither shape nor position in the heavens accorded with that of any star of magnitude.

"It was certainly," so said Reuben Harmer, who had some knowledge of the heavenly bodies, "no star, but one of those travelling meteors or comets which are seen from time to time, and which from remote ages have been declared to foretell calamity to the lands over which they appear to travel."

The Harmer family were godly people of somewhat Puritanic leaning, yet they were by no means entirely free from the superstition of their times, nor would Rachel have called it superstition to regard this manifestation as a warning from God. Why should He not send some such messenger before He proceeded to take vengeance upon an ungodly city? Was not even guilty Sodom warned of its approaching doom?

All faces then were grave, but that of the Master Builder wore a look of fear as well.

"I must to my wife," he said. "If she sees this comet, she will be vastly put about. I must to her side to reassure her. Pray Heaven that no calamity be near to us!"

"Amen!" replied Harmer, gravely; and then the Master

Builder retreated down the staircase, whilst from a room below a cheerful voice was heard announcing that supper was ready.

The party therefore all moved downstairs towards the kitchen, where all the meals were taken in company with the apprentices, shopmen, and serving wenches.

Dorcas, the maiden who had brought news of the comet, slipped her. hand within Reuben's arm, and asked him in a whisper:

"Thinkest thou, Reuben, that it betides evil to the city?"

"Nay, I know not what to think," he answered. "It is a strange thing, and men often say it betides ill; but I have no knowledge of mine own. I never saw the like before."

"They spoke of it at my Lady Scrope's today," said Dorcas. "I was behind her chair, with her fan and essence bottles, and the lap dogs, when in comes one and another of the old beaux who beguile their leisure with my lady's sharp speeches; and they spoke of this thing, and she laughed them to scorn, and called them fools for listening to old wives' fables. It is her way thus to revile all who come anigh her. She said she had lived through a score of such scares, and would snap her fingers at all the comets of the heavens at once. Sometimes it makes me tremble to hear her talk; but methinks she loveth to raise a shudder in the hearts of those who hear her. She is a strange being. Sometimes I almost fear to go to and fro there, albeit she treats me well, and seldom speaks harshly to me. But men say she is above a hundred years old, and she leads so strange a life in her lonely house. Fancy being there alone of a night, with only that deaf old man and his aged wife within doors! It would scare me to death. But she will not let one other of her

Evelyn Everett-Green

servants abide there with her!"

"Ay, it is her whimsie. Women folks are given to such," answered Reuben, tolerantly. "She is a strange creature, albeit I doubt not that men make her out stranger than she is. Well, well, the comet at least will do us no hurt of itself; and if it be God's way of warning us of peril to come, we need not fear it, but only set ourselves to be ready for what He may send us."

Below stairs there was a comfortable meal spread upon the table, simple and homely, but sufficient for the appetites of all. The three rosy-faced apprentices, of whom a son of the house made one, formed a link at table between the family and the shopmen and serving wenches. All sat down together, and Rebecca, the daughter who lived at home, served up the hot broth and puddings. The eldest daughter was a serving maid in the household of my Lady Howe, and was seldom able to get home for more than a few hours occasionally, even when that fashionable dame was in London. Dorcas spent each night under the shelter of her father's roof, and went daily to the quaint old house close beside Allhallowes the Less, where lived the eccentric Lady Scrope, her mistress, of whom mention has been made. The youngest son was also from home, being apprenticed to a carpenter in the service of the Master Builder next door, and he lived, as was usual, in the house of his employer. Thus four out of Harmer's seven children lived always at home, and Dan the sailor was with them whenever his ship put into the river after a voyage.

No talk of either comet or plague was permitted at table; indeed the meal was generally eaten in something approaching to silence. Sometimes the master of the house would address a question to one of the family, or suppress by a glance the giggling of the lads at the lower end of the table.

Joseph's presence there rather encouraged hilarity, for he was a merry urchin, and stood not in the same awe of his father as did his comrades. Kindness was the law of the house, but it was the kindness of thorough discipline. Neither the master nor the mistress believed in the liberty that brings licence in its train.

Life went very quietly, smoothly, and monotonously within the walls of that busy house. Trade was brisk just now. The fashion lately introduced amongst fine ladies of having whole dresses of gold or silver lace, brought more orders for the lace maker than he well knew how to accomplish in the time. He and his son and his apprentices were hard at work from morning to night; and glad enough was the master of the daily-increasing daylight, which enabled him and those who were glad to earn larger wages to work extra hours each day.

Being thus busy at home, he went less than was his wont abroad, and heard but little either of the sullen comet which hung night after night in the sky, or of the whispers sometimes circulating in the city of fresh cases of the distemper.

These last, however, were growing fewer. The scare of a few weeks back seemed to be dying down. People said the pest had been stamped out, and the brighter, hotter weather cheered the hearts of men, albeit in case of sickness it might be their worst enemy, as some amongst them well knew.

"I never believed a word of it!" said the wife of the Master Builder, as she sat in her fine drawing room and fanned herself with a great fan made of peacock's feathers. She was very handsomely dressed, far muore like a fine Court dame than the wife of a simple citizen. Her comnpanion was a very pretty girl of about nineteen, whose abundant chestnut hair was dressed after a fashionable mode, although she refused to have it frizzed over her head as her mother's was, and would have preferred to dress it quite simply. She wished she might have plain clothes suitable to her station, instead of being tricked out as though she were a fine lady. But her mother ruled her with a rod of iron, and girls in those days had not thought of rising in rebellion.

The Master Builder's wife considered that she had gentle blood in her veins, as her grandfather had been a country squire who was ruined in the civil war, so that his family sank into poverty. Of late she had done all in her power to get her neighbours to accord her the title of Madam Mason, which she extorted from her servants, and which was given to her pretty generally now, although as much in mockery, it must be confessed, as in respect of her finery. She did not look a very happy woman, in spite of all the grandeur about her. She had frightened away her simpler neighbours by her airs of condescension and by the splendour of her house, and yet she could not yet see any way of inducing other and finer folks to come and see her. Sometimes her husband brought in a rich patron and his wife to look at the fine room, and examnine the furniture in it, and these persons would generally be mighty civil to her whilst they stayed; but then they did not come to see her, but only in the way of business. It was agreeable to be able to repeat what my lord this or my lady that said about the cabinets and chairs; but after all she was half afraid that her boasting deceived nobody, and Gertrude would never come to her aid with any little innocent fibs about their grand visitors.

"I never did believe a word of it," repeated Madam, after a pause. "Gertrude, why do you not answer when I speak to you? You are as dull as a Dutch doll, sitting there and saying nothing. I would that Frederick were at home! He can speak when he is spoken to; but you are like a deaf mute!"

"I beg your pardon, ma'am. I was reading—I did not hear."

"That is always the way—reading, reading, reading! Why, what good do you think reading will do you? Why don't you get your silk embroidery or practise upon the spinnet? Such advantages as you have! And all thrown away on a girl who does not know when she is well off. I have no manner of patience with you, Gertrude. If I had had such opportunities in my girlhood, I should never have been a mere citizen's wife now."

A slightly mutinous look passed across Gertrude's face. Submissive in word and manner, as was the rule of the day, she was by no means submissive in mind, and had her mother's ears been sharper she might have detected the undertone of irony in the reply she received.

"I think nobody would take you for a citizen's wife, ma'am. As for me, I am not made to shine in a higher sphere than mine own. I have not even the patience to learn the spinnet. I would sooner be baking pies with Rebecca next door, as we used to do when we were children, before father grew so rich."

Madam's face clouded ominously. She heartily wished she had never admitted her children to intimacy with the Harmers next door. It had done no harm in the case of Frederick. He was his mother's son, every inch of him, and was as ready to turn up a supercilious nose at his old comrades as ever Madam could wish.

But Gertrude was different—she was excessively provoking at times. She did not seem able to understand that if one intended to rise in the world, one must cut through a number of old ties, and start upon a fresh track. It was not easy in those times to rise; but still the wealthier citizens did

Evelyn Everett-Green

occasionally make a position for themselves, and get amongst the hangers-on of the Court party, especially if they were open handed with their money.

Madam often declared that if they only moved into another part of the town, everything she wanted could be attained; but on that point her husband was inexorable. He loved the old bridge house. There he had been born, and there he meant to die, and he had not the smnallest intention of removing elsewhere to please even the wife to whom he granted so many indulgences.

"You are a fool!" cried Madam, angrily; "you say those things only to provoke me. I wish you had some right feeling and some conversation. You are as dull as ditch water. You care for nothing. I don't believe it would rouse you to hear that the plague was in the next street!"

"Well, we shall see," answered Gertrude, with a calmness that was at least a little provoking, "for people say it is spreading very fast, and may soon be here."

"What!" cried Madam, in a sudden panic; "who says that? What do you mean, girl?"

"It was Reuben who told me," answered Gertrude, with a little blush which she tried to conceal by turning her face towards the window.

But her ruse was in vain. Madam's hawk eye had caught the rising colour, and her brow contracted sharply.

"Reuben! what Reuben? Have I not told you a hundred times that I would have none of that sort of talk any more? Reuben, indeed! as though you were boy and girl together! Pray tell me this, you forward minx, does he dare to address you as

Gertrude when he has the insolence to speak to you in the streets, where alone I presume he can do so?"

Gertrude's face was burning with indignation. She had to clasp her hands tightly together to restrain the hot words which rose to her lips.

"We have been children together—and friends," she said, "the Harmers and I. How should we forget that so quickly— even though you have forgotten! My father does not mind."

Madam's face was as red as her daughter's. She was about to make some violent retort, when the sound of a footstep on the stairs checked the words upon her lips.

"There is Frederick!" she said.

CHAPTER II

LONDON'S YOUNG CITIZENS

The door of the room where mother and daughter sat was flung wide open with scant ceremony, and to the accompaniment of a boisterous laugh. Into the room swaggered a tall, fine-looking young man of some three-and-twenty summers, dressed in all the extravagance of a lavish and extravagant age. Upon his head he wore an immense peruke of ringlets, such as had been introduced at Court the previous year, and which was almost universal now with the nobles and gentry, but by no means so amongst the citizens. The periwig was surmounted by a high-crowned hat adorned with feathers and ribbons, and ribbons floated from his person in such abundance that to unaccustomed eyes the effect was little short of grotesque. Even the absurd high-heeled shoes were tied with immense bows of ribbon, whilst knees, wrists, throat, and even elbows displayed their bows and streamers. The young dandy wore the full "petticoat breeches" of the period, with a short doublet, a jaunty cloak hung from the shoulders, and an abundance of costly lace ruffles adorned the neck and wrists of the doublet, he wore at his side a short rapier, and had a trick of laying his hand upon the hilt, as though it would take very little provocation to make him draw it forth upon an adversary.

His step was not altogether so steady as it might have been, as he swaggered into his mother's presence. His handsome face was deeply flushed. He was laughing boisterously; but there was that in his aspect which made his sister turn away with a look of repulsion, though his mother's glance rested on him with a look of admiring pride that savoured of adoration. In her fond and foolish eyes he was perfection, and the more he copied the vices and the follies of the gallants about the person of the King, the prouder did his vain and weak mother become of him.

"Ho! ho! ho! such a bit of fun!"

It is impossible to give Frederick Mason's words verbatim, as he seldom opened his lips without an oath, and inter-larded his talk with coarse jests in English and fragments of ribaldry in vile French, till it would scarce be intelligible to the reader of today.

"Such a prime bit of fun! Who would have thought that little Dorcas next door would grow up such a marvelous pretty damsel! By my troth, what a slap she did give me in return for my kiss!"

Gertrude suddenly turned upon her brother with flashing eyes.

"Think shame of yourself, Frederick! You disgrace your boasted manhood. How dare you annoy with your coarse gallantry the daughter of our father's oldest friend, and that too in the open streets!"

"How dare you speak so to your brother, girl?" cried Madam, bristling up like an angry mother hen. "What call have you to chide him? Is he answerable to you for his acts?"

Evelyn Everett-Green

Gertrude subsided into silence, for she could not answer back as she would have liked. It was not for her to argue with her mother; and Madam, having vanquished her daughter, turned upon her son.

"You must have a care how you vex our neighbours, for your father would take it ill an he heard of it. Nay, I would not myself that you mixed yourself up too much with them. They are honest good folks enow, but scarce such as are fitting company for us. What of this girl Dorcas? Is not she the one who is waiting maid to that mad old witch woman in Allhallowes, Lady Scrope?"

"That may well be. I saw her come forth from a grim portal hard by Allhallowes the Less. I knew not who it was, but I gave chase, and ere she put her foot upon the bridge, I had plucked the hood from off her pretty curls, and had kissed her soundly on both cheeks. And at that she gave me such a cuff as I feel yet, and ran like a fawn, and I after her, till she vanished within the door of our neighbour's house; and then it came to me that it was Dorcas, grown wondrous pretty since I last took note of her. If she comes always home at this hour, I'll waylay my lady again and take toll of her."

"You had better be careful not to let Reuben get wind of it" said Gertrude, with suppressed anger in her voice. "If he were to catch you insulting his sister, it is more than a slap or a cuff you would get."

Frederick burst into a boisterous laugh.

"What! do you think a dirty shopman would dare lay hands upon me? I'd run him through the body as soon as look at him. He'd better keep out of reach of my sword arm. You can tell him so, fair sister, if you have a tendresse for the young counter jumper."

Gertrude's sensitive colour flew up, and her brother laughed loud and long, pointing his finger at her, and adding one coarse jest to another; but the mother interposed rather hastily, being uneasy at the turn the talk was taking.

"Hist, children, no more of this!"

"I would not that this tale came to your father's ears, Frederick; it were better to have a care where our neighbours are concerned. Let the wench alone. There are many prettier damsels than she, who will not rebuff you in such fashion."

"Ay, verily, but that is the spice of it all. When the wench gives you kiss for kiss, it is sweet, but flavourless. A box on the ear, and a merry chase through the streets afterwards, is a game more to my liking. I'll see the little witch again and be even with her, or my name's not Frederick Mason the Scourer!"

"Your father will like it ill if it comes to his ears," remarked Madam, with a touch of uneasiness; "and for my part, the less we have to do with our neighbours the better. They are no fit associates for us."

"Say that we are no fit associates for them," murmured Gertrude, beneath her breath.

Her heart was swelling with sorrow and anger. In her eyes there was no young man in all London town to be compared with Reuben Harmer. From the day when in childhood they had playfully plighted their troth, she had never ceased to regard him as the one man in the world most worthy of love and reverence, and she knew that he had never ceased to look upon her with the same feelings.

Latterly they had had but scant opportunities of meeting.

Evelyn Everett-Green

Madam threw every possible obstacle in the way of her daughter's entering the doors of that house, and kept her own closed against those of her former friends whom she now chose to regard as her inferiors. Madam had never been liked. She had always held her head high, and shown that she thought herself too good for the place she occupied. Her house had never been popular. No neighbours had ever been in the habit of running in and out to exchange bits of news with her, or ask for the loan of some recipe or household convenience. It had not been difficult to seclude herself in her gradually increasing dignities, and only her daughter had keenly felt the difference when she had intimated that she wished the intimacy between her family and that of the Harmers to cease.

Frederick had long since taken to himself other associates of a more congenial kind. The Master Builder went to and fro as before, permitting his wife full indulgence of her fads and fancies, but resolved to exercise his own individual liberty, and quite unconscious of the blow that was being inflicted upon his daughter, who was naturally tied by her mother's commands, and forced to abide by her regulations.

Madam had been quick to see that if she did not take care Reuben Harmer would shortly aspire to the hand of her daughter, and she was not sure but that her husband would be weak enough to let the foolish girl please herself in the matter, and throw away what chance she had of marrying out of the city, and rising a step in life.

Madam pinned her main hopes of a social rise for herself in the marriages of her children. She fondly believed that Frederick, with his good looks and his wealth, could take his pick even amongst high-born ladies, and not all the good-natured ridicule of her husband served to weaken this conviction. She was not a great admirer of her daughter's charms, but she knew that the girl was admired, and had been noticed more than once by the fine ladies who had come to look at her furniture and hangings. She had a plan of her own for getting Gertrude into the train of some fine Court dame, and once secured in such a position, her fair face and ample dowry might do the rest. If her son and daughter were well married, she would have two houses where she could make a home for herself more to her liking. No end of ambitious dreams were constantly floating in her shallow brain, and as all these were more or less bound up with the future of her son and daughter, it was natural that she should desire to put down with a strong hand the smallest indication of a love affair between Gertrude and Reuben. She had even persuaded her husband that Gertrude ought to make a good marriage; and as he was able to give her an ample dowry, and was proud of her good looks, he himself was of opinion that she might do something rather brilliant, even if she did not realize her mother's fond dreams.

All this was very well known to poor Gertrude by this time, and it was seldom now that she did more than catch a passing glimpse of Reuben, or exchange a few hasty words with him in the street. The young man was proud, and knew that he was looked down upon by the Master Builder and his wife. This made him very reticent of showing his feelings, and reduced Gertrude often to the lowest ebb of depression.

So the coarse jests of her brother were a keen pain to her, and she presently rose and left the room in great resentment, followed by a mocking laugh from the ill-conditioned young man.

Having lost one victim, that amiable youth next turned his attention to his mother, and began to torment her with the same zest as he had displayed in the baiting of his sister.

Evelyn Everett-Green

"All the town is talking of the plague," he remarked, in would-be solemn tones. "They say that in St. Giles' and St. Andrew's parishes they are burying them by the dozen every day;" and as his mother uttered a little scream, and shrank away even from him, he went on in the same tone, "All the fine folks from that end of the town are thinking of moving into the country. The witches and wizards are declaring openly in the streets that the whole city is to be destroyed. Some folks say that soon the Lord Mayor and the Magistrates will have all the infected houses shut up straitly, so that none may go in or come forth when it is known that the distemper has appeared there. The door will be marked with a red cross, and the words 'Lord, have mercy upon us!' writ large above it. So, good mother, when I come home one day with the marks of the distemper upon me, the whole house will be closed, and none will be able to go forth to escape it. So we shall all perish together, as a loving family should do."

The blasphemies and ribald jokes with which this good-for-nothing young man adorned his speech made it sound tenfold more hideous than I can do. Even his mother shrank away from him, in terror and amaze at his levity, and cried aloud in her fear so that instantly the door opened, and her husband entered to know what was amiss.

Frederick looked a little uneasy then, for he still held his father in a wholesome awe; but the mother made no complaint of her son, but only said she had been affrighted by hearing that there were more deaths from the plague than she had thought would ever be the case after all the care the Magistrates had taken, and was it true that the Lord Mayor had spoken of shutting up the houses, and so causing the sound ones to become diseased and to perish with the stricken ones?

The Master Builder answered gravely enough; for he had himself but just come in from hearing that the weekly Bills of Mortality were terribly high, and that the deaths in certain of the western parishes had been beyond all reckoning since the last years when the plague had visited the city. True, there were not many put down as having died of the plague; but it was known how much was done to get other diseases set down in the bills, so that there was not much comfort to be got out of that.

The Master Builder thought that the houses would not be shut up unless things became much worse. The matter had been spoken of, as he himself had heard; but the people were much against it, and it would be a measure most difficult to enforce, and would tend to make men conceal from the authorities any case of distemper which appeared amongst them. But he said it was true enough that persons of high degree were beginning to move into the country, at least from the western part of the town; but that all felt very sure the distemper would speedily be checked, and would not come within the city walls at all, nor extend eastward beyond its boundaries.

Madam breathed a little more freely on hearing this, but made an eager suggestion to her husband that they should go away if the distemper began to spread.

But the Master Builder shook his head impatiently.

"A fine thing to run away from a chance ill, and court a certain ruin! How do you think business will thrive if all the men run away from their shops like affrighted sheep? No, no; it is often safest to stay at home with closed doors than to run helter skelter to strange places where one knows not who may have been last. Keep indoors with your perfumes and spices, and keep the wench close with you. That is the best

Evelyn Everett-Green

way of outwitting the enemy. Besides, it has come nowhere near us yet."

Madam had certainly no mind to be ruined, nor was she one who loved change or the discomforts of travel. So she thought on the whole her husband's advice was good. It would be much more comfortable to stay here with closed doors, surrounded by the luxuries of home.

Now as Frederick sat with outstretched legs in one of the easiest chairs in the room, and heard his father speak of these things, a thought came into his head which tickled his fancy so vastly that throughout the evening he kept bursting into smothered laughter, so much so that his sister threw him many suspicious glances, and divined that he had some evil purpose in his head.

The May light lasted long in the sky; but as it failed Frederick went out, as was his wont, and for many hours he spent his time with a number of kindred spirits in a neighbouring tavern, quaffing large potations, and dicing and gaming after the fashion of the Court gallants.

The bulk of the young roisterers thus assembled belonged to one of those bands of Scourers of which Frederick claimed to be the head. They were the worthy successors to the "Roaring Boys" or Bonaventors of past centuries, and their favourite pastime was, after spending the night in revelry and play, to start forth towards dawn and scour the streets, upsetting the baskets or carts of the early market folks bringing their wares into the town, scattering the merchandise in the gutter, kissing the women, cuffing the men, wrenching off knockers from house doors, and getting up fights with the watch or with some rival band of Scourers which resulted in broken heads and sometimes in actual bloodshed.

The Magistrates treated these misdemeanours with wonderful tolerance when the culprits were from time to time brought before them, and the nuisance went on practically unchecked—the people being used to wild and dissolute ways and much brawling—and looking on it as one of the necessary ills of life.

But upon this bright May morning, before the streets began to awaken, even before the market folks were astir, Frederick led forth his band intent upon a new sort of mischief. Some of the number carried pots of red paint in their hands, and others pots of white paint.

Up and down the empty streets paraded these worthies, pausing here and there at the door of some citizen that presented a tempting surface. One of their number would paint upon it the ominous red cross, whilst another who had skill enough (for writing was not the accomplishment of every citizen even then) would add in staring white letters the legend, "Lord, have mercy upon us!"

It was a brutal jest at such a time, when the dread visitor had actually appeared as it were in their midst, and all sober men were in fear of what might betide, and of the methods already spoken of for the suppression of the distemper. But it was its very wickedness which gave it its charm in the opinion of the perpetrators, and as they went from street to street, Frederick suddenly exclaimed:

"Ha! we are close to Allhallowes. Let us adorn the door of the old madwoman, Lady Scrope. They say she lives quite alone, and that her servants come in the morning and leave at night. Sure they will none of them have courage to pass the threshold when that sign adorns it, and the old hag will have to come forth herself to seek them. An excellent joke! I will watch the house, and give her a kiss as she comes forth."

Whereupon the whole crew burst into shouts of drunken laughter, and made a rush to the door, which stood flush in a grim-looking wall just beneath the shadow of the church of Allhallowes the Less.

Frederick had the paint pot in his hand, and he traced a fine red cross upon the door, all the while making his ribald jests upon the old woman within, he and his companions alike, far too drunk with wine and unholy mirth to have eyes or ears for what was happening close beside them. They did not hear the sound of an opening window just above them. They did not see a nightcapped head poked forth, the great frilled cap surrounding a small, wizened, but keenly-courageous face, in which the eyes were glittering like points of fire.

None of them saw this. None of them heeded, and the head was for a moment silently withdrawn. Then it was again cautiously protruded, and the next minute there descended on the head of Frederick a black hot mass of tar and bitumen. It scalded his face, it blinded his eyes. It choked and almost poisoned him by its vaporous pungency. It matted itself in his voluminous periwig, and plastered it down to his shoulders; it clotted his lace frills, and ran in filthy rivulets down his smart clothes. In a word, it rendered him in a moment a disgusting and helpless object, unable to see or hear, almost unable to breathe, and quite unable to rid himself of the sticky, loathsome mass in which he had suddenly become encased.

Then from the window above came a shrill, jeering cry:

"To your task, bold Scourers—to your task! Scour your own fine friend and comrade. Scour him well, for he will need it. Scour him from head to foot. A pest upon you, young villains! I would every citizen in London would serve you the same!"

Then the window above was banged to. The mob of roisterers fled helter skelter, laughing and jeering. Not one amongst them offered to assist their wretched leader. They left him alone in his sorry plight to get out of it as best he might. They had not the smallest consideration for one even of their own number overtaken by misfortune. Roaring with laughter at the frightful picture he presented, they dispersed to their own homes, and the wretched Frederick was left alone in the street to do the best he could with his black, unsavoury plaster.

He strove in vain to clear his vision, and to remove the peruke, which clung to him like a second skin. He was in a horrible fright lest he should be seen and recognized in this ignominious plight; and although he felt sure his comrades would spread the story of his discomfiture all over the town, he did not wish to be seen by the watch, or by any law-abiding citizens who knew him.

But how to get home was a puzzle, blind and half suffocated as he was; and he scarce knew whether anger or relief came uppermost to his mind when he felt his arm taken, and a voice that he knew said in his ear:

"For shame, Frederick! It is a disgrace to London the way you and your comrades go on. And now of all times to jest when the foe is at our doors. Shame upon you! The old dame has given you no more than your due. But come with me, and I will get you home ere the town be awake; and have a care how you offend again like this, for the Magistrates will not suffer jests of such a kind at such a time. Know you not that it is almost enough to frighten a timid serving wench into the distemper to see such signs upon the doors? And if it break out in the midst of us, who can say where it will end?"

It was Reuben Harmer who spoke, as Frederick very well

Evelyn Everett-Green

knew. The young men had been boys together, and as Reuben was two years the elder, he assumed a tone in speaking which Frederick now keenly resented. But it was no time to repel an overture of help, and he sullenly forced himself to accept Reuben's good offices. The great clotted periwig was with some difficulty got off, and then it was possible to remove the worst of the tar from face and eyes. Frederick at last could see clearly and breathe freely, but presented so lamentable an object that he only longed to get safe home to the shelter of his father's house.

The costly periwig of curls had perforce to be left in the gutter, hopelessly ruined, and Frederick, who had given more money for it than he could well afford, shook his fist at the house which contained the redoubtable old woman who had thus fooled and bested him.

"You Scourers will find that you can play your meddlesome games too often," remarked Reuben sternly, his eyes upon the red cross and the half-completed words above. "I would that all the city were of the same spirit as Lady Scrope. She always keeps a quantity of hot pitch or tar beside her bed, with a lamp burning beneath it, in case of attacks from robbers. You may thank your stars that it descended not boiling hot upon your head. Had she been so minded to punish you, she would have done so fearlessly. You may be thankful it was no worse."

Frederick sullenly picked up his hat, which he had laid aside while painting the door, and which had thus escaped injury, pulled it as far over his face as it would go, and turned abruptly away from Reuben.

"I'll be revenged on the old hag yet!" he muttered between his teeth. "I've got a double debt to pay to this house now. I'll not forget it either."

He turned abruptly away and scuttled home by the narrowest alleys he could find, whilst Reuben went about looking for the red crosses, and giving timely notice to the master of the house, that they might be erased, as quietly and quickly as possible.

Accident had led Reuben early abroad that day, but he made use of his time to undo as far as he was able the mischievous jesting of Frederick's band of Scourers.

CHAPTER III

DRAWING NEARER

"Brother Reuben, I cannot think what can be the reason, but my Lady Scrope has bidden me beg of thee to give her speech upon the morrow. All this day she has been in a mighty pleasant humour: she gave me this silken neckerchief when I left today, and bid me bring my brother with me on the morrow—and she means thee, Reuben."

"What can be the meaning of that?" asked Rachel Harmer, with a look of curiosity. "Doth she often speak to thee of thy kindred, child?"

"If the whim be on her, and she has naught else to amuse her, she will bid me tell of the life at home, and of our neighbours and friends," answered Dorcas. "But never has she spoke as she did today. Nor can I guess why she would have speech with Reuben."

"I can guess shrewdly at that," said the young man. "It so befell this morning that I found a party of roisterers at her door, who were marking it with a red cross, as though it were a plague-stricken house—as the Magistrates talk of marking them now if the distemper spreads much further and wider. The bold lady had herself put these fellows to the rout by pouring pitch upon them from a window above; but I stopped to rebuke the foremost of them myself, and to erase their handiwork from the door. I did not know that I was either seen or known; but methinks my Lady Scrope has eyes in the back of her head, as the saying goes."

"You may well say that!" cried Dorcas, with a laugh and a shrug. "Never was there such a woman for knowing everything and everybody. But she spoke not to me of any roisterers. Would I had been there to see her pouring her filthy compound over them! She always has it ready. How she must have rejoiced to find a use for it at last!"

"It is an evil and a scurvy jest at such a time to mock at the peril which is at our very doors, and which naught but the mercy of God can avert from us," said the master of the house, very gravely.

Then, looking round upon his assembled household, he added in the same very serious way, "I have been this day into the heart of the city. I have spoken with many of the authorities there. The Lord Mayor and the Magistrates are in great anxiety, and I fear me there can be no longer any doubt that the distemper is spreading fearfully. It has not yet appeared within the city nor upon the other side of the river; but in the western parishes it is spreading every way, and they say that all who are able are fleeing away from their houses. Perchance for those who can do so this may be the safest thing to do. But soon they will not be permitted to leave, unless they have a bill of health from the Lord Mayor, as in the country beyond the honest folks are taking alarm, and are crying out that we are like to spread the plague all over the kingdom."

"I, too, have heard sad tales of the mortality," said Dinah, raising her calm voice and speaking very seriously. "I met a

Evelyn Everett-Green

good physician, under whom I often laboured amongst the sick, and he tells me that there be poor stricken wretches from whom all the world flee in terror the moment it appears they have the distemper upon them. Many have died already untended and uncared for, whilst others have in the madness of the fever and pain burst out of the rooms in which they have been shut up, and have run up and down the streets, spreading terror in their path, till they have dropped down dead or dying, to be carried to graveyard or pest house as the case may be. But who can tell how many other victims such a miserable creature may not have infected first?"

"Ay, that is the terror of it," said Harmer. "All are saying that nurses must be found to care for the sick, and many are very resolved that the houses where the distemper is found should be straitly shut up and guarded by watchmen, that none go forth. It is a hard thing for the whole to be thus shut in with the infected; but as men truly say, how shall the whole city escape if something be not done to restrain the people from passing to and fro, and spreading the distemper everywhere?"

"I have thought," said Dinah, very quietly, "that it may be given to me to offer myself as a nurse for these poor persons. I have passed unscathed through many perils before now. Once I verily believe I was with one who died even of this distemper, albeit the physician called it the spotted fever, which frights men less than the name of plague. There be many herbs and simples and decoctions which men say are of great value in keeping the infection at bay. And even were it not so, we must not be thinking only at such times of saving our own lives. There be some that must be ready to risk even life, if they may serve their brethren. The good physicians are prepared to do this, to say nothing of the Magistrates and those who have the management of this great city at such a time. And it seems to me that women must always be ready to tend the sick even in times of peril. I seem to hear a call that bids me offer myself for this work; but none else shall suffer through me. If I go, I return hither no more. I shall live amongst the sick until this judgment be overpast, or until I myself be called hence, as may well be."

All faces were grave and full of awe. Yet perhaps none who knew Dinah were overmuch surprised at her words. Her life had been lived amongst the sick for many years. She had never shrunk from danger, or had spared herself when the need was pressing. Her sister Rachel, although the tears stood in her eyes, said nothing to dissuade her.

Nor indeed was there much time for discussion then, for the Master Builder looked in at that moment with a face full of concern. He brought the news that fresh revelations were being hourly made as to the terrible rapidity with which the plague was spreading in the parishes without the walls; and he added that even the gay and giddy Court had been at last alarmed, and that the King had been heard to say he should quit Whitehall and retire with his Court and his minions to Oxford in the course of a week or a fortnight, unless matters became speedily much better.

"Ay, that is ever the way," said Harmer, sternly. "The reckless monarch and his licentious Court draw down upon the city the wrath of God in judgment of their wickedness, and those who have provoked the judgment flee from the peril, leaving the poor of the city to perish like sheep."

"Well, well, well; fine folks like change, and it is easy for them to go elsewhere. I would do the same, perchance, were I so placed," said the Master Builder; "but we men of business must stick to our work as long as it sticks to us.

"What about your mistress, Lady Scrope, Dorcas? Has she

Evelyn Everett-Green

said aught of leaving London? She is one who could easily fly. Not but what I trust the distemper will be kept well out of the city by the care taken."

"She has spoken no word of any such thing," answered Dorcas. "She reads and hears all that is spoken about the plague, and makes my blood run cold by the stories she tells of it in other lands, and during other outbreaks which she can remember. Methinks sometimes the very hair on my head is standing up in the affright her words bring me. But she only laughs and mocks, and calls me a little poltroon. I trow that she would never fly; it would not be like her."

"Men and women do many things unlike themselves in stress of particular and deadly peril," said the Master Builder. "Lady Scrope would do well to consider leaving whilst the city has so good a bill of health; it may be less easy by-and-by, should the distemper spread."

"Thou canst speak to her of this thing, Reuben, when thou dost see her on the morrow," observed his father. "Perchance she has not considered the peril of being detained if she puts off flight too long."

Reuben said he would name the matter to the lady; and when Dorcas set forth upon the morrow for her daily walk, her brother accompanied her, and told her in confidence what he had not told to his family—how Frederick Mason had been served by the irate old lady, and what a sorry spectacle he had presented afterwards.

Dorcas laughed heartily at the story. She had no love for Frederick, and she told her brother that she suspected he had been the half-tipsy gallant who had striven to kiss her in the streets, and had partially succeeded. This put Reuben into a great wrath, and he promised whenever he could do so to come and escort his sister home from the house in Allhallowes. True, the distance was but very short, yet the lane to the bridge head was lonely and narrow, and Frederick was known for a most ill-conditioned young man.

Lady Scrope received Reuben in a demi-toilet of a peculiar kind, and a very strange and wizened object did she appear. She thanked him for the rebuke she had heard him administer to the roisterer, enjoyed a hearty laugh over his wretched appearance, and then proceeded to indulge her insatiable taste for gossip by demanding of him all the city news, and what all the world there was talking about.

"Since this plague bogey has got into men's minds I see nobody and hear nothing," she said. "All the fools be flying the place like so many silly sheep; or, if they come to sit awhile, their talk is all of pills and decoctions, refuses and ointments. Bah! they will buy the drugs of every foolish quack who goes about the streets selling plague cures, and then fly off the next day, thinking that they will be the next victim. Bah! the folly of the men! How glad I am that I am a woman."

"Still, madam," said Reuben, taking his cue, "there be many noble ladies who think it well to remove themselves for a time from this infected city. Not that for the time being the city itself is infected, and we hope to keep it free—"

"Then men are worse fools than I take them for," was the sharp retort. "Keep the plague out of the city! Bah! what nonsense will they talk next! Is it not written in the very heavens that the city is to be destroyed? Heed not their idle prognostications. I tell you, young man, that the plague is already amongst us, even though men know it not. In a few more weeks half the houses in the very city itself will be shut up, and grass will be growing in the streets. We may be thankful if there are enough living to bury the dead. Keep it out of the city, forsooth! Let them do it if they can; I know better!"

Dorcas paled and shrank, fully convinced that her redoubtable mistress possessed a familiar spirit who revealed to her the things that were coming; but Reuben fancied that the old lady was but guessing, and he saw no reason to be afraid at her words. Saying such things would not bring them to pass.

"Then, madam," he answered, "if such be the case, would it not be well to consider whether you do not remove yourself ere these things comne to pass? Pardon me if I seem to take it upon mnyself to advise you, but I was charged by my father, who is like to be appointed for a time one of the examiners of health whom the Mayor and Magistrates think it well to institute at this time, that soon it may not be so easy to get away from the city as it is now; wherefore it behoves the sound whilst they are yet sound to bethink them whether or not they will take themselves away elsewhere. Also my mother wished me to ask the question of your ladyship, forasmuch as she would like to know whether my sister in such case would be required to accompany you."

Lady Scrope nodded her head several times, an odd light of mockery gleaming in her keen black eyes.

"Tell your worthy father, good youth, that I thank him for his good counsel; but also tell him that nothing will drive me from this place—not even though I be the only one left alive in the city. Here I was born, and here I mean to die; and whether death comes by the plague or by some other messenger what care I? I tell thee, lad, I am far safer here than gadding about the country. Here I can shut myself up at pleasure from all the world. Abroad, I am at the muercy of any plague-stricken vagabond who comes to ask an alms. Let all sensible folks stay at home and shut themselves up, and let the fools go gadding here, there, and all over. As for Dorcas, let her come and go as long as she safely may; but if your good mother would keep her at home, then let her abide there, and return to me when the peril is overpast. I like the wench, and if she likes to abide altogether with me she may do so. Let her mother choose."

Dorcas, however, had no wish to live in that lonely house altogether, and for the present there was no reason why she should not go backwards and forwards to her father's abode. Her parents were grateful to Lady Scrope for her offer, but for the present there was no reason for making any change.

The weather during these bright days of May had been cool and fresh, and in spite of all evil auguries, sanguine persons had tried hard to believe and to make others believe that the peril of a visitation of the plague had been somewhat overrated. Yet the choked thoroughfares leading out of London gave the lie to these suppositions, and for many weeks the bridge was a sight in itself, crowded with carriages and waggons all filled with the richer folks and their goods, hastening to the pleasant regions of Surrey to forget their fears and escape the pestilential atmosphere of the city.

Then towards the end of the month a great heat set in, and at once, as it were, the infection broke out in a hundred different and unsuspected places, not only without but within the city walls. How the distemper had so spread none then dared to guess. It seemed everywhere at once, none knew why or how. Doubtless it was in innumerable instances the tainted condition of the wells from which the bulk of the people still drew their water; but men did not think of these things long ago. They looked each other in the face in fear and terror, none knowing but that his neighbour in the street

Evelyn Everett-Green

might be carrying about with him the seeds of the dread distemper.

It now behoved all careful citizens to bethink them well what they would do, with the fearful foe knocking as it were at their very doors, and the matter was brought home right early to the Harmer household, by a thing that befell them at the very outset of the access of hot weather which told so fatally upon the city almost imumediately afterwards.

Rachel Harmer was awakened from sleep one night by the sound of something rattling upon the bed-chamber floor, as though it had fallen from the open casement, and as she came to her waking senses, she heard a voice without calling in urgent accents:

"Mother! mother! mother!"

Rising in some alarm, she went to the window which projected over the lower stories of the house, as was usual at that time, and on putting out her head she beheld a female figure standing in the roadway below. When the moonlight fell upon the upturned face, she saw it was that of her daughter Janet, who was in the service of Lady Howe, and was her waiting maid, living in her house not far from Whitehall, and earning good wages in that gay household.

In no little alarm at seeing her daughter out alone in the street at night, she spoke her name and bid her wait at the door till she could let her in, which she would do immediately; but Janet instantly replied:

"Nay, mother, come not to the door; come to the little window at the corner, where I can speak quietly till I have told you all. Open not the door till you have heard my lamentable tale. I know not even now that I am right to come hither at all."

In great fear and anxiety the mother cast a loose wrapper about her, and descended quickly to the little storeroom close against the shop, where there was a tiny window which opened direct upon the street. At this window, but a few paces away, she found her daughter awaiting her, and by the light of the rush candle that she carried she saw that the girl's face was deadly white.

"Child, child, what ails thee? Come in and tell me all. Thou must not stand out there. I will open the door and fetch thee in."

"No, mother, no—not till thou hast heard my tale," pleaded Janet; "for the sake of the rest thou must be cautious. Mother, I have been with one who died of the plague at noon today!"

"Mercy on us, child! How came that about?"

"It was my fellow servant and bed fellow," answered Janet. "We were like sisters together, and if ever I ailed aught she tended me as fondly as thou couldst thyself, mother. Today, when we rose, she complained of headache and a feeling of illness; but we went down and took our breakfast below with the rest. At least I took mine as usual, though she did but toy with her food. Then all of a sudden she put her hand to her side and turned ghastly white, and fell off her chair. A scullery wench set up a cry, 'The plague! the plague!' and forthwith they all fled this way and that—all save me, who could not leave her thus. I made her swallow some hot cordial which I think they call alexiteric water, and which is said to be very beneficial in cases of the distemper; and she was able to crawl upstairs after a while to her bed once more, where I put her. I knew not for some hours what was passing in the house, though I heard a great commotion there, and presently there stole in a mincing physician who attends my lady, holding a handkerchief steeped in vinegar to his nose, and smelling like an apothecary's shop. He looked at poor Patience, who lay in a stupor, heeding none, and he directed me to uncover her neck for him to see if she had the tokens upon her. There had been none when I put her to bed again, so that I had hoped it was but a colic or some such affection; but, alas, when I looked at his direction, there were the black swellings plainly to be seen. Forthwith he fled with indecent haste, and only stopped to say he would send a nurse and such remedies as should be needful."

"O my child! and thou wast with her all the time!—thou didst even touch and handle her?"

"Mother, I could not leave her alone to die. And hardly had the doctor gone than the fever came upon her, and it was all I could do to keep her from rushing out of the room in her pain. But it lasted only a brief while—for the poison must have gotten a sore hold on her—and just after noon she fell back in mine arms and died.

"O mother, I see her face now—so livid and terrible to look upon! O mother, mother, shall I too look like that when my turn comes to die?"

"Hush, hush, my child! God is very merciful. It may be His good pleasure to spare thee. Thy aunt doth go to and fro amongst the smitten ones, and she is yet in her wonted health. But ere I call thy father and ask counsel what we are to do, tell me the rest of thy tale. Who came to thy relief? and how camest thou hither so late?"

"I could not come before. I dared not go forth by day, lest I bore about the seeds of the distemper. The nurse came at three o'clock, and finding her patient already dead, wrapped her in a sheet, and said that a coffin would be sent at dark, and that the bearers would fetch her for burying when the cart came round, and that when I heard the bell ring I must call to them from the window and let them in. I asked why the porter should not do that, but she told me that already every person in the house had fled. My lady had fallen into an awful fright on hearing that one of her servants was smitten, and before any knowledge could have been received of it by the authorities, she had applied for and obtained a clean bill for herself and her household, and every one of them had fled. The house was empty, save for me and the poor dead girl; and I was bidden to stay till her corpse was removed, for the nurse said she was wanted in a dozen places at once, and that she had too much to do with the sick to attend upon the dead."

"And thou wert willing to wait?"

"I could not leave her alone. Besides, I feared to walk the streets till night. The nurse bid me not linger after the body was taken, for no man knows when the houses will be shut up, so that none can go forth who have been with an infected person. But it is not so done yet, and I was free. But I dared not come home amongst you all to bring, perhaps, death with me. I waited in the house till the men and the cart came, and they brought a coffin and took poor Patience away. They told me then that soon there would be no more coffins, and that they would have to bury without them."

Janet paused and shuddered strongly.

"O mother, mother, mother!" she wailed, "what shall I do? What will become of me? Shall I have to die in the streets, or to go to the pest house? Oh, why do such terrible things befall us?"

The mother was weeping now, but the next moment she felt

the touch of her husband's hand upon her shoulder, and his voice said in its quiet and authoritative way:

"What means all this coil and to do? Why does the child speak thus? Tell me all; I must hear the tale."

"Janet, my girl, never ask the why and the wherefore of any of the Lord's just judgments. It is for us to bow our heads in repentance and submission, trusting that He will never try us above what we are able to bear."

Comforted by the sound of her father's voice, Janet repeated her tale to him in much the same words as before, the father listening in thoughtful silence, without comment or question; till at the conclusion of the tale he said to his wife:

"Go upstairs and bring down with thee my heavy riding cloak which hangs in the press;" and when she had obeyed him, he added, "Now go up to thy room, and shut thyself in till I call thee thence."

Implicit obedience to her husband was one of Rachel's characteristics. Although she longed to know what was to be done, she asked no questions, but retired upstairs and fell on her knees in prayer. The master of the house went to a great cask of vinegar which stood in the corner, and after pretty well saturating the heavy cloak in that pungent liquid, he unbarred the door, and beckoning to his daughter to approach, threw about her the heavy mantle and bid mer follow him.

He led her through the house and up to a large spare guest chamber, rather away from the other sleeping chambers of the house, and he quickly brought to her there a bath and hot water, and certain herbs specially prepared—wormwood, woodsorrel, angelica, and so forth. He bid her wash herself all over in the herb bath, wrapping all her clothing first in the cloak, which she was to put outside the door. Then she was to go to bed, whilst all her clothing was burnt by his own hands; and after that she must submit to remain shut up in that room, seeing nobody but himself, until such time should have gone by as should prove whether or not she had become infected by the distemper.

Janet wept for joy at being thus received beneath her father's roof, having heard so many fearsome tales of persons being turned out of doors even by their nearest and dearest, were it but suspected that they might carry about with them the seeds of the dreaded distemper. But the worthy lace maker was a godly man, and brave with the courage that comes of a lively faith. He had learned all that could be told of the nature of the distemper; and after he had burnt all his daughter's clothing with his own hands, and had assured himself that she felt sound and well, and had also fumigated his own house thoroughly, he felt that he had done all in his power against the infection, and that the rest must be left in the hands of Providence.

The mother hovered anxiously about, but came not near her husband till permitted by him. She did not enter the room where her daughter now lay comfortably in a soft bed, but she prepared some good food for her, which was carried in by the father later on, and promised her that by the morning she should have clothing to put on, and that she should have every care and comfort during the days of her captivity.

Janet thanked God from the very bottom of her heart that night for having given to her such good and kindly parents, and earnestly besought that she might be spared, not only for her own unworthy sake, but for their sakes who had risked so much rather than that she should be an outcast from home at such a time of peril and horror.

CHAPTER IV

JAMES HARMER'S RESOLVE

It was with a grave face, yet with a brave and cheerful mien, that the worthy Harmer met his household upon the following morning. He had passed the remainder of that strangely interrupted night in meditation and prayer, and had arrived now at a resolution which he intended to put into immediate effect.

His household consisted, it will be remembered, of his own family, together with apprentices, shopmen, and serving wenches. To all of these he now addressed himself, told the story which his daughter had related of the treatment received in the house of the high-born lady by the poor girl stricken by the pestilence, and how it had made even his own child almost fear to enter her father's house.

"My friends," said the master, looking round upon the ring of grave and eager faces, "these things ought not to be. In times of common trouble and peril the hearts of men should draw closer together, and we should remember that God's command to us is to love our neighbour as ourself. If we were to lie stricken of mortal illness, should we think it a Christ-like act for all men to flee away from us? But inasmuch as we ought all of us to take every care not to run into needless peril, so must we take every right and reasonable precaution to keep from ourselves and our homes this just but terrible visitation, which God has doubtless sent for our admonition and chastisement."

After this preface, Harmer proceeded to tell his household what he had himself resolved upon. His two apprentices— other than his own son Joseph—were sons of a farmer living in Greenwich; and he purposed that very day to get his sailor son Dan to take them down the river in a boat, that he might deliver the lads safe and sound to their parents before further peril threatened, advising them to keep them at home till the distemper should have abated, and arranging with them for a regular supply of fresh and untainted provisions, to be conveyed to his house from week to week by water, so long as there should be any fear of marketing in the city. He foresaw that very soon trade would come almost to a standstill. The scare and the pestilence together were emptying London of all its wealthier inhabitants. There would be soon no work for either shopmen or apprentices, and he counselled the former, if they had homes out of London to go to, to remain no longer in town, but to take their wages and seek safety and employment elsewhere, until the calamity should be overpast. He also gave the same liberty to the serving wenches, one of whom came from Islington and the other from Rotherhithe. And all of these persons having home and friends, decided to leave forthwith, to be out of the danger of infection, and of that still more dreaded danger of being shut up in an infected house with a plague-stricken person.

The master gave liberally to each of his servants according to their past service, and promised that if he should escape the pestilence, and continue his business in more prosperous times, he would take them back into his house again.

For the present, however, it seemed good to him that only his own family should remain with him. His wife and three daughters could well manage the house, and he did not desire that any other person should be imperilled through the course of action he himself intended to take.

When he took boat with his apprentices, he offered to Joseph to accompany his companions and remain under the charge of the farmer and his wife at Greenwich; but the boy begged so earnestly to remain at home with the rest, that he was permitted to do so. Truth to tell, Joseph was more fascinated than alarmed by the thought of the advance of the dreaded plague, and was by no means anxious to be taken away from the city when all the world was saying that such strange things would be seen ere long. The lad felt so safe beneath the care of wise and loving parents, that he would never of his own will consent to leave them.

The moment the party had started by boat, the shop being that day shut for the first time, albeit for some days nothing had been stirring in the way of custom—Joseph darted away down a network of alleys hard by in search of his younger brother Benjamin, who was apprenticed to a carpenter in Lad Lane, off Wood Street, and therefore much nearer to the infected parishes than the house on the bridge. Benjamin was sure to know the latest news as to the spread of the pestilence. Joseph was of opinion that it was all rather fine fun, especially since it seemed like to get him a spell of unwonted holiday.

Already as he passed through the streets he noted a great many empty and shut-up houses. Men were going about with grave and anxious faces. Often they would look askance at some passerby who might be walking a little feebly or unsteadily, and once Joseph saw a man some fifty paces in advance of him stagger and fall to the ground with a lamentable cry.

Instead of flying to his assistance, all who saw him fled in terror, crying one to the other, "It is the pestilence! Send for the watch to get him away!"

And presently there came two men who lifted him up and carried him away, but whether he was then alive or dead the boy did not know, and a great awe fell upon him; for he had never seen such a thing before, and could not understand how death could come so suddenly.

"Is it always so with them?" he asked of a woman who was craning her head out of a window to see where the bearers were taking him.

"I cannot tell," she answered. "They say that there be many walking about amongst us daily in the streets who carry death to all in their breath and in their touch, and yet they know it not themselves, and none know it till they fall as yon poor man did, and die ofttimes in a few minutes or hours. If such be so, who knows when he is safe? May the Lord have mercy upon us all! There be seven lying dead in this street today, and though folks say they died of other fevers and distempers, who can tell? They bribe the nurses and the leeches to return them dead of smaller ailments, but I verily believe the pestilence is stalking through our very midst even now."

She shut down the window with a groan, and Joseph pursued his way with somewhat modified feelings, half elated at being in the thick of so much that was terrible and awesome, and yet beginning to understand somewhat of the horror that was possessing the minds of all. He found himself walking in the middle of the street, and avoiding too close contact with the passersby; indeed all seemed disposed to give strangers a wide berth just now, so that it was not difficult to avoid contact.

Evelyn Everett-Green

Yet crowds were to be seen, too, at many open spaces. Sometimes a fervid preacher would be declaiming to a pale-faced group on the subject of God's righteous judgments upon a wicked and licentious city. Sometimes a wizened old woman or a juggling charlatan would be seen selling all sorts of charms and potions as specifics against the plague. Joseph pressing near in curiosity to one of these vendors, found him doing a brisk trade in dried toads, which he vowed would preserve the wearer from all infection. Another had packets of dried herbs to which he gave terribly long names, and which he declared acted as an antidote to the poison. Another had small leaflets on which directions were given for applying a certain ointment to the plague spots, which at once cured them as by magic. The leaflets were given away, but the ointment had to be bought. Those, however, who once read what the paper said, seldom went away without a box of the precious specific.

Joseph would have liked one himself, but had no money, and was further restrained by a sense of conviction that his father would say it was all nonsense and quackery.

Church bells were ringing, and many were tolling—tolling for the dead, and ringing the living into the churches, where special prayers were being offered and many excellent discourses preached, to which crowds of people listened with bated breath. Joseph crept into one church on his way for a few minutes, but was too restless to listen long, and soon came forth again.

He was now near to Lad Lane, and hastening his steps lest he might be further delayed, came quickly upon the back premises of the carpenter's shop, where the sound of hammer and chisel and saw made quite a clamour in the quiet air.

"They are busy here at all events," muttered Joseph, as he

pushed open the gate of the yard, and in truth they were busy within; but yet the sight that presented itself to his eyes was anything hut a cheerful one, for every man in the large number assembled there was at work upon a coffin. Coffins in every stage of construction stood everywhere, and the carpenters were toiling away at them as if for dear life. Nothing but coffins was to be seen; and scarcely was one finished, in never so rude a fashion, but it was borne hurriedly away by some waiting messenger, and the master kept coming into the yard to see if his men could not work yet faster.

"They say they must bury the corpses uncoffined soon," Joseph heard him whisper to his foreman as he passed by. "No bodies may wait above ground after the first night when the cart goes its round. Six orders have come in within the last hour. No one knows how many we shall have by nightfall, or how many men we shall have working soon. I sent Job away but an hour since. I hope it was not the distemper that turned his face so green! They say it has broken out in three streets hard by, and that it is spreading like wildfire."

Joseph shuddered as he listened and crept away to the corner where his brother was generally to be found. And there sure enough was Benjamin, a pretty fair-haired boy, who looked scarce strong enough for the task in hand, but who was yet working might and main with chisel and hammer. His face brightened at sight of his brother, yet he did not relax his efforts, only saying eagerly:

"How goes it at home with them all, Joseph? I trow it is the coffin makers, not the lace makers, who have all the trade nowadays! We are working night and day, and yet cannot keep up with the orders."

Benjamin was half proud of all this press of business, but he did not look as though it agreed with him. His face was pale, and when at last he threw down his hammer it was with a gasp of exhaustion. The day was very hot, and he had been at work before the dawn. It was no wonder, perhaps, that he looked wan and weary, yet the master passing by paused and cast an uneasy glance at him. For it was from the very next stool that he had recently dismissed the man Job of whom he had spoken, and of whose condition he felt grave doubts.

Seeing Joseph close by he gave him a nod, and said:

"Hast come to fetch home thy brother? Two of my apprentices have been taken away since yesterday. He is a good lad, and does his best; but he may take a holiday at home if he likes. You are healthier at your end of the town, and they say the distemper comes not near water.

"Wilt thou go home to thy mother, boy? We want men rather than lads at our work in these days."

Joseph had had no thought of fetching home his brother when he started, but it seemed to him that Benjamin would be much better at home than in this crowded yard, where already the infection might have spread. The boy confessed to a headache and pains in his limbs; and so fearful were all men now of any symptom of illness, however trifling, that the master sent him forth without delay, bidding Joseph take him straight home to his mother, and keep him there at his father's pleasure. A young boy was better at home in these days, as indeed might well be the case.

Benjamin was well pleased with this arrangement, having had something too much of over hours and hard work.

"He thinks perchance I have the distemper upon me," he

remarked slyly to Joseph, "but it is not that. It is but the long hours and the heat and noise of the yard. I shall be well enough when I get home to mother."

And this indeed proved to be the case. The child was overdone, and wanted but a little rest and care and mothering; and right glad were both his parents to have him safe under their own wing.

Upon that hot evening, almost the first in June, James Harmer had the satisfaction of feeling that he had every member of his family under his own roof, and that his household contained now none who were not indeed his very own flesh and blood. Janet had slept peacefully almost the whole day, and had conversed happily and affectionately through the closed door with her sisters, who were rejoiced to have her there. She spoke of feeling perfectly well but desired to remain in seclusion until certain that she could injure none beside. She was not therefore able to be present when her father unfolded his plans to the rest of the family, though she was quickly apprised of the result later on.

"My dear wife and dutiful children," said the master of the house, as he sat at table and looked about him at the ring of dear faces round him, "I have been thinking much as to what it is right for us to do in face of this peril and scourge which God has sent upon the city; and albeit I am well aware that it is the duty of every man to take reasonable care of himself and his household, yet I also feel very strongly that in the protection of the Lord is our greatest strength and safeguard, and that our best and strongest defence is in throwing ourselves upon His mercy, and asking day by day for His merciful protection for a household which looks to Him as the Lord of life and death."

Then the good man proceeded to quote from Holy Writ

Evelyn Everett-Green

certain passages in which the pestilence is represented as being the scourge of the Lord, and is spoken of as being an angel of the Lord with a drawn sword slaying right and left, yet ever ready to spare where the Lord shall bid.

"I shall then," continued Harmer, "daily and nightly confide those of this household into the keeping of Almighty God, and pray to Him for His protection and special blessing. It may be (since His ears are always open to the supplication of His children) that He will send His angel of life to watch over us and keep us from harm; and having this confidence, and using such means as seem wise and reasonable for the protection of all, I shall strive—and you must all strive with me—to dismiss selfish terrors and the horror that begets cruelty and callousness, that we may all of us do our duty towards those about us, and show that even the scourge of a righteous and offended God may become a blessing if taken in meekness and humility."

Then the good man proceeded to say what precautions he was about to take for the preservation of his family. He did not propose to fly the city. He had many valuable goods on the premises, which he might probably lose were he to shut up his house and leave. He had no place to go to in the country, and believed that the scourge might well follow them there, were every householder to seek to quit his abode. Moreover, never was there greater need in the city for honest men of courage and probity to help to meet the coming crisis and to see carried out all the wise regulations proposed by the Mayor and Aldermen. He had resolved to join them— since business was like to be at a standstill for a while—and do whatsoever a man could do to forward that good work. His son Reuben was of the same mind with him; whilst his wife would far rather face the peril in her own house than go out, she knew not whither, to be perhaps overtaken by the plague on the road. Her heart had yearned over the sick ever since she had heard her daughter's harrowing tale, and knew that her sister was at work amongst the stricken. She knew not what she might be able to do, but she trusted to her husband for guidance, and would be entirely under his direction.

Some citizens spoke of victualling their houses as for a siege, and entirely secluding themselves and their families till the plague was overpast—and indeed this was many times done with success, although the plan broke down in other cases—but this was not Harmer's idea. He did indeed advise his wife and daughters to be careful how they adventured themselves abroad, and where they went. He had arranged at the farm near Greenwich for a regular supply of provisions to be brought by water to the stairs hard by the bridge; and since their house was supplied by water from the New River, they were sure of a constant fresh supply. But he had no intention of incarcerating himself or any of his household, and preventing them from being of use to afflicted neighbours, whilst he himself anticipated having to go into many stricken homes and into infected houses. All the restriction he imposed was that any person sallying forth into places where infection might be met should change his raiment before going out, in a small building in the rear of the shop which he was about to fit up for that purpose, and to keep constantly fumigated by the frequent burning of certain perfumes, of oil of sulphur, and of a coarse medicated vinegar which was said to be an excellent disinfectant. On returning home again, the person who had been exposed would doff all outer garments in this little room, would resume his former clothing, and hang up the discarded garments where they would be subjected to this disinfecting fumigation for a number of hours, and would be then safe to wear upon another occasion. He intended burning regularly in his house a fire of pungent wood such as pine or cedar, which was to be constantly fed with such spices and perfumes and disinfectants as the physicians should pronounce most efficacious. Perfect cleanliness he did not need to insist upon, for his wife could not endure a speck of dust upon anything in the house.

A careful diet, regular hours, and freedom from needless fears would, he was assured, do much towards maintaining them all in health, and he concluded his address by kneeling down in the midst of his sons and daughters, and commending them all most fervently to the protection of Heaven, praying for grace to do their duty towards all about them, and for leading and guidance that they ran not into needless peril, but were directed in all things by the Spirit of God.

They had hardly risen from their knees before a knock at the door announced the arrival of a visitor, and Joseph running to answer the summons—since there was now no servant in the house—came back almost immediately ushering in the Master Builder, whose face wore a very troubled look.

"Heaven guard us all! I think my wife will go distraught with the terror of this visitation, if it goes on much longer. What is a man to do for the best? She raves at me sometimes like a maniac for not having taken her away ere the scourge spread as it is doing now. But when I tell her that if she is bent upon it she must e'en go now, she cries out that nothing would induce her to set her foot outside the house. She sits with the curtains and shutters fast closed, and a fire of spices on the hearth, till one is fairly stifled, and will touch nothing that is not well-nigh soaked in vinegar. And each time that Frederick comes in with some fresh tale, she is like to swoon with fear, and every time she vows that it is the pestilence attacking her, and is like to die from sheer fright. What is a man to do with such a wife and such a son?"

"Surely Frederick will cease to repeat tales of horror when he sees they so alarm his mother," said Rachel; but the Master Builder shook his head with an air of more than doubt.

"It seems his delight to torment her with terror; and she appears almost equally eager to hear all, though it almost scares her out of her senses. As for Gertrude, the child is pining like a caged bird shut up in the house and not suffered to stir into the fresh air. I am fair beset to know what to do for them. Nothing will convince Madam but that there be dead carts at every street corner, and that the child will bring home death with her every time she stirs out. Yet Frederick comes to and fro, and she admits him to her presence (though she holds a handkerchief steeped in vinegar to her nose the while), and she gets no harm from him."

"Poor child!" said Rachel, thinking of Gertrude, whom once she had known so well, running to and fro in the house almost like one of her own. "Would that we could do somewhat for her. But I fear me her mother would not suffer her to visit us, especially since poor Janet came home last night from a plague-stricken house."

Reuben's eyes had brightened suddenly at his mother's words, but the gleam died out again, and he remained quite silent whilst the story of Janet's appearance at home was told. The Master Builder listened with interest and sighed at the same time. Perhaps he was contrasting the nature of his neighbour's wife with that of his own. How would Madam have acted had her child come to her in such a plight?

Harmer then told his neighbour the rules he was about to lay down for his own household, all of which the Master Builder, who was a keen practical man, cordially approved. He was himself likely soon to be in a great strait, for most probably he would be appointed in due course to serve as an

Evelyn Everett-Green

examiner of health, and would of necessity come into contact with those who had been amongst the sick, even if not with the infected themselves, and how his wife would bear such a thing as that he scarce dared to think. Business, too, was at a standstill, all except the carpentering branch, and that was only busy with coffins. If London became depopulated, there would be nothing doing in the building and furnishing line for long enough. Some prophets declared that the city was doomed to a destruction such as had never been seen by mortal man before. Even as it was the plague seemed like to sweep away a fourth of the inhabitants; and if that were so, what would become of such trades as his for many a year to come? Already the Master Builder spoke of himself as a half-ruined man.

His neighbour did all he could to cheer him, but it was only too true that misfortune appeared imminent. Harmer had always been a careful and cautious man, laying by against a rainy day, and not striving after a rapid increase of wealth. But the Master Builder had worked on different lines. He had enlarged his borders wherever he could see his way to doing so, and although he had a large capital by this time, it was all floating in this and that venture; so that in spite of his appearance of wealth and prosperity, he had often very little ready money. So long as trade was brisk this mattered little, and he turned his capital over in a fashion that was very pleasing to himself. But this sudden and totally unexpected collapse of business came upon him at a time when he could ill afford to meet it. Already he had had to discharge the greater part of his workmen, having nothing for them to do. The expenses which he could not put down drained his resources in a way that bid fair to bring him to bankruptcy, and it was almost impossible to get in outstanding accounts when the rich persons in his debt had fled hither and thither with such speed and haste that often no trace of them could be found, and their houses in town were shut up and absolutely empty.

"As for Frederick, he spends money like water—and his mother encourages him," groaned the unhappy father in confidence to his friend. "Ah me! when I look at your fine sons, and see their conduct at home and abroad, it makes my heart burn with shame. What is it that makes the difference? for I am sure I have denied Frederick no advantage that money could purchase."

"Perhaps it is those advantages which money cannot purchase that he lacks," said James Harmer, gravely—"the prayers of a godly mother, the chastisement of a father who would not spoil the child by sparing the rod. There are things in the upbringing of children, my good friend, of far more value than those which gold will purchase."

The Master Builder gave vent to a sound almost like a groan.

"You are right, Harmer, you are right. I have not done well in this thing. My son is no better than an idle profligate. I say it to my shame, but so it is. Nothing that I say will keep him from his riotous comrades and licentious ways. I have spoken till I am weary of speaking, and all is in vain. And now that this terrible scourge of God has fallen upon the city, instead of turning from their evil courses with fear and loathing, he and such as he are but the more reckless and impious, and turn into a jest even this fearful visitation. They scour the streets as before, and drink themselves drunk night by night. Ah, should the pestilence reach some amongst them, what would be their terrible doom! I cannot bear even to think of it! Yet that is too like to be the end of my wretched boy, my poor, unhappy Frederick!"

CHAPTER V

THE PLOT AND ITS PUNISHMENT

Strange as it may appear, the awful nature of the calamity which had overtaken the great city had by no means the subduing influence upon the spirits of the lawless young roisterers of the streets that might well have been expected. No doubt there were some amongst these who were sobered by the misfortunes of their fellows, and by the danger in which every person in the town now stood; but it seemed as if the very imminence of the peril and the fearful spread of the contagion exercised upon others a hardening influence, and they became even more lawless and dissolute than before. "Let us eat and drink; for tomorrow we die," appeared to be their motto, and they lived up to it only too well.

So whilst the churches were thronged with multitudes of pious or terrified persons, assembled to pray to God for mercy, and to listen to words of godly counsel or admonition; whilst the city authorities were doing everything in their power to check the course of the frightful contagion, and send needful relief to the sufferers, and many devoted men and women were adventuring their lives daily for the sake of others, the taverns were still filled day by day and night by night with idle and dissolute young men, tainted with all the vices of a vicious Court and an unbelieving age—drinking, and making hideous mockery of the woes of their townsmen, careless even when the gaps amid their own ranks showed that the fell disease was busy amongst all classes and ranks. Indeed, it was no unheard of thing for a man to fall stricken to the ground in the midst of one of these revels; and although the master of the house would hastily throw him out of the door as if he had staggered forth drunk, yet it would ofttimes be the distemper which had him in its fatal clutches, and the dead cart would remove him upon its next gloomy round.

For now indeed the pestilence was spreading with a fearful rapidity. The King, taking sudden alarm, after being careless and callous for long, had removed with his Court to Oxford. The fiat for the shutting up of all infected houses had gone forth, and was being put in practice, greatly increasing the terror of the citizens, albeit many of them recognized in it both wisdom and foresight. Something plainly had to be done to check the spread of the infection. And as there was no means of removing the sick from their houses—there being but two or three pest houses in all London—even should their friends be prompt to give notice, and permit them to be borne away, the only alternative seemed to be to shut them up within the doors of the house where they lay stricken; and since they might already have infected all within it, condemn these also to share the imprisonment. It was this that was the hardship, and which caused so many to strive to evade the law by every means in their power. It drove men mad with fear to think of being shut up in an infected house with a person smitten with the fell disease. Yet if the houses were not so closed, and guarded by watchmen hired for the purpose, the sick in their delirium would have constantly been getting out and running madly about the streets, as indeed did sometimes happen, infecting every person they met. Restraint of some sort was needful, and the closing of the houses seemed the only way in which this could be accomplished.

It may be guessed what hard work all this entailed upon such of the better sort of citizens as were willing to give themselves to the business. James Harmer and his two elder sons, Reuben and Dan, offered themselves to the Lord Mayor to act as examiners or searchers, or in whatever capacity he might wish to employ them. Dan should by this time have been at sea, but his ship being still in the docks when the plague broke out remained yet unladed. None from the infected city would purchase merchandise. The sailing master had himself been smitten down, and Dan, together with quite a number of sailors, was thrown out of employment.

Many of these poor fellows were glad to take service as watchmen of infected houses, or even as bearers and buriers of the dead. At a time when trade was at a standstill, and men feared alike to buy or to sell, this perilous and lugubrious occupation was all that could be obtained, and so there were always men to be found for the task of watching the houses, though at other times it might have been impossible to get enough.

Orders had been sent round the town that all cases of the distemper were to be reported within a few hours of discovery to the examiner of health, who then had the house shut up, supplied it with a day and a night watchman (whose duty it was to wait on the inmates and bring them all they needed), and had the door marked with the ominous red cross and the motto of which mention has been made before. Plague nurses were numerous, but too often these were women of the worst character, bent rather upon plunder than desirous of relieving the sufferers. Grim stories were told of their neglect and rapacity. Yet amongst them were many devoted and excellent women, and the physicians who bravely faced the terrors of the time and remained at their post when others fled from the peril, deserve all honour and praise; the more so that many amongst these died of the infection, as indeed did numbers of the examiners and searchers who likewise remained at their post to the end.

It will therefore be well understood that good Master Harmer and his sons had no light time of it, and ran no small personal risk in their endeavours to serve their fellow citizens in this crisis. Although the pestilence had not as yet broken out in this part of the town with the virulence that it had shown elsewhere, still there were fresh cases rumoured day by day; and it often appeared that when one case in a street was reported, there had been many others there before of which no notice had been given, and that perhaps half a dozen houses were infected, and must be forthwith shut up. At first neglectful persons were brought before the Magistrates; but soon these persons became too numerous, and the Magistrates too busy to hear their excuses. An example was made of one or another, to show that the laws must be kept; but Newgate itself becoming infected by the disease, it was not thought fit to send any malefactor there except for some heinous offence.

Dan joined the force of the constables, and day by day had exciting tales to tell about determined persons who had escaped from infected houses either by tricking or over-powering the watchman. All sorts of clever shifts were made to enable families where perhaps only one lay sick to escape from the house, leaving the sick person sometimes quite alone, or sometimes in charge of a nurse. Dan said it was heartrending to hear the cries and lamentations of miserable creatures pleading to be let out, convinced that it was certain death to them to remain shut up with the sick. Yet, since they might likely be themselves already infected, it was the greater peril and cruelty to let them forth; and he had ghastly tales to tell of the visitation of certain houses, where the watchmen reported that nothing had been asked for for long, and where, when the house was entered by searchers or constables, every person within was found either dead or dying.

The precautions duly observed by the Harmer family had hitherto proved efficacious, and though the father and his sons going about their daily duties came into contact with infected persons frequently, yet, by the use of the disinfectants recommended by the College of Physicians, and by a close and careful attention to their directions, they went unscathed in the midst of much peril, and brought no ill to those at home when they returned thither for needful rest and refreshment. Janet had had a slight attack of illness, but there were no absolute symptoms of the distemper with it. Her father was of opinion that it might possibly be a very mild form of the disease, but the doctor called in thought not, and so their house escaped being shut up, and after a prudent interval Janet came down and took her place in the family as before. Mother and daughters worked together for the relief of the sick poor, making and sending out innumerable dainties in the way of broth, possets, and light puddings, which were gratefully received by poor folks in shut-up houses, who, although fed and cared for at the public expense when not able to provide for themselves, were grateful indeed for these small boons, and felt themselves not quite so forlorn and wretched when receiving tokens of goodwill from even an unknown source.

The harmony, tranquillity, and goodwill that reigned in this household, even in the midst of so much that was terrible, was a great contrast to the anguish, terror, and ceaseless recriminations which made the Masons' abode a veritable purgatory for its luckless inhabitants. As the news of the spreading contagion reached her, so did Madam's terror and horror increase. As her husband had said long since, she sat in rooms with closed windows and drawn curtains, burned fires large enough to roast an ox, and half poisoned herself with the drugs she daily swallowed, and which she would have forced upon her whole household had they not rebelled against being thus sickened. As a natural consequence of her folly and ungovernable fears, Madam was never well, and was for ever discovering some new symptom which threw her into an ecstasy of terror. She would wake in the night screaming out in uncontrollable fear that she had gotten the plague—that she felt a burning tumour here or there upon her person—that she was sinking away into a deadly swoon, or that something fatal was befalling her. By day she would fall into like passions of fear, call out to her daughter to send for every physician whose name she had heard, and upbraid and revile her in the most unmeasured terms if the poor girl ventured to hint that the doctors were beginning to be tired of coming to listen to what always proved imaginary terrors.

The only times when husband or daughter enjoyed any peace was when Frederick chose to make his appearance at home. On these occasions his mother would summon him to her presence, although in mortal fear lest he should bring infection with him, and make him tell her all the most frightful stories which he had picked up about the awful spread of the disease, about the iniquities and abominations practised by nurses and buriers, of which last there was plenty of gossip (although probably much was set down in malice and much exaggerated) and all the prognostications of superstitious or profane persons as to the course the pestilence was going to take. Eagerly did she listen to all of these stories, which Frederick took care should be very well spiced, as it was at once his amusement to frighten his mother and spite his sister; for Gertrude in private implored him not to continue to alarm their mother with his frightful tales, and also begged him for his own sake to relinquish his evil habits of intemperance, which at such a time as this might lead to fatal results.

The good-for-nothing youth only mocked at her, and derided his father when he gave him the same warning. He had become perfectly unmanageable and reckless, and nothing that he heard or saw about him produced any impression. Although taverns and ale houses were closely watched, and ordered to close at nine o'clock, and the gatherings of idle and profligate youths of whatever condition of life sternly reprobated and forbidden by the authorities, yet these worthies found means of evading or defying the regulations, and their revels continued as before, so that Frederick was seldom thoroughly sober, and more reckless and careless even than of old. In vain his father strove to bring him to a better mind; in vain he warned him of the peril of his ways and the danger to his health of such constant excesses. Frederick only laughed insolently; whereupon the Master Builder, who had but just come from his neighbour's house, and was struck afresh with the contrast presented by the two homes, asked him if he knew how Reuben Harmer was passing his time, and made a few bitter comparisons between his son and those of his neighbour.

This was perhaps unfortunate, for Frederick, like most men of his type, was both vain and spiteful. The mention of the Harmers put him instantly in mind of his grudge against Reuben and his suddenly-aroused admiration for rosy-cheeked Dorcas, both of which matters had been put out of his head by recent events. He had discovered also that Reuben generally accompanied his sister home from Lady Scrope's house in the evening, so that it had not been safe to pursue his attempted gallantries towards the maid. But as he heard his father's strictures upon his conduct, coupled with laudations of his old rival Reuben, a gleam of malice shone in his eyes, and he at once made up his mind to contrive and carry out a project which had been vaguely floating in his brain for some time, and which might be the more easily arranged now that the town was in a state of confusion and distress, and the streets were often so empty and deserted.

In that age of vicious licence, it seemed nothing but an excellent joke to Frederick and his boon companions to waylay a pretty city maiden returning to her home from her daily duties. Frederick meant no harm to the girl; but he had been piqued by the way in which his compliments and kisses had been received, and above all he was desirous to do a despite to Reuben, whose rebukes still rankled in his heart, though he had quickly forgotten his good offices on the occasion of his escapade before Lady Scrope's door. Moreover, he owed that notable old woman a grudge likewise, and thought he could pay off scores all round by making away with pretty Dorcas, at any rate for a while. So he and his comrades laid their plans with what they thought great skill, resolved that they should be carried out upon the first favourable opportunity.

For a while Dorcas had been rather nervous of leaving the house in Allhallowes unless Reuben was waiting for her. But as she had seen no more of the gallant who had accosted her, and as it was said on all hands that these had left London in hundreds, she had taken courage of late, and had bidden her brother not incommode himself on her account, if it were difficult for him to be her escort home.

Of late he had oftentimes been kept away by pressure of other duties. Sometimes Dan had come in his stead. Sometimes she had walked back alone and unmolested. Persons avoided each other in the streets now, and hurried by with averted glances. Although upon her homeward route, which was but short, she had as yet no infected houses to pass, she always hastened along half afraid to look about her. But her father's good counsel and his daily prayers for his household so helped her to keep up heart, that she had not yet been frightened from her occupation, although her mistress always declared on parting in the evening that she never expected to see her back in the morning.

"If the plague does not get you, some coward terror will. Never mind; I can do without you, child. I never looked for you to have kept so long at your post. All the rest have fled long since."

Which was true indeed, only Dorcas and the old couple who lived in the house still continuing their duties. Fear of the pestilence had driven away the other servants, and they had sought safety on the other side of the water, where it was still believed infection would not spread.

"I will come back in the morning. My father bids us all do our duty, and sets us the example, madam," said Dorcas, as she prepared to take her departure.

It was a dark evening for the time of year; heavy thunder-clouds were hanging low in the sky and obscuring the light. The air was oppressive, and seemed charged with noxious vapours. Part of this was due to the cloud of smoke wafted along from one of the great fires kept burning with the object of dispelling infection. But Dorcas shivered as she stepped out into the empty street, and looked this way and that, hoping to see one of her brothers. But nobody was in sight and she had just descended the steps and was turning towards her home when out from a neighbouring porch there swaggered a very fine young gallant, who made an instant rush towards her, with words of welcome and endearment on his lips.

In a moment Dorcas recognized him not only as the gallant

who had addressed her once before, but also as Frederick Mason, her brothers' old playfellow, of whom such evil things were spoken now by all their neighbours on the bridge.

Uttering a little cry of terror, the girl darted back, turned, and commenced running like a hunted hare in the opposite direction, careless where she went or what she did provided she only escaped from the address and advances of her pursuer. But fleet as were her own steps, those in pursuit seemed fleeter. She heard her tormentor coming after her, calling her by name and entreating for a hearing. She knew that he was gaining upon her and must soon catch her up. She was in a lonely street where not a single passerby seemed to be stirring. She looked wildly round for some way of escape, and just at that moment saw a man come round a corner and fit a key into the door of one of the houses.

Without pausing to think, Dorcas made a rush towards him, and so soon as the door was opened she dashed within the house, and fled up the staircase—fled she knew not whither—uttering breathless, frightened cries, whilst all the time she knew that her pursuer was close behind, and heard his voice mingled with angry cries of remonstrance from the man they had left below.

Suddenly a door close to Dorcas opened, and a new terror was revealed to her horror-stricken gaze. A gaunt, tall figure, wrapped in a long white garment that looked like grave clothes, sprang out into the stairway with a shriek that was like nothing human. Dorcas sank, almost fainting with terror, to the ground; but the spectre—for such it seemed to her— paid no heed to her, but sprang upon her pursuer, who had at that moment come up, and the next moment had his arms wound about him in a bearlike embrace, whilst all the time he was laughing an awful laugh. Then lifting the unfortunate young man off his feet with a strength that was almost superhuman, he bore him rapidly down the stairs and rushed out with him into the street.

All this happened in so brief a moment of time that Dorcas had not even time to regain her feet, or to utter the scream of terror which came to her lips. But as she found breath to utter her cry, another door opened and a scared face looked out, whilst a woman's voice asked in lamentable accents:

"What do you here, maiden? What has happened to bring any person into this shut-up house? Child, child, how didst thou obtain entrance here? The plague is in this house, and we are straitly shut up!"

Before Dorcas could answer for fright and the confusion of her faculties, a pale-faced watchman came hurrying up the stairs.

"Where is the maid?" he asked, and then seeing Dorcas he grasped her by the wrist and cried, "Unless you wish to be shut up for a month, come away instantly. This is a stricken house. What possessed you to seek shelter here? Better anything than that.

"As for your son, mistress, he is fled forth into the street; I could not hinder him. We are undone if the constable comes. But if we can get him back again ere that, all may be well. I will let you forth to lead him hither if he will listen to your voice."

From the room whence the sick man had appeared a frightened face looked forth, and a half-tipsy old crone whimpered out:

"The fault was none of mine. I had but just dropped asleep

for a moment. But when a man has the strength of ten what can one poor old woman do?"

Without paying any heed to this creature, the watchman and the mother of the plague-stricken man, together with Dorcas, who hurriedly told her tale as they moved, ran down the dark staircase and out into the street. There, a little way off, was the tall spectre-like figure, still hugging in bearlike embrace the hapless Frederick, and dancing the while a most weird and fantastic dance, chanting some awful words which none could rightly catch, but the burden of which was, "The dance of death! the dance of death! None who dances here with me will dance with any other!"

"For Heaven's sake release him from that embrace!" cried the mother, who knew that her son was smitten to death. "If all be true that the maid hath said, he is not fit to die, and that embrace is a deadly one!—O my son, my son! come back, come back!

"Mercy on us, here is the watch! We are undone!"

Indeed the trampling of many hasty feet announced the arrival of a number of persons upon the scene. It seemed like enough to be the constables or the watch; but the moment the newcomers appeared round the corner, Dorcas, uttering a little shriek of joy and relief, threw herself upon the foremost man, who was in fact none other than Reuben himself—Reuben, followed closely by his brother Dan, and they by several young roisterers, the boon companions of Frederick.

It had chanced that almost as soon as Dorcas had run from Lady Scrope's door, hotly pursued by Frederick, her brothers had come up to fetch her thence. It was also part of that worthy's plan that they should hear she had been carried off, though not by himself. His half-tipsy comrades, therefore, who had come to see the sport, immediately informed the young men that the maid had been pursued by a Scourer in such and such a direction; and so quickly had the brothers pursued the flying footsteps of the pair—guided by the footmarks in the dusty and untrodden streets—that they had come upon this strange and ghastly scene almost at its commencement, and in a moment their practised eyes took in what had happened.

The open door marked with the ominous red cross, the troubled face of the watchman, the ghastly apparition of the delirious plague-stricken man, the horror depicted in the face of the mother—all this told a tale of its own. Scenes of a like kind were now growing common enough in the city; but this was more terrible to the young men from the fact that the face of the unhappy and half-fainting Frederick was known to them and that they understood the awful peril into which this adventure had thrown him. They knew the strength of delirious patients, and the peril of contagion in their touch. To attempt to loosen that bearlike clasp might be death to any who attempted it.

Reuben looked about him, still holding his sister in his arms as though to keep her away from the peril; and Dan, who had taken one step forward towards the sheeted spectre, paused and muttered between his teeth:

"The hound! he has but got his deserts!"

"True," said Reuben, for he was certain now that it had been Frederick who was Dorcas's pursuer; "yet we must not leave him thus. He will be strangled or choked by the pestilential smell if we cannot get him away. Take Dorcas, Dan. Let me see if I can do aught with him."

But even as Reuben spoke, and Dorcas clung closer than

ever to him in fear that he was about to adventure himself into greater peril, the delirious man suddenly flung Frederick from him, so that he fell upon the pavement almost as one dead; and then, with a hideous shriek that rang in their ears for long, fled back to the house as rapidly as he had left it, and fell down dead a few moments later upon the bed from which he had so lately risen.

That fact they learned only the next day. For the moment it was enough that the patient was safely within doors again, and that the watchman could make fast the door. The roisterers had fled at the first sight of the plague-stricken man with their hapless leader in his embrace, and now the darkening street contained only the prostrate figure on the pavement, the two brothers, and the white-faced Dorcas, who felt like to die of fear and horror.

As chance or Providence would have it, up at that very moment came the Master Builder himself, and seeing his son in such a plight, shook his head gravely, thinking him drunk in the gutter. But Reuben went up and told all the tale, as far as he knew or guessed it, and Dorcas having confirmed the same more by gestures than words, the unhappy father smote his brow, and cried in a voice of lamentation:

"Alas that I should have such a son! O unhappy, miserable youth! what will be thy doom now?"

At this cry Frederick moved, and got slowly upon his feet. He had been stunned by the violence of his fall, and for the first moment believed himself drunk, and caught at his father's arm for support.

"Have a care, sir," said Reuben, in a low voice; "he may be infected already by the contact."

But the Master Builder only uttered a deep sigh like a groan, as he answered, "I fear me he is infected by a distemper worse then the plague. I thank you, lads, for your kindly thoughts towards him and towards me, but I must e'en take this business into mine own hands. Get you away, and take your sister with you. It is not well for maids to be abroad in a city where such things can happen. Lord, indeed have mercy upon us!"

CHAPTER VI

NEIGHBOURS IN NEED

Gertrude Mason sat in the topmost attic of the house, leaning out at the open window, and drinking in, as it were, great draughts of fresh air, as she watched the lights beginning to sparkle from either side of the river, and the darkening volume of water slipping silently beneath.

This attic was Gertrude's haven of refuge at this dread season, when almost every other window in the house was shuttered and close-curtained; when she was kept like a prisoner within the walls of the house, and half smothered and suffocated by the fumes of the fires which her mother insisted on burning, let the weather be ever so hot, as a preventive against the terrible infection which was spreading with fearful rapidity throughout all London.

But Madam Mason's feet never climbed these steep ladder-like stairs up to this eyrie, which all her life had been dear to Gertrude. In her childhood it had been her playroom. As she grew older, she had gradually gathered about her in this place numbers of childish and girlish treasures. Her father bestowed gifts upon her at various times. She had clever fingers of her own, and specimens of her needlework and her painting adorned the walls. At such times as the fastidious

Evelyn Everett-Green

mistress of the house condemned various articles of furniture as too antiquated for her taste, Gertrude would get them secretly conveyed up here; so that her lofty bower was neither bare nor cheerless, but, on the contrary, rather crowded with furniture and knick-knacks of all sorts. She kept her possessions scrupulously clean, lavishing upon them much tender care, and much of that active service in manual labour which she found no scope for elsewhere. Her happiest hours were spent up in this lonely attic, far removed from the sound of her mother's plaints or her brother's ribald and too often profane jesting. Here she kept her books, her lute, and her songbirds; and the key of her retreat hung always at her girdle, and was placed at night beneath her pillow.

This evening she had been hastily dismissed from her father's presence, he having come in with agitated face, and bidden her instantly take herself away whilst he spoke with her mother. She had obeyed at once, without pausing to ask the questions which trembled on her lips. That something of ill had befallen she could not doubt; but at least her father was safe, and she must wait with what patience she could for the explanation of her sudden dismissal.

She knew from her brother's reports that already infected houses were shut up, and none permitted to go forth. But so straitly had she herself been of late imprisoned within doors, that she felt it would make but little difference were she to hear that a watchman guarded the door, and that the fatal red cross had been painted upon it.

"Our neighbours are not fearful as we are. They go to and fro in the streets. They seek to do what they can for the relief of the sick. My father daily speaks of their courage and faith. Why may not I do likewise? I would fain tend the sick, even though my life should be the forfeit. We can but live once and die once. Far sooner would I spend a short life of usefulness to my fellow men, than linger out a long and worthless existence in the pursuit of idle pleasures. It does not bring happiness. Ah! how little pleasure does it bring!"

Gertrude spoke half aloud and with some bitterness, albeit she strove to be patient with the foibles of her mother, and to think kindly of her, her many faults notwithstanding. But the terror of these days was taking with her a very different form from what it did with Madam Mason. It was inflaming within her a great desire to be up and doing in this stricken city, where the fell disease was walking to and fro and striking down its victims by hundreds and thousands. Other women, in all lands and of all shades of belief, had been found to come forward at seasons of like peril, and devote themselves fearlessly to the care of the sick. Why might not she make one of this band? What though it should cost her her life? Life was not so precious a thing to her that she should set all else aside to preserve it!

She was awakened from her fit of musing by an unwonted sound—a hollow tapping, tapping, tapping, which seemed to come from a corner of the attic where the shadows gathered most dun and dark. The girl drew in her head from the window with a startled expression on her face, and was then more than ever aware of the strange sound which caused a slight thrill to run through her frame.

What could it be? There was no other room in their house from which the sound could proceed. She was not devoid of the superstitious feelings of the age, and had heard before of ghostly tappings that were said to be a harbinger of coming death or misfortune.

Tap! tap! tap! The sound continued with a ceaseless regularity, and then came other strange sounds of wrenching and tearing. These were perhaps not quite so ghostly, but equally alarming. What could it be? Who and what could be behind that wall? Gertrude had heard stories of ghastly robberies, committed during these past days in plague-stricken houses, which were entered by worthless vagabonds, when all within were dead or helpless, and from which vantage ground they had gained access into other houses, and had sometimes brought the dread infection with them.

Gertrude was by nature courageous, and she had always made it a point of duty not to add to her mother's alarms by permitting herself to fall a victim to nervous terrors. Frightened though she undoubtedly was, therefore, she did not follow the impulse of her fear and run below to summon her father, who was, she suspected, bent on some serious work of his own; but she stood very still and quiet, pressing her hands over her beating heart, resolved if possible to discover the mystery for herself before giving any alarm.

All at once the sounds grew louder; something seemed to give way, and she saw a hand, a man's hand, pushed through some small aperture. At that she uttered a little cry.

"Who is there?" she cried, in a shaking voice; and imme-diately the hand was withdrawn, whilst a familiar and most reassuring voice made answer:

"Is anybody there? I beg ten thousand pardons. I had thought the attic would be hare and empty."

"Reuben!" cried Gertrude, springing forward towards the small aperture in the wall. "Oh, what is it? Is it indeed thou? And what art thou doing to the wall?"

"Gertrude! is that thy voice indeed? Nay, now, this is a good hap. Sweet Mistress Gertrude, have I thy permission to open once again betwixt thy home and mine that door which as children thy brother and we did contrive, but which was presently sealed up, though not over-strongly?"

"Ah, the door!" cried Gertrude, coming forward to the place and feeling with her hands at the laths and woodwork; "I had forgot, but it comes to me again. Yes, truly there was a rude door once. Oh, open it quickly! I will get thee a light and hold it. Dost thou know, Reuben, what has befallen to make my father look as he did but now? I trow it is something evil. My heart is heavy within me."

"Ay, I know," answered Reuben; "I will tell thee anon, sweet mistress, if thou wilt let me into thy presence."

"Nay, call me not mistress," said Gertrude, with a little accent of reproach in her voice. "Have we not played as brother and sister together, and do not times like this draw closer the bonds of friendship? Thou canst not know how lonesome and dreary my life has been of late. I pine for a voice from the world without. Thou wilt indeed be welcome, good Reuben."

Gertrude was busying herself with the tedious preparations for obtaining a light, and being skilful by long practice, she soon had a lamp burning in the room; and in a few minutes more, by the diligent use of hammer and chisel, Reuben forced open the little rough door which long ago had been contrived between the boys of the two households, and which had not been done away with altogether, although it had been securely fastened up by the orders of Madam Mason when she found her son Frederick taking too great advantage of this extra means of egress from the house, though she had other motives than the one alleged for the checking of the great intimacy which was growing up between her children and those of her neighbour.

The door once opened, Reuben quickly stood within the attic, and looked around him with wondering and admiring eyes.

"Nay, but it is a very bower of beauty!" he cried, and then he came forward almost timidly and took Gertrude by the hand, looking down at her with eyes that spoke eloquently.

"Is this thy nest, thou pretty songbird?" he said. "Had I known, I should scarce have dared to invade it so boldly."

Gertrude clung to him with an involuntary appeal for protection that stirred all the manhood within him.

"Ah, Reuben, tell me what it all means!" she cried, "for methinks that something terrible has happened."

Still holding the little trembling hand in his, Reuben told her of the peril her brother had been in. He spoke not of Dorcas, not desiring to pain her more than need be, but he had to say that her brother was, in a half-drunken state, pursuing some maiden in idle sport, and that, having been so exposed to contagion, there was great fear now for him and for his life.

Gertrude listened with pale lips and dilating eyes; her quick apprehension filled up more of the details than Reuben desired.

"It was Dorcas he was pursuing," she cried, recoiling and putting up her hands to her face; "I know it! I know it! O wretched boy! why does he cover us with shame like this? I marvel that thou canst look kindly upon me, Reuben. Am I not his most unhappy sister?"

"Thou art the sweetest, purest maiden my eyes ever beheld," answered Reuben, his words seeming to leap from his lips against his own will. Then commanding himself, he added more quietly, "But he is like to be punished for his sins, and it may be the lesson learned will be of use to him all his life. It will be a marvel if he escapes the distemper, having been so exposed, and that whilst inflamed by drink, which, so far as I may judge, enfeebles the tissues, and causes a man to fall a victim far quicker than if he had been sober, and a temperate liver."

"My poor brother!" cried Gertrude, beneath her breath. "Oh, what has my father done with him? What will become of him?"

"Your father brought him hither at once—not within the house, but into one of his old offices where in past times his goods were wont to be stored. He has now gone to consult with your mother whether or not the poor lad should be admitted within the house or not. If your mother will not have him here, he will remain for a while where he is; and if he falls sick, he will be removed to the pest house."

"Oh no! no! no!" cried Gertrude vehemently, "not whilst he has a sister to nurse him—a roof, however humble, to shelter him. Let him not die amongst strangers! I fear not the infection. I will go to him this minute. Already I have thought it were better to die of the plague, doing one's duty towards the sick and suffering, than to keep shut up away from all. They shall not take him away to die amidst those scenes of horror of which one has heard. Even my mother will be brave, methinks, for Frederick's sake. I trow she will open her doors to him."

"That is what your father thinks. It may be that even now he is bringing him within. But, sweet mistress, if Frederick comes here, it may well be that in another week this house will be straitly shut up, with the red cross upon the door, and the watchman before the portal day and night. That is why I have come hither at once, to open the little door between our houses; for I cannot bear the thought of knowing naught that befalls you for a whole long month. And since, though my work takes me daily into what men call the peril of infection, I am sound and bring no hurt to others, I am not afraid that I shall bring hurt to thee. I could not bear to have no tidings of how it fared with thee. Thou wilt not chide me for making this provision. It came into my head so soon as I knew that peril of infection was like to come within these walls. We must not let thee be shut quite away from us. We may be able to give thee help, and in times of peril neighbours must play a neighbourly part."

The tears stood in Gertrude's eyes. She was thinking of the unkindly fashion in which her mother had spoken of late years of these neighbours, and contrasting with that the way in which they were now coming forward to claim the neighbour's right to help in time of threatened trouble. The tears were very near her eyes as she made answer:

"O Reuben, how good thou art! But if our house be infected, how can it be possible for thee to come and go? Would it not be a wrong against those who lay down these laws for the preservation of the city?"

Then Reuben explained to her that, though the magistrates and aldermen were forced to draw up a strict code for the ordering of houses where infection was, these same personages themselves, together with doctors, examiners, and searchers of houses, had perforce to go from place to place; yet by using all needful and wise precautions, both for themselves and others, they had reasonable hope of doing nothing to spread the contagion. Reuben, as a searcher under his father, had again and again been in infected houses, and brought face to face with persons dying of the malady; yet so far he had escaped, and by adopting the wise precautions ordered at the outset by their father, no case of illness had appeared so far amongst them. If every person who could be of use excluded himself from all chance of contagion, there would be none to order the affairs of the unhappy city, or to carry relief to the sufferers. There must be perforce some amongst them who were ready to run the risk in order to assist the sufferers, and they of the household of James Harmer were all of one mind in this.

"We do naught that is rash. We have herbs and drugs and all those things which the doctors think to be of use; and thou shalt have a supply of all such anon—if indeed thy mother be not already amply provided. But I cannot bear for thee to be straitly shut up; I must be able to see how it goes with thee. And should it be that thou wert thyself a victim, thou shalt not lack the best nursing that all London can give."

She looked up at him with fearless eyes.

"Do men ever recover when once attacked by the plague?"

"Yes, many do—though nothing like the number who die. Amongst our nurses and bearers of the dead are numbers who have had the distemper and have survived it. They go by the name of the 'safe people.' Yet some have been known to take it again, though I think these cases are rare."

"If Frederick takes it, will he be like to live?" asked Gertrude; and Reuben was silent.

Both knew that the unhappy young man had long been given to drunkenness and debauchery, and that his constitution was undermined by his excesses. The girl pressed her hands together and was silent; but after a few moments' pause she looked up at Reuben, and said, "You have given me courage

Evelyn Everett-Green

by this visit. Come again soon. I must to my mother now. I must ask her what I can do to help her and my unhappy brother."

"Take this paper and this packet before you go," said Reuben. "The one contains directions for the better lodging and tending of the sick. The other contains prepared herbs which are useful as preventives—tormentil, valerian, zedoary, angelica, and so forth; but I take it that pure vinegar is as good an antidote to infection as anything one can find. Keep some always about you. Let your kerchief be always steeped in it. Then be of a cheerful courage, and take food regularly, and in sufficient quantities. All these things help to keep the body in health; and though the most healthy may fall victims, yet methinks that it is those who are underfed or weakened by disease or dissipation upon whom the malady fastens with most virulent strength. I will come anon and learn what is betiding. Farewell for the nonce, sweet mistress, and may God be with you."

Greatly cheered and strengthened by this unexpected interview, Gertrude descended to the lower part of the house in search of her mother, and found her, with her face tied up in a cloth soaked in vinegar, bending over the unhappy Frederick, who lay with a face as white as death upon a couch in one of the lower rooms.

To her credit be it said, the motherhood in the Master Builder's wife had triumphed over her natural terror at the thought of the infection. When her husband had brought her the news that Frederick was in one of the old shop buildings, awaiting her permission (after what had occurred) to enter the house; when she knew that should he sicken of the plague he would be taken away to the pest house to be tended there, and as she believed assuredly to die, she burst into wild weeping, and declared that she would risk everything sooner than that should happen. So it had been speedily arranged that the unhappy youth should be provided with a vinegar and herb bath and a complete change of raiment out there in the disused shop, and that then he should come into the house, his mother being willing to take the risk rather than banish him from home.

This had been quickly done, under the direction of good James Harmer, who as one of the examiners of health was well qualified to give counsel in the matter. He also told his neighbour that should the young man be attacked by the plague, he would strive if possible to gain for him the services of his sister-in-law, Dinah Morse, who was one of the most tender and skilful nurses now working amongst the sick. She was always busy; but so fell was the action of the plague poison, that her patients died daily, despite her utmost care, and she was constantly moving from house to house, sometimes leaving none alive behind her in a whole domicile. A certain number recovered, and these she made shift to visit daily for a while; but her main work lay amongst the dying, whose friends too often left them in terror so soon as the fatal marks appeared which bespoke them sickening of the terrible distemper.

The Master Builder received this promise with gratitude, having heard gruesome stories of the evil practices of many of those who called themselves plague nurses, but who really sought their own gain, and often left the patient alone and untended in his agony, whilst they coolly ransacked the house from which the other inmates had often contrived to flee before it was shut up.

Frederick, utterly unnerved and overcome by the horror of the thing which had befallen him, looked already almost like one stricken to death. His mother was striving to get him to swallow some of the medicines which were considered as

Evelyn Everett-Green

valuable antidotes, and to sip at a cup of so-called plague water—a rather costly preparation much in vogue amongst the wealthier citizens at that time. But the nausea of the horrible smell of the plague patient was still upon him, sickening him to the refusal of all medicine or food, and to Gertrude's eyes he looked as though he might well be smitten already.

Her father was the only person who had eyes to notice her approach, and he strode forward and took her by the hands as though to keep her away.

"Child, thou must not come here. Thy brother has been in a terrible danger—half strangled by a creature raving in the delirium of the distemper. It may be death to approach him even now. I would have had thy mother keep away. Come not thou near to him. Let us not increase the peril which besets us."

Gertrude stood quite still, neither resisting her father, nor yet yielding to the pressure which would have forced her from the room.

"Dear sir," she said, with dutiful reverence, "I must fain submit to thee in this thing. Yet I prithee keep me not from my brother in the hour of his extremity. Methinks that a more terrible thing than the plague itself is the cruel fear which it inspires, whereby families are rent asunder, and the sick are neglected and deserted in the hour of their utmost need. If indeed Frederick should fall a victim, this house will be straitly shut up; and if it be true what men say, the infection will spread through it, do what we will to keep it away. Then what can it matter whether the risk be a little more or less? Is it not better that I should be with my mother and my brother, than that I should seek my own safety by shutting myself up apart from all, a readier prey to grief and terror? Methinks I should the sooner fall ill thus shut away from all. Prithee let me take my place beside Frederick, and relieve my mother when she be weary; so do I think it will be best for me and her."

The father's face quivered with emotion as he took his daughter in his arms and kissed her tenderly.

"Thou shalt do as thou wilt, my sweet child," he said. "These indeed are fearful days, and it may be that happier are they who let their heart be ruled by love instead of by fear. Fear has become a cruel thing, from what men tell us. Thou shalt do thy desire. Yet methinks thy brother has scarce deserved this grace at thy hands."

"Let us not think of that," said Gertrude, with a look of pain in her eyes; "let us only think of his peril, and of the terrible retribution which may fall upon him. God grant that he may find repentance and peace at the last!"

"Amen!" said the Master Builder, with some solemnity, thinking of the fashion in which his son's time had been spent of late, and of the very escapade which had brought this evil upon him.

All that night mother and sister watched beside the bed of the unhappy young man, who moaned and tossed, and too often broke into blasphemous railings at the fate which had overtaken him. He gave himself up for lost from the first, and having no hope or real belief as regards the future life, was full of darkness and bitterness of heart. He would not so much as listen when Gertrude would have spoken to him of the Saviour's love for sinners, but answered with mocking and profane words which made her heart die within her.

Towards morning he fell into a restless sleep, from which he

Evelyn Everett-Green

wakened in a high fever, not knowing any of those about him. The father coming in, went towards him with a strange look in his eyes, and after bending over him a few seconds, turned a haggard face towards his wife and daughter, saying:

"May the Lord have mercy upon us! he has the tokens upon him!"

Instantly the mother uttered a scream of lamentation, and fell half senseless into her husband's arms; whilst Gertrude stood suddenly up with a white face and said:

"Let me take word to our neighbours next door. Master Harmer is an examiner. We must needs report it to him; and they will tell us what we must do, and give us help if any can."

"Ay, that they will," answered the Master Builder, with some emotion in his voice. "Go, girl, and report that the distemper has broken out in the house, and that we submit ourselves to the orders of the authorities for all such as be infected."

Gertrude sped upstairs. She preferred that method of transit to the one by the street door. But she had no need to go further than her attic; for upon opening the door she saw two figures in the room, and instantly recognized Reuben and his sister Janet. The latter came forward with outstretched hands, and would have taken Gertrude into her embrace, but that she drew back and said in a voice of warning:

"Take heed, Janet; touch me not. I have passed the night by the bedside of my brother, and he is stricken with the plague!"

"So soon?" quoth Reuben, quickly; whilst Janet would not be denied her embrace, saying softly:

"I have no longer a fear of that distemper myself, for I have been with it erstwhile, and my aunt Dinah tells me that I have had a very mild attack of the same ill, and that I am not like to take it again."

"If indeed Frederick is smitten, we must take precautions to close the house," said Reuben. "Is there aught you would wish to do ere giving the notice to my father?"

"Nay, I was on my way to him," said Gertrude, speaking with the calmness of one upon whom the expected blow has at last fallen. "Let what must be done be done quickly. Can we have a nurse? for methinks Frederick must needs have tendance more skilled than any we can give him. But let it not be one of those women"—Gertrude paused and shuddered, as though she knew not how to finish her sentence.

"Trust me to do all for you that lies in my power," answered Reuben, in a voice of emotion; "and never feel shut up altogether from the world; even when the outer door be locked and guarded by a watchman. I have already hung a bell within our house, and the cord is tied here upon this nail. In any time of need you have but to ring it, and be sure that the summons will be speedily answered."

A mist rose before Gertrude's eyes and a lump in her throat. She pressed Janet's hand, and said to Reuben in a husky voice:

"I have no words today. Some day I will find how to thank you for all this goodness at such a time."

Before many hours had passed Dinah Morse was installed beside the sick man. Strong perfumes were burnt in and about his room, and the terrible tumours which bespoke the poison in his blood were treated skilfully by poultices and medicaments, applied by one who thoroughly understood the nature of the disease and the course it ran.

But from the first it was apparent to a trained eye that the young man was doomed. There was too much poison in his blood before, and his constitution was undermined by his reckless and dissolute life. All that was possible was done to relieve the sufferings and abate the fever of the patient. One of the best and most devoted of the doctors who remained courageously at his post during this terrible time was called in. But he shook his head over the patient, and bid his parents make up their minds for the worst.

"You have the best nurse in all London," said Dr. Hooker. "If skill and care could save him, he would be saved. But I fear me the poison has spread all over. Be cautious how you approach him, for he breathes forth death to those who are not inoculated. I would I could do more for you, but our skill avails little before this dread scourge."

And so, with looks and words of friendly compassion and goodwill, the doctor took his departure; and before nightfall Frederick was called to his last account.

Just as the hour of midnight tolled, a sound of wheels was heard in the street below, a bell rang, and a lugubrious voice called out:

"Bring forth your dead! bring forth your dead!"

Directed by Reuben, who was on the alert, the bearers themselves entered the house and removed the body, wrapped in its linen swathings, but without a coffin, for by this time there was not such a thing to be had for love or money; nor could the carts have contained their loads had each corpse been coffined.

Gertrude alone, from an upper window, saw the body of her brother laid decently and reverently, under Reuben's direction, in the ominous-looking vehicle. For the mother of the dead youth was weeping her heart out in her husband's arms, and was not allowed to know at what hour nor in what manner her son's body was conveyed away.

"Will they fling him, with never a prayer, into some great pit such as I have heard spoken of?" asked Gertrude of Dinah, who stood beside her at the window, fearful lest she should be overwhelmed by the horror of it all.

She now drew her gently and tenderly back into the room, whilst the cart rumbled away upon its mournful errand, and smoothing the tresses of the girl, and drawing her to rest upon a couch hard by, she answered:

"Think not of that, dear child. For what does it matter what befalls the frail mortal body? With whatsoever burial we may be buried now, we shall rise again at the last day in glory and immortality! That is what we must think of in these sorrowful times. We must lift our hearts above the things of this world, and let our conversation and citizenship be in heaven."

Then the tears gushed out from Gertrude's eyes, and she wept freely and fully the healing tears of youth.

CHAPTER VII

SISTERS OF MERCY

"Father, dear father, prithee let me go!"

"What, my child? Have I not lost all but thee? Am I to send thee forth to thy death in this terrible city, stricken by the hand of God?"

Into Gertrude's face there crept a wonderful light and brightness. Her eyes shone with the intensity of her feeling.

"Father," she said, "it is even because I hold the city to be smitten by God that I ask thy permission to go forth to minister to the sick and stricken ones. It seems to me as though in my heart a voice had spoken, saying, 'Go, and I will be with thee.' Father, listen, I pray thee. I heard that voice first, methought, upon the terrible night when they came and took Frederick away. When mother was next laid low, and as I watched beside her, and watched likewise how Dinah soothed and comforted and assuaged her anguish of mind and body, the voice in my heart grew ever louder and louder. Whilst she lived, I knew my place was beside her; but it has pleased God to take her away. No tie binds me here now. If I stay, I shall but eat out my heart in fruitless longing, shut into these walls, and by no means permitted to sally forth. From a plague-stricken house I may only go to those smitten with the distemper. Father, let me go! prithee let me go! Dinah will take me; she will let me be with her. Ask her; she will tell thee."

As the girl made her appeal to her father, the grave-faced, gentle woman who had remained with this household for nigh fourteen days stood quietly by. Dinah Morse had not quitted the house since the day upon which the hapless Frederick had been stricken down by the fell disease. For hardly had his remains been borne from the house before the mother fell violently ill of a wasting fever. At first there were no special indications of the plague in her malady; but after a week's time these suddenly developed themselves. From the first she had declared herself smitten by the distemper, and whether this conviction helped to develop the germs of the malady none could say. But be that as it might, the dreaded tokens appeared upon her body at last, and within three days from that time she lay dead.

All that the kindness of friends and neighbours could avail had been done. The Harmer family, in particular, had showed so much attention and sympathy in this trying time, that Gertrude was often overcome with shame as she recalled in what uncivil fashion they had been treated by her mother of late years, and how they were now returning good for evil, just at a time when so many men were finding themselves forsaken even by their nearest and dearest in the hour of their affliction.

The whole experience through which she had passed had made a deep and lasting impression upon Gertrude. She had already watched two of the beings nearest and dearest to her fall victims to the dire disease which was raging in the city and laying low its thousands daily. It seemed to her that there was but one thing to be done now by those whose

Evelyn Everett-Green

circumstances permitted it, and that was to go forth amid the sick and smitten ones, and do what lay within human power to mitigate their sufferings, and to afford them the solace and comfort of feeling that they were not altogether shut off from the love and sympathy of their fellow men.

"Father," she urged, as she saw that her parent still hesitated, "what would have become of us without Dinah? What should we have done had no help come to us in our hour of need? Think of the hundreds and thousands about us longing for some such tendance and love as she brought hither to us! What would have become of us had no kind neighbours befriended us? And are we not bidden to do unto others as we would have them do unto us in like case?"

"But the risk, my child, the risk!" he urged. "Am I to lose my last and only stay and solace?"

"Mother died in this house, which is now doubly infected. I was with her and with Frederick both, and yet I am sound and whole, and thou also. Why should we so greatly fear, when no man can say who will be smitten and who will escape? Methinks, perchance, those who seek to do their duty to the living, as our good neighbours and the city aldermen and magistrates and doctors are doing, will be specially protected of God. Father, let me go! Truly I feel that I have been bidden. Here I should fret myself ill in fruitless longing. Let me go forth with Dinah. Let me obey the call which methinks God has sent me. Truly I think I shall be the safest so. And who can say in these days, take what precaution he will, that he may not already have upon him the dreaded tokens? If we must die, let us at least die doing good to our fellow men. Did not our Lord say to those who visited the sick in their necessity, 'Ye have done it unto me'?"

"Child," said the Master Builder, in a much-moved voice, "it shall be as you desire. Go; and may the blessing of God go with you. I will offer myself for any post, as searcher or examiner, which may be open, if indeed I may go forth from this house ere the twenty-eight days be expired. If Dinah will take you, and if the Harmers will let you both sally forth from the house, I will not keep you back. It may be indeed that God has called you; and if so, may He keep and bless you both."

Father and daughter embraced each other tenderly.

In those times the shadow of death was so very apparent that no one knew from day to day what might befall him ere the morrow. Strong men, leaving their homes apparently in their usual health, would sink down in the streets an hour afterwards, and perhaps die before the very eyes of the passersby, none of whom would be found willing so much as to approach the sufferer with a kind word. Men would hasten by with vinegar-steeped cloths held closely over their faces; and later on some bearer with a cart or barrow would be sent to carry away the corpse and fling it into the nearest pit, of which there was now an ever-increasing number in the various parishes.

It will well be understood that in such days as these the need for nurses for the sick was terribly great. The majority of those so-called nurses were women of the lowest class, whose motive was personal gain, not a loving desire to mitigate the sufferings of the stricken.

Whether all the dismal tales told by the miserable beings shut up in their houses, and left to the mercy of watchmen and nurses, were true may be well open to doubt. Many poor creatures became half demented by terror, and scarcely knew what they said. But enough was from time to time substantiated to prove how very terrible were the scenes

Evelyn Everett-Green

which sometimes went on within these sealed abodes; and more than once some careless watchman or thieving and neglectful nurse had been whipped through the streets for misdemeanours brought home to them by the authorities.

But now things were growing too pressing for individual cases to attract much attention. Do as men would to cope with the evil, the spread of the fell disease was something terrible to witness. Up till quite recently, the cases in the southern and eastern parishes and within the city walls had been few as compared with those in the north and west; but now the scourge seemed to have fallen upon the city itself, and the resources of the authorities were taxed to the uttermost.

The Harmer family welcomed back Dinah with joy; but when they heard of Gertrude's resolve, they looked grave and awed. Then Janet stepped forward suddenly, and addressing her father, said:

"Dear father, what Gertrude has desired for herself is nothing less than what I myself have often wished. Let me go forth also to tend the sick. If our neighbour can dare to let his only child do this thing, surely thou wilt spare me. Every day brings terrible tales of the woe and the pressing need of hundreds and thousands around us. Let me go, too. I am like to be safer than many, seeing that I may already have been touched by the distemper, though I knew it not."

The example of his neighbour was not without effect upon the worthy citizen. Moreover, it seemed to him that those who went about their daily duties, and shrank not from contact with the sick when it was needful, fared better than many who shut themselves up at home, and feared to look forth even from their windows. As an examiner of health he was frequently brought into contact with the sick, and his son even oftener, and yet both kept their health wonderfully. True, there were many amongst those who filled these perilous offices who did fall victims, but not more in proportion than others who shunned all contact with peril. Steady nerves and a stout heart seemed as good preventives as any antidote; and the physicians who laboured ceaselessly and devotedly amongst the stricken ones seemed seldom to suffer. Moreover, after all these weeks of terror, the minds of persons of all degrees were growing used to the sense of uncertainty and peril, and Janet's request aroused no very strenuous opposition from any member of her family.

"She shall please herself," said her father, after some discussion on the subject. "God has been very merciful to us so far. We will put our trust in Him during all this time. If the girl has had a call, let her do her duty, and He will he with her."

That night the three devoted women slept beneath the roof of the bridge house. Upon the morrow they sallied forth to their strange task, but were told by the master of the house that they might return thither at any time they chose, provided they took the prescribed precautions with regard to their clothing before they entered.

The sun was blazing hotly down on the streets as they opened the door to go forth. Sultry weather had now set in, no rain fell through the long, scorching days, and the heat was a terrible factor in the spread of the epidemic. Dinah, who had been nigh upon fourteen days shut up in one house, looked about her with grave, watchful eyes. Already she saw a great difference in the look of the bridge. Four houses were marked with the ominous red cross; and the tide of traffic, bearing the stream of persons out from the stricken city, had almost ceased. Bills of health were difficult to obtain now. The country villages round were loth to receive inmates of

London. All roads were watched, and many hapless stragglers sent back again who had thought to escape from the city of destruction. Myriads had already left, and others were still flying—they could make shift to escape. But the continuous stream had ceased to cross the bridge. Foot passengers were few, and all walked in the middle of the road, avoiding contact with one another. Many kept a handkerchief or cloth pressed to their faces. Strangers eyed each other askance, none knowing that the other might not be already sickening of the disease. Between the stones of the streets blades of grass were beginning to grow up. Dinah pointed to these tokens and gave a little sigh.

Just before they turned off from the bridge a flying figure was seen approaching, and Janet exclaimed quickly:

"Why, it is Dorcas!"

Since her fright of a fortnight back, Dorcas had remained an inmate of Lady Scrope's house by her own desire. Although she knew that poor Frederick would annoy her no more, she had come to have a horror of the very streets themselves. She had never forgotten the apparition of that white-robed figure, clad in what seemed like its death shroud; and as Lady Scrope was by no means ill pleased to keep her young maiden by night as well as by day, her father was glad that she should be saved the risk even of the short walk to and fro each day.

But here she was, flying homewards as though there were wings to her feet; and she would almost have passed them in her haste, had not Janet laid hold of her arm and spoken her name aloud. Then she gave a little cry of relief and happiness, and turning upon her aunt, she cried:

"Ah, how glad I am to see thee! I was praying thou mightst

still be at home. Lady Scrope has been suddenly seized by some malady, I know not what. Everyone in the house but the old deaf man and his wife has fled. Three servants left before, afraid of passing to and fro. The rest only waited for the first alarm to seize whatever they could lay hands upon and fly. I could not stop them. I did what I could, but methinks they would have rifled the house had it not been that the mistress, ill as she was, rose from her bed and chased them forth. They feared her more than ever when they thought she had the plague upon her. And now I have come forth for help; for I am alone with her in the house, and I know not which way to turn.

"Ah, good aunt, come back with me, I prithee. I am at my wit's end with the fear of it all."

Without a moment's delay the party turned towards the house in Allhallowes, and speedily found themselves at the grim-looking portal, which Dorcas opened with her key. The house felt cool and fresh after the glare of the hot streets. Although by no means a stately edifice outside, it was roomy and commodious within, and the broad oak staircase was richly carpeted—a thing in those days quite unusual save in very magnificent houses. Doors stood open, and there were traces of confusion in some of the rooms; but Dorcas was already hurrying her companions up the stairs, and the silence of the house was broken by the sound of a shrill voice demanding in imperious tones who were coming and what was their business.

"Fear not, mistress, it is I!" cried Dorcas, springing forward in advance of the others.

She disappeared within an open door, and her companions heard the sharp tones of the answering voice saying:

"Tush, child! who talks of fear? It is only fools who fear! Dost think I am scared by this bogey talk of plague? A colic, child—a colic; that is all I ail. I have always suffered thus in hot weather all my life. Plague, forsooth! I could wish I had had it, that I might have given it as a parting benediction to those knaves and hussies who thought to rob me when I lay a-dying, as many a woman has been robbed before! I only hope they may sicken of pure fright, as has happened to many a fool before now! Ha! ha! ha! how they did run! They thought I was tied by the leg for once. But I had them—I had them! I warrant me they did not take the worth of a sixpence from my house!"

The chuckling laugh which followed bespoke a keen sense of enjoyment. Certainly this high-spirited old lady was not much like the ordinary plague patient. Dinah knocked lightly at the door, and entered, the two girls following her out of sheer curiosity.

"Heyday! and who are these?" cried Lady Scrope.

That redoubtable old dame was sitting up in bed, her great frilled nightcap tied beneath her chin, her hawk's eyes full of life and fire, although her face was very pinched and blue, and there were lines about her brow and lips which told the experienced eyes of the sick nurse that she was suffering considerable pain.

Dinah explained their sudden appearance, and asked if they could be of any service. The old lady gazed at them all in turn, and her face relaxed as she broke into rather a grim laugh.

"Plague nurses, by all the powers! Certes, this is very pretty company! If all that is said be true, ye be the worst harpies of all. I had better have my own minions to rob me than be left to your tender mercies. Three of you, too! Verily, 'wheresoever the carcase is, there will the eagles be gathered together,'" and the patient laughed again, as though tickled at her own grim pleasantry.

Dorcas would have expostulated and explained and apologized, but her mistress cut her short with a sharp tap of her fan.

"Little fool, hold thy peace! as though I didn't know an honest face when I see it!"

"Come, good people, look me well over, and you'll soon see I have none of the tokens. It is but a colic, such as I am well used to at this season of the year; but in these days let a body's finger but ache, and all the world runs helter skelter this way and that, calling out, 'The plague! the plague!' The plague, forsooth! as though I had not lived through a score of such scares of plague. If men would but listen to me, there need never be any more plagues in London. But the fools will not hear wisdom."

"What is your remedy, madam?" asked Dinah, who saw very clearly that the old lady had gauged her symptoms aright; and although she had alarmed her attendants by a partial collapse an hour before, was mending now, and had no symptom of the distemper upon her.

"My remedy is too simple for fools. Fill up every well in London—which is just a poison trap—and drink only New River water, and make every house draw its supply from thence, and we shall soon cease to hear of the plague! That's my remedy; but when I tell men so, they gibe and jeer and call me fool for my pains. Fools every one of them! If it would only please Providence to burn their city about their ears and fill up all the old wells with the rubbish, you would soon see an end of these scares of plague. Tush! if men will drink rank poison they deserve to have the plague—that is all I have to say to them."

Such an idea as this was certainly far in advance of the times, and it was small wonder that Lady Scrope found no serious listeners when she propounded her scheme. Dinah did not profess to have an opinion on such a wide question. Her duties were with the sick. Others must seek for the cause of the outbreak. That was not the province of women.

Something in her way of moving about and performing her little offices pleased the fancy of the capricious old woman, as did also the aspect of the two girls, who were assisting Dorcas to set the room to rights after the confusion of the morning, when the mistress had suddenly been taken with a violent colic, which had turned her blue and rigid, and had convinced her household that she was taken for death, and that by a seizure of the prevailing malady.

She asked Dinah of herself and her plans, and nodded her head with approval as she heard that the two girls were to attend the sick likewise under her care.

"Good girls, brave girls—I like to see courage in old and young alike. If I were young myself, I vow I would go with you. It's a fine set of experiences you will have.

"Young woman, I like you. I shall want to hear of you and your work. Listen to me. This house is my own. I have no one with me here save the child Dorcas, and I don't think she is of the stuff that would be afraid; and I take good care of her, so that she is in no peril. Come back hither to me whenever you can. This house shall be open to you. You can come hither for rest and food. It is better than to go to and fro where there be so many young folks as in the place you come from. Bring the girls with you, too. They be good, brave maidens, and deserve a place of rest. I have victualled my house well. I have enough and to spare. I like to hear the news, and none can know more in these days than a plague nurse.

"Come, children, what say you to this? Go to and fro amongst the sick; but come home hither and tell me all you have done. What say you? Against rules for persons to pass from infected houses into clean ones? Bah! in times like these what can men hope to do by their rules and regulations? Plague nurses and plague doctors are under no rules. They must needs go hither and thither wherever they are called. If I fear not for myself, you need not fear for me. I shall never die of the plague; I have had my fortune told me too many times to fear that! I shall never die in my bed—that they all agree to tell me. Have no fears for me; I have none for myself.

"Make this house your home, you three good women. I am not a good woman myself, but I know the kind when I see them. They are rare, but all the more valued for that. Come, I say; you will not find a better place!"

Dorcas clasped her hands in rapture and looked from one to the other. The fear of the distemper was small in comparison with the pleasure of the thought of seeing her sister and aunt and friend at intervals, now that she was so completely shut up in this lonely house, and that the servants had all fled never to return.

It was just such an eccentric and capricious whim as was eminently characteristic of Lady Scrope. She had had nothing but her own whims to guide her through life, and she indulged them at her pleasure. She had taken a fancy to Dinah from the first moment. She knew all about the family of her young companion, from having listened to Dorcas's chatter when in the mood. Keenly interested in the spread of the plague, which had driven away all her fashionable friends, she was eager for news about it, and the more ghastly the tales that were told, the more did she seem to revel in them. To have news first hand from those who actually tended the sick seemed to her a capital plan; and Dinah recognized at once the advantage of having admittance for herself and the two girls to this solitary and commodious house, where rest and refreshment could be readily obtained, and where their coming and going would not be likely to be observed or to hurt any one.

"If your ladyship really means it—" she began.

"My ladyship generally does mean what she says—as Dorcas will tell you if you ask her," was the rather short, sharp reply. "Say no more, say no more; I hate chitter-chatter and shilly-shally. The thing's settled, and there's an end of it. Go your ways, go your ways; I'm none too ill for Dorcas to look to, now that the little fool is assured that I haven't got the plague. But you may have brought it here yourself, so you are bound in duty to come back and look after us the first moment you can. Go along with you all, and bring me word what London is doing, and what the streets are like. They say there be courts down in the worst parts of the town where not a living person remains, and where there be none left to give notice of the deaths. You go and bring me word about all that.

"A fine thing truly for our grand city! The living soon will not be enough to bury the dead! Go! go! go! I shall wait and watch for your return. None will interfere with anything that goes on in my house. You can come and go at will. Dorcas will give you a key. I will trust you. You have a face to be trusted."

"It is quite true—nobody ever dares interfere with her," said Dorcas, as she led the way downstairs. "They think she is a witch; and truly, methinks she is the strangest woman that ever drew breath! But I shall love her for what she has said and done today. I pray you be not long in coming again. None can want you much more sorely than I do!"

CHAPTER VIII

IN THE DOOMED CITY

The clocks in the church steeples were chiming the hour of ten as Dinah and her two companions started forth a second time upon their errand of mercy and charity. It was an hour at which in ordinary times all the city should be alive, the streets filled with passersby, wagons lumbering along with heavy freights, fine folks in their coaches or on horseback picking their way from place to place, and shopmen or their apprentices crying their wares from open doorways.

Now the streets were almost empty. The shops were almost all shut up. Here and there an open bake house was to be seen, orders having been issued that these places were to remain available for the public, come what might; and women or trembling servant maids were to be seen going to and fro with their loads of bread or dough for baking.

But each person looked askance at the other. Neighbours were afraid to pause to exchange greetings, and hurried away from all contact with one another; and children breaking away from their mothers' sides were speedily called back, and chidden for their temerity.

Some of the churches stood wide open, and persons were

seen to hurry in, lock themselves for a few minutes into separate pews, and pour out their souls in supplication. Often the sound of lamentation and weeping was heard to issue from these buildings. At certain hours of the day such of the clergy as were not scared away through fear of infection, or who were not otherwise occupied amongst the sick, would come in and address the persons gathered there, or read the daily office of prayer; but although at first these services had been well attended—people flocking to the churches as though to take sanctuary there—the widely-increased mortality and the fearful spread of the distemper had caused a panic throughout the city. The magistrates had issued warnings against the assembling of persons together in the same building, and the congregations were themselves so wasted and decimated by death and disease that each week saw fewer and fewer able to attend.

From every steeple in the city the bells tolled ceaselessly for the dead. But it was already whispered that soon they would toll no more, for the deaths were becoming past all count, and there might likely enough be soon no one left to toll.

At one open place through which Dinah led her companions, a tall man, strangely habited, and with a great mass of untrimmed hair and beard, was addressing a wild harangue to a ring of breathless listeners. In vivid and graphic words he was summing up the wickedness and perversity of the city, and telling how that the wrath of God had descended upon it, and that He would no longer stay His hand. The day of mercy had gone by; the day of vengeance had come—the day of reckoning and of punishment. The innocent must now perish with the guilty, and he warned each one of his hearers to prepare to meet his Judge.

The man was gazing up overhead with eyes that seemed ready to start from their sockets. Every face in the crowd

Evelyn Everett-Green

grew pale with horror. The man seemed rooted to the spot with a ghastly terror. They followed the direction of his gaze, but could see nothing save the quivering sunshine above them.

Suddenly one in the crowd gave a shriek which those who heard it never forgot, and fell to the ground like one dead.

With a wild, terrible laugh the preacher gathered up his long gown and fled onwards, and the crowd scattered helter skelter, terrified and desperate. None seemed to have a thought for the miserable man smitten down before their very eyes. All took care to avoid approaching him in their hasty flight. He lay with his face upturned to the steely, pitiless summer sky. A woman coming furtively along with a market basket upon her arm suddenly set up a dolorous cry at sight of him, and setting down her basket ran towards him, the tears streaming down her face.

"Why, it is none other than good John Harwood and his wife Elizabeth!" cried Janet, making a forward step. "Oh, poor creatures, poor creatures! Good aunt, prithee let us do what we can for their relief. I knew not the man, his face was so changed, but I know him now. They are very honest, good folks, and have worked for us ere now. They live hard by, if so be they have not changed their lodgings. Can we do nothing to help them?"

"We will do what we can," said Dinah. "Remember, my children, all that I have bidden you do when approaching a stricken person. Be not rash, neither be over-much affrighted. The Lord has preserved me, and methinks He will preserve you, too."

With that she stepped forward and laid a hand upon the shoulder of the poor woman, who was weeping copiously over her husband, and calling him by every name she could think of, though he lay rigid with half-open eyes and heeded her not.

"Good friend," said Dinah, in her quiet, commanding fashion, "it is of no avail thus to weep and cry. We must get your goodman within doors, and tend him there. See, there is a man with a handcart over yonder. Go call him, and bid him come to our help. We must not let your goodman lie out here in the streets in this hot sunshine."

"God bless you! God bless you!" cried the poor distracted woman, unspeakably thankful for any help at a time when neighbours and friends were wont alike to flee in terror from any stricken person. "But alas and woe is me! Tell me, is this the plague?"

"I fear so," answered Dinah, who had bent over the smitten man; "but go quickly and do as I have said. There be some amongst the sick who recover. Lose not heart at the outset, but trust in God, and do all that thou art bidden."

The woman ran quickly, and the man, who was indeed one of those forlorn creatures who, for a livelihood, were even willing to scour the streets and remove from thence those that were stricken down by death as they went their way amongst their fellows, came with her at her request, and lifting her husband into his cart, wheeled him away towards a poor alley where lay her home.

As she turned into it she looked at the three women who followed, and said:

"God have mercy upon us! I would not have you adventure yourselves here. There be but three houses in all the street where the distemper has not come, and of those, mine, which was one, must now be shut up. Lord have mercy upon us indeed, else we be all dead men!"

Dinah paused for a brief moment, and looked at her young charges.

"My children," she said, "needs must that I go where the need is so great. But bethink you a moment if ye have strength and wish to follow. I know not what sad and terrible sights we may have to encounter. Think ye that ye can bear them? Have ye the strength to go forward? If not, I would have you go back ere you have reached the contamination."

Janet looked at Gertrude, and Gertrude looked at Janet; but though there was great seriousness and awe in their faces, there was no fear. Gertrude had gone through so much already within the walls of her home that she had no fear greater than that of remaining in helpless idleness there, alone with her own thoughts and memories. As for Janet, she had much of the nature of her aunt—much of that eager, intense sympathy and compassion for the sick and suffering which has induced women in all ages to go forth in times of dire need, and risk their lives for their stricken and afflicted brethren.

So after one glance of mutual comprehension and sympathy, they both answered in one breath:

"No, we will not turn back. We will go with you. Where the need is sorest, there would we be, too."

"God bless you! God bless you for angels of mercy!" sobbed the poor woman, who heard their words, and knowing both Dinah and Janet, understood something of the situation, "for we be perishing like sheep here in this place, shut away from all, and with never a nurse to come nigh us. There be some rough fellows placed outside the houses to see that none go in or out, and perchance they do their best to find nurses; but at such a time as this it is small wonder if ofttimes none are to be found. And some they have brought are worse than none. The Lord protect us from the tender mercies of such!"

The narrow court into which they now turned was cool in comparison with the sunny street; but there was nothing refreshing in the coolness, for fumes of every sort exhaled from the houses, and at the far end there burned a fire of resinous pine logs, the smoke from which, when it rolled down the court, was almost choking.

"They say it will check the spread of the distemper to the streets beyond," said the woman, "but methinks it does as much harm as good. If the Lord help us not, we be all dead men. The cart took away a score or more of corpses last night. Pray Heaven it take not away my poor husband tonight!"

The bearer of the handcart stopped at the door indicated by the woman, and lifted the stricken man in his arms. It was one of the very few doors all down that street which did not bear the ominous red cross.

As Gertrude looked up and down the court her heart sank within her for pity. The houses were closed. Watchers lounged at the doors, drinking and smoking and jesting together, being by this time recklessly and brutally hardened to their office. They knew not from day to day when their own turn might come; but this knowledge seemed to have an evil rather than a sobering effect upon them.

The better sort of watchmen were employed, as a rule, to keep the better sort of houses. When these crowded courts and alleys were attacked, the authorities had to send whom

Evelyn Everett-Green

they could rather than whom they would. Indefatigable and courageously as they worked, the magnitude of the calamity was such that it taxed their resources to the utmost; and had it not been for the bountiful supplies of money sent in by charitable people, from the king downwards, for the relief of the city in this time of dire need, thousands must have perished from actual want, as well as those who fell victims to the plague itself. Yet do as these brave and devoted men could, the sufferings of the poor at this time were terrible.

As the sound of voices was heard in the street below, windows were thrown up, and heads protruded with more or less of caution. From one of the windows thus thrown up there issued a lamentable wailing, and a woman with a white, wild face cried out in tones of passionate entreaty:

"Help! help! help! good people. Ah, if that be a nurse, let her come hither. There be five dying and two dead in the house, and none but me to tend them, and methinks I am stricken to the death!"

"Janet," said Dinah, with a searching glance at her niece, "methinks I must needs answer that cry. Go with this good woman, and do what thou canst for her husband. Thou dost know what is best to be done. I will come to thee anon; but thou wilt not fear to be thus left? There is but one sick in this house. The need is sorer elsewhere."

"Go, I will do my best. At least I can make a poultice, and see that he is put to bed. I have medicaments in my bag. I would not hinder thee. Sure there is work for all in this terrible place!"

"And this is only one of many scattered throughout the city!" breathed Gertrude softly, her heart swelling within her.

Ever since she had halted before this house she had been aware of the sound of plaintive weeping and wailing proceeding from the adjoining tenement; and as Dinah moved away towards the door opposite, she asked Elizabeth Harwood what the sound meant, and if there was trouble in the next house.

"Trouble?—trouble and death everywhere!" was the answer. "The man was taken away in the cart yesternight. God alone knows who is alive in the house now. There be seven little children there with their mother, but which of them be living and which dead by now no one knows. I have heard nothing of the woman's voice these many hours. Pray Heaven she be not dead—and the little helpless children all alone with the dead corpse!"

"Oh, surely that could not be!" cried Gertrude. "Surely the watchman would go to them! Oh, that must not be! I will go and speak with him. He would not leave them to perish so!"

The woman shook her head, and hurried up the stairs whither her husband had been carried. Her heart was too full of her own anxious misery to have room for more than a passing sympathy for the needs and troubles of others.

But Gertrude could not rest. She neither followed Janet into this house nor her aunt across the street. She went to the door of the next house, upon which the red cross had been painted; and seeing her so stand before it, a man detached himself from a group hard by and asked her business, since the house was closed.

"I am a nurse," answered Gertrude, boldly. "I have come to nurse the sick. Let me into this house, I pray, for I hear the need is very sore."

"Sore enough, mistress," answered the man, fumbling with his key, for of course there was admittance to plague nurses and doctors into infected houses; "but if you take my advice, you'll not venture within the door. The dead cart has had four from it these last two days. Like enough by this time they are all dead. They have asked for nothing these past ten hours—not since the cart came last night."

With a shudder of pity and horror, but without any personal shrinking, Gertrude signed to the man to open the door, which he proceeded to do in a leisurely manner. Then she stepped across the threshold, the door was closed behind her, and she heard the key turn in the lock.

Truly her work had now begun. She was incarcerated in a plague-stricken house, and this time by her own will.

For the first few seconds she stood still in the dark entry, unable to see her way before her; but soon her eyes grew used to the dim light, and she saw that there was a door on one side of the passage and a steep flight of stairs leading upwards, and it was from some upper portion of the house from which the sound of crying proceeded.

Just glancing into the lower room, which she found quite empty, and which was unexpectedly clean, she mounted the rickety staircase, the wailing sound growing more distinct every step she took. The house was a very tiny one even for these small tenements, and there were only two little rooms upon the upper floor. It was from one of these that the crying was proceeding, but Gertrude could not be sure which.

With a beating heart she opened the first door, and saw a sight which went to her heart. Upon a narrow bed lay two little forms wrapped in the same sheet, rigidly still, waiting their last transit to the common grave. Except for the two dead children the room was empty, and Gertrude, softly closing the door, and breathing a silent prayer, she scarce knew whether for herself, for the living, or for the dead, she opened the other, and came upon a scene, the pathos and inexpressible sadness of which made a lasting impression upon her, which even after events did not efface from her memory.

There was a bed in this room too, and upon it lay the emaciated form of a woman; asleep, as the girl first thought—dead, as she afterwards quickly discovered. By her side there nestled a little child, hardly more than an infant, wailing pitifully with that plaintive, persistent cry which had attracted her attention at the outset. Three children, varying in age from four to eight, sat huddled on the floor in a corner, their tear-stained faces all turned in wondering expectancy upon the newcomer. Stretched upon the floor beside the bed was another child, so still that Gertrude felt from the first that it, too, was dead, and when she lifted up the little form, she saw the dreaded death tokens upon the waxen skin.

With a prayer in her heart for grace and strength and guidance, Gertrude laid the dead child beside its dead mother—for she saw that the woman was cold and stiff in death; and then she gathered the living children round her, and taking the infant in her arms, she led them all down into the lower room, and quickly kindled the fire that was laid ready in the grate.

She found nothing of any sort in the house, and the children were crying for food; but the watchman quickly provided what was needful, being, perhaps, a little ashamed of the condition in which this household had been found.

Gertrude tended and fed and comforted the little ones, her heart overflowing with sympathy. They clung about her and

Evelyn Everett-Green

fondled her as children will do those who have come to them in their hour of dire necessity; and as their hunger became appeased, and they grew confident of the kindness of their new friend, they told their pathetic tale with the unconscious graphic force of childhood.

There had been a large household only a few days before. Father, mother, two grownup sons, and one or two daughters—evidently by a former marriage. The big brothers had gone away—probably to act as bearers or watchmen— and the little ones knew nothing of them. One of the sisters had been in service, but came home suddenly, complaining of illness, sat down in a chair, and died almost before they realized she was ill. They had kept that death a secret, had obtained a certificate of some other ailment than the distemper, and for a week all had gone on quietly, when suddenly three became ill together.

Numbers of houses were shut up all round them. Theirs was reported and closed. For a few days there had been hope. Then the father sickened, and all the grownup persons had died almost together, save the mother, and had been taken away the night before last.

What had happened since was dim and confused to the children. Their mother had seemed like one stunned—had hardly noticed them, or attended to their wants. Then two of them had been taken away into the other room. They had heard their mother weeping aloud for a while, but she would not let them in to her. By and by she had come back to them, and had taken the baby in her arms and lain down upon the bed. She had never moved after that—not even when little Harry had called to her, and had lain crying and moaning on the floor. The children thought she was asleep, and by and by Harry had gone to sleep too. They had slept together on the floor, huddled together in helpless misery and confusion of mind, until awakened by the ceaseless wailing of the baby, which never roused their mother. They were too much bewildered and weakened to make any attempt to call for help, and were just waiting for what would happen, when Gertrude had come amongst them like an angel of mercy.

Her tears fell fast as the story was told, but the children had shed all theirs. They were comforted now, feeling as though something good had happened, and they crept about her and clung round her, begging her not to leave them.

Nor had she any wish to do so. It seemed to her as though this must surely be her place for the present—amongst these helpless little ones to whom Providence had sent her in the hour of their extreme necessity.

The baby was sleeping in her arms. She looked down into its tiny face, and wondered if it would be possible that its life could be saved. For a whole night it had lain at its dead mother's side. Could it have escaped the contagion? The three older children appeared well, and even grew merry as the hours wore slowly away.

From time to time Gertrude looked out into the street, but there was nothing to be seen save the men on guard; and only from time to time was the silence broken by the cry of some delirious patient, or a shriek for mercy from some half-demented woman driven frantic by the terrors by which she was surrounded.

When afternoon came, she prepared more food for the children, and partook of it with them, and wondered how and where she should spend the night. The infant in her arms had grown strangely still and quiet. It could not be roused, and breathed slowly and heavily.

"Harry looked just like that before he went to sleep," said the eldest of the children, coming and peeping into the small waxen face; and Gertrude gave a little involuntary shiver as she thought of the four still forms lying sleeping upstairs, and wondered whether this would make a fifth for the bearers to carry forth at night.

Just as the dusk began to fall, there came the sound of a slight parley without. Then the key turned in the house door, and the next minute, to Gertrude's unspeakable relief, Dinah entered the room.

"My poor child, did you think I was never coming to you?"

"I did not know if you could," answered Gertrude. "Oh, tell me, what must I do for all these little ones—and for the baby? Is he dying too? It is so long since he has moved. I am afraid to look at him lest I disturb him, but—but—"

Dinah bent over the little form, and lifted it gently from Gertrude's arms.

"Poor little lamb, its troubles are all over," she said, after a few moments. "The little ones often go like that—quite peacefully and quietly. It has not suffered at all. It has been a gentle and merciful release. You need not weep for it, my child."

"I think my tears are for the living rather than for the dead," answered Gertrude, with brimming eyes. "There are but three left out of seven living yesterday, and what is to become of them?"

"We must report their case to the authorities. There are numbers of poor children left thus orphaned, and it is hard to know what will become of them. I will send at once to my brother-in-law, and report the matter to him. He will know what it were best to do. Meantime I shall remain here with you. Janet is busy next door. Her patient is mending, and none besides in the house is sick. But oh, the things I have seen and heard this day! There is not one living now in the house to which I went first, and I have seen ten men and women die since I saw you last.

"God alone knows how it is to end. It seems as though His hand were outstretched, and as though the whole city were doomed!"

CHAPTER IX

JOSEPH'S PLAN

"Ben, boy, I am sick to death of sitting at home doing naught, and seeing naught of all the sights that be abroad, and of which men are for ever speaking. What boots it to be alive, if one is buried or shut up as we are? Art thou afraid to come forth? or shall I go alone?"

"Where wilt thou go, brother?" asked Ben, looking up from a bit of wood carving upon which he was engrossed, with an eager light in his eyes. Perhaps these two young lads had felt the calamity which had befallen the city more than any one else in the house; for whilst the father, mother, sisters, and two elder sons were all hard at work doing all in their power for the relief of the sick, the younger lads were kept at home, to be as far as possible out of harm's way, and they had felt the confinement and idleness as most irksome. Their mother employed them about the house when she could, but it was not much she could find for them to do. To be sure there was some amusement to be found in watching the life on the river; for though traffic was suspended, many whole families were living on board vessels moored on the river, and hoped by this device to keep the plague away from them. Yet the time hung very heavy on their hands, and the stories of the increasing ravages of the plague could not but depress them, seeming as they did to lengthen out indefinitely the time of their captivity.

Three of the sisters were practically living away from the house (of which more anon), and the loneliness of the silent house was becoming unbearable. To lads used to an active life and plenty of exercise, the distemper itself seemed a less evil than this close confinement between four walls. The bridge houses did not even possess yards or strips of garden, and without venturing out into the streets—which had for some weeks been forbidden by their father—the boys could not stir beyond the walls of their home.

August had now come, a close, steaming, sultry August, and the plague was raging with a virulence that threatened to destroy the whole city. The Bills of Mortality week by week were appalling in magnitude; and yet those who knew best the condition of the lower courts and alleys were well aware that no possible record could be kept of those crowded localities, where whole households and families, even whole streets, were swept away in the course of a few days, and where there were sometimes none left to give warning and notice that there were dead to be borne away. So the registered deaths could only show a certain proportionate accuracy; for even the dead carts could keep no reckoning of the numbers they bore to the common grave, and the bearers themselves were too often stricken down in the performance of their ghastly duties, and shot by their comrades into the pit amongst those whom they had carried forth an hour before.

It was small wonder that the father had forbidden his younger sons to adventure themselves in the streets, where the pestilence seemed to hang in the very air. But the magnitude of the peril was beginning to rob even the most cautious persons of any confidence in their methods, for it seemed as if those working hardest amongst the sick and dead were quite as much preserved from peril as those who shunned their neighbours and never came abroad unless dire necessity compelled them. Indeed, despite many deaths of individuals, it began to be noted that the magistrates, aldermen, examiners of health, and nurses of the plague-stricken sickened and died less, in proportion, than almost any other class. And of the physicians who remained at their posts to tend the sick, not many died, although some few here and there were stricken, and of these a certain proportion succumbed. But, as a whole, the workers who toiled with a good heart and gentle spirit amongst the sick (not just for daily bread or love of gain) fared better in the prevailing mortality than many others who held themselves aloof and lived in deadly fear of the pestilence. Wherefore it was not strange that at the last a sort of recklessness was bred amongst the citizens, and they kept themselves less close now when things were in so terrible a pass than they had done when the deaths were fewer and the conditions less fatal.

James Harmer had always been one of those who had put his confidence more in the providence of God than in any merely human precautions, and although he had always insisted upon prudence and care, he had steadily discouraged in his household any of that feeling of panic or of despair which he believed had been a strong factor in the spread of the distemper in its earlier stages. He also agreed in part with Lady Scrope's views regarding the water supply of the city— the old wells and the contaminated river water. He let nothing be drunk in his house save what was supplied from the New River, and he impressed the same advice upon all his neighbours.

But to return to the boys and their weariness of the shut-up life of the house. The heat had grown intolerable, their pining after fresh air and liberty was become too strong for resistance. Benjamin's eyes glowed at the very thought of escape from the region of streets and shut-up houses, and he drank in the sense of his brother's words eagerly.

"Hark ye," cried Joseph, in a rapid undertone, for they did not wish their mother to overhear them, she being by many degrees more fearful than their father, as was but natural, "why should we stay pent up here day after day and week after week, when even the girls be permitted abroad, and go into the very heart of the peril? We cannot be nurses to the sick, I know right well; neither can we help to search houses, or do such like things, as the elder ones. But why do we tarry at home eating our hearts out, when the whole world is before us, and there be such wondrous things to see?

"Listen, Ben. I have a plan. Let us but once get free of this house, and be our own masters, and we will wander about London as we will, and see those things of which all men be speaking. I long to look into one of those yawning pits where they shoot the dead, and to see the grass growing in the city, and to hear some of those strange preachers who go about prophesying in the streets. I long for liberty and freedom. I would sooner die of the plague at last than fret my heart out shut up here. And we may be smitten as well at home as abroad, as even father says himself."

"Why, so we may; and methinks more are smitten so than those who go forth and breathe the air without!" cried Benjamin. "Our aunt lives amongst the dying, but she is not smitten; and the girls are ever in peril, but they live on, whilst others are taken. But will our father let us go forth? For I would not like to go unless he bid us."

"Nay, nor I," answered Joseph quickly, for reverence for their father was a strong sentiment in all James Harmer's sons and daughters; "we will strive to win his consent and blessing to our going forth; but we need not say all that we purpose doing when we are free. For, indeed, it may well be that we shall meet with many hindrances. They say that the roads leading away from the city are all closely watched, that no infected person is able to pass, and that many sound ones are turned back lest they bring the infection with them."

"Then how shall we get out?" asked Benjamin; but Joseph nodded his head wisely, and said he had a plan.

Before, however, he could further enlighten his brother they heard their father's footfall on the stair, and he came in looking weary and sad, as it was inevitable that he should, coming as he did into personal contact with so much misery, sickness, and death.

There was always refreshment ready for the workers at any hour of the day when they should come in to seek it. The boys rushed off to get him such things as their mother had ready, and whilst he partook of the wholesome and appetising meal prepared for him, Joseph burst out with his pent-up weariness of the shut-up life, his longing to be free of the house and the city, and his earnest desire that his father would permit him and Benjamin to go forth and shift for themselves in the country until the terrible visitation was past.

The father listened with a grave face. He too began to have a great fear that the whole city was doomed to be swept away, and although upheld in his resolve to do his duty, so long as he was able, by his strong and fervent faith in the goodness and mercy of God, he was disposed to the opinion that all who remained would in turn be carried off victims to the fearful pestilence. Had he known from the beginning how terrible it would become in time, he sometimes said to himself, he would at least have made shift to send his family away; but now that they were engrossed in works of piety and charity, he could not feel it right to bid them cease their labours of love, nor did he feel any temptation to quit his own post. Yet this made him the more ready to listen to the eager petition of his boys, and to consider the project which had formed itself in the quick brain of Joseph.

"Father, I have thought of it so much these past days. We are sound in health. Thou couldst get us the papers without which men say none can pass the watch upon the roads. With them we can sally forth, with a small provision of money and food, and make our way either by boat to the farm at Greenwich where the other 'prentice boys live, and where there would be a welcome for us always, or else northward to our aunt beyond Islington, who will be hungering for news of us, and who will be rejoiced, I am very sure, to give us a welcome and to hear of the welfare of all, even though we come to her from the land of the shadow of death."

"Ay, verily do ye!" exclaimed the father, whose phrase Joseph had picked up and quoted. "Heaven send that my poor sister be yet numbered among the living. I know not whether the fell disease has wrought havoc beyond the limits of the city in that direction; but at the first it raged more fiercely north and west than with us, and God alone knows who are taken and who are left!"

"Then, father, may we go?" asked Benjamin, eagerly.

The father looked from one boy to the other with the glance of one who thinks he may be looking his last upon some loved face. Men had begun to grow used to the thought that when they left their homes in the morning they might return to them no more, or that they might return to find that one or more of their dear ones had been struck down and carried off in the course of a few hours. So terrible was the malignity of the disease, that often death supervened after a few hours,

Evelyn Everett-Green

although others would linger—often in terrible suffering—for many days before death (or much more rarely, recovery) relieved them of their pain. This good man knew that if he let the lads go, he might never see them again. He or they might be victims before they met, and might see each other's face no more upon earth.

Yet he did not oppose the boys' plan. He knew how bad for them was this shut-up life, and how the very sense of fret and compulsory inactivity might predispose them to the contagion. If they could once get beyond the limits of the city, they might be far safer than they could be here. It would be a relief to have them gone—to think of them as living in safety in the fresh air of the country. Moreover, it pleased him to think of sending a message of loving assurance to his favourite sister, who dwelt in the open country beyond the hamlet of Islington. He felt assured that if she still lived she would have a warm welcome for his boys; and if the lads were well provided with money and wholesome food, they had wits enough to take care of themselves for a while, until they had found some asylum. In all the surrounding villages, as he well knew, were only too many empty houses and cottages. He knew that there was risk; but there was risk everywhere, and he felt sympathy with the lads for their eager desire to get free of their prison.

The mother felt more fear, but she never interfered with the decisions of her husband. Her tears fell as she packed up in very small compass a few articles of clothing and some provisions for the lads. Their father furnished them with money, the bulk of which was sewn up in their clothing, and with those health passes which were so needful for those leaving the infected city.

The summer's night was really the best time in which to commence a journey. The heat of the streets by day was intolerable, the danger of encountering infected persons was greater, whilst although it was at night that the dead carts went about, these could be easily avoided, as the warning bell and mournful cry gave ample notice of their approach.

Last thing of all, after the boys had partaken of an ample supper, and had shed a few natural tears at the thought that it might be the last meal ever eaten beneath the roof of the old home, the father knelt down and commended them solemnly to the care of Him in whose hands alone lay the issues of life and death. Then he blessed the boys individually, charged them to take every reasonable care, and finally escorted them down to the door, which he carefully opened, and after ascertaining that the road was quite clear, he walked with them as far as the end of the bridge, and dismissed them on their way with another blessing.

Much sobered by the scenes through which they had passed, yet not a little elated by the quick and successful issue to their demand, the boys looked each other in the face by the light of the great yellow moon, and nipped each other by the hand to make sure it was not all a dream.

How strange the sleeping city looked beneath that pale white light! The boys had hardly ever been abroad after nightfall, and never during this sad strange time, when even by day all was so different from what they had been used to see. Now it did indeed look like a city of the dead, for not even an idle roisterer, or a drunkard stumbling homewards with uncertain gait, was to be seen. The watchmen, sleeping or trying to sleep within the porches or upon the doorsteps of certain houses, were the only living beings to be seen; and even they were few and far between in this locality, for almost every house was shut up and empty, the inhabitants of many having fled before the distemper became so bad, and others having all died off, leaving the houses utterly vacant.

"Let us go and see the house where Janet and Rebecca and Mistress Gertrude dwell," said Benjamin, as they watched their father's figure vanish in the distance, and felt themselves quite alone in the world; "perchance one of them may be waking, and may look forth from the window if we throw up a pebble. I would fain say a farewell word to them ere we go forth, for who knows whether we may see them again?"

"Ay, verily, we may be dead or else they," said Joseph, but in the tone of one who has grown used to the thought. "This way then; the house lies hard by, next door to my Lady Scrope's. Who would have thought that that cross old madwoman would have turned so kindly disposed towards the poor and sick as she hath done?"

There were many amongst her former friends and acquaintances who would have asked that question, had they been there to ask it. Lady Scrope had never been credited with charitable feelings; and yet it was her doing that a large house, her own property, next door to the small one she chose to inhabit, had been made over to the magistrates and authorities of the city at this time, for the housing of orphaned children whose parents had perished of the plague, and who were thrown upon the charity of strangers, or upon those entrusted with the care of the city at this crisis.

True, the house was standing empty and desolate. Its tenants had fled, taking their goods with them. All that was left of plenishing belonged to Lady Scrope. Pallets were easily provided by the officers of health, and the place was speedily filled with little children, who were tenderly cared for by Gertrude, Janet, and Rebecca (who had joined her sister in this labour of love), all three having given themselves up to this work, and finding their hands too full to desire other occupation abroad.

Joseph and Benjamin had of course heard all about this, and knew exactly where to find the house. It was marked with the red cross, for, as was inevitable, many of the little inmates were carried off by the fell disease after admission, and the numbers were constantly thinning and being replaced by fresh ones. But hitherto the nurses themselves had been spared, and toiled on unremittingly at their self-chosen work.

There was no watchman at the door as the boys stole up, but they had scarcely been there ten seconds before a window was thrown up, and Janet's voice was heard exclaiming, "Andrew, art thou yet returned?"

"There is nobody here, sister," answered Joseph, "save Ben and me. We are come to say farewell, for we are going forth this night from the city, to seek safety with our aunt in Islington. Can we do aught for you ere we go?"

"Alas, it is the dead cart of which we have need tonight," answered Janet. "We sent the watchman for physic, but it is needed no longer. The little ones are dead already—three of them, and only one ill this morning.

"Ah, brothers, glad am I to hear ye be going. God send you safety and health; and forget not to pray for us in the city when ye are far away. May He soon see fit to remove His chastening hand! It is hard to see the little ones suffer."

Janet's voice was quiet and calm, but Benjamin burst into tears at the sound of her words, and at the thought of the little dead children; but she leaned out and said kindly:

"Nay, nay, weep not, Ben, boy; let us think that they are taken in mercy from the evil to come. But linger not here, dear brothers. Who knows that contagion may not dwell in the very air? Go forth with what speed you may.

"Ah, there is the bell! The cart is on its way! And here comes good Andrew back. Now he will do all that we need. Fare you well, brothers. Rebecca is sleeping tonight, and I would not wake her. I will give her your farewell love tomorrow."

She waved them away, and they withdrew; but a species of fascination kept them hanging round the spot. Moreover, they feared to meet the death cart in that narrow thoroughfare, and the porch of the church of Allhallowes the Less was in close proximity. The iron gate was open, and they were quickly able to hide themselves in the porch, from whence by peeping out they could see all that passed.

Nearer and nearer came the sound of the rumbling wheels and the bell, and now the cry, "Bring forth your dead! bring forth your dead!" was clearly to be heard through the still air. Round the corner came the strange conveyance, drawn by two weary-looking horses; and at some signal from the inmates it drew up at the door of the house in front of which the boys had been standing a minute before.

The watchman brought out three little shrouded forms. They were laid upon the top of the awful pile, and the cart with its heavy load rumbled away, the bell no longer ringing, because there was no room for more upon that journey.

The boys stood with hands closely locked together, for although they had heard of these things before, they had never seen the sight. Their bedroom at home looked out upon the river, and the dead cart only went about at night. They trembled at the thought which came to them, that had they been numbered amongst the dead during this terrible visitation they too had been carried in that fashion to their last resting place.

"Come, Ben, let us be going," said Joseph, recovering

himself first; "we need not linger in the city if we like it not. There may be strange things to see in all truth; but if we have no stomach for them, why let us make our way northward with all speed. We can leave all this behind us by daybreak an we will."

Taking hands, and feeling their courage return as they walked on, the brothers passed along the silent streets. Sometimes a window would be opened from above, and a doleful voice would cry aloud in grief or anguish of mind, or some command would be shouted to the watchman beneath, or there would be a piercing cry for the dead cart as it rumbled by. The boys at last grew used to the sound of the bell and the wheels. Go where they would they could not avoid hearing one or another as the men went about their dismal errand. It seemed less terrible after a time than it had done at first, and the bold spirit within them came back.

They wended their way northward, avoiding the narrower thoroughfares and keeping to the broader streets. Even these were often very narrow and ill smelling, so that the brothers had recourse to their vinegar bottle or swallowed a spoonful of Venice treacle before venturing down. Once they were forced to turn aside out of their way to avoid a heap of corpses that had been brought out from a narrow alley to wait for the cart. They had heard of such things before, but to see them was tenfold more terrible. Yet the spirit of adventure took possession of them as they passed along, and they were less afraid even of the most terrible things than they had been of lesser ones at starting.

In passing near to the little church of St. Margaret's, Lothbury, they were attracted by the sound of a voice crying out as if in excitement or fear. Being filled with curiosity in spite of their fears, they turned in the direction of the sound, and came upon a man clutching hard at the railings of the little churchyard, which like all others in that part was now filled to overflowing, and closed for burials, the dead being taken to the great pits dug in various places. Night though it was, there was a small crowd of persons gathered round the railings, all peering in with eager faces, whilst the voice of the man at the corner kept calling out:

"See! see! there she goes! She stands there by yon tall tombstone waving her arms over her head! Now she is wringing her hands, and weeping again.

"O my wife, my wife! do you not know me? I am here, Margaret, I am here! Weep not for the children who are dead; weep for unhappy me, who am left alive. Ay, it is for the living that men should weep and howl. The dead are at peace—their troubles are over; but our agony is yet to come.

"Margaret! Margaret! look at me! pity me!"

"Ah, she will not hear! She turns away! See, she is gliding hither and thither seeking the graves of her children—

"Margaret! I could not help it. They would not let them lie beside thee! They took them away in the cart. I would have sprung in after them, but they held me back.

"Ah, woe is me! woe is me! There is no place for me either among the living or the dead. All turn from me alike!"

The tears rolled down the poor man's face, his voice was choked with sobs. He still continued to point and to cry out, and to address some imaginary being whom he declared was wandering amongst the tombs. The boys pressed near to look, for some in the crowd suddenly made exclamations as though they had caught a glimpse of the phantom; but look as they would the brothers saw nothing, and Joseph asked of an elderly man in the little crowd what it all meant.

"Methinks it means only that yon poor fellow has lost his reason," he answered, shaking his head. "His wife was one of the first to die when the distemper broke out; and men called it only a fever, though some said she had the tokens on her. She was buried here. And it is but a week since the last of his children was taken—six in two weeks; and he has escaped out of his house, and wanders about the streets, and comes here every night, saying that he sees his dead wife, and that she is looking for her children, and cannot find them because they are lying in the plague pit. He is distraught, poor fellow; but many men gather night by night to hear him.

"For my part, I will come no more. Men are best at home in their own houses; and you lads had best go home as fast as you can. It is no place and no hour for boys to be abroad."

Joseph and Benjamin said a civil goodnight to the man, and taking hands bent their steps northward once again. They were now close to the open Moor Fields; and although there was still another region of houses to be passed upon the other side, they felt that when once they had passed the gate and the walls they should have left the worst of the peril behind them.

CHAPTER X

WITHOUT THE WALLS

Only one trifling incident befell the boys before they found themselves without the city gate. They were proceeding down Coleman Street towards Moor Gate, where they knew they should have to show their pass, and perhaps have some slight trouble in getting through, and were rehearsing such things as they had decided to tell the guard at the gate, when the sound of a dismal howling smote upon their ears, and they paused to look about them, for the street was very still, and almost every house seemed deserted and empty.

The sound came again, and Joseph remarked:

"'Tis some poor dog who perchance has lost master and home. There be only too many such in the city they say. They throw them by scores into the river to be rid of them; but I have heard father say that it is an ill thing to do, and likely to spread the contagion instead of checking it. Alive, the poor beasts do no ill; but their carcasses poison both the water and the air. Beshrew me, but he makes a doleful wailing!"

Going on cautiously through the darkness, for the moon was veiled behind some clouds, the brothers presently saw, lying just outside a shut-up house, a long still form wrapped in a winding sheet, put out ready for one of the many carts that passed up the street on the way to the great pits in Bunhill and Finsbury Fields. Whether the corpse was that of a man or a woman the boys could not tell. They made a circuit round it to avoid passing near.

But beside the still figure squatted a little dog of the turnspit variety, and he was awakening the echoes of the quiet street by his lugubrious howls.

Both the brothers were fond of animals, and particularly of dogs, and they paused after having passed by, and tried to get the creature to come to them; but though he paused for a moment in his wailing, and even wagged his tail as though in gratitude for the kind words spoken, he would not leave his post beside the corpse, and the boys had perforce to go on their way.

"The dumb brute could teach a lesson in charity to many a human being," remarked Joseph, gravely; "he will not leave his dead master, and they too often flee away even from the living. Poor creature, how mournful are his cries! I would that we could comfort him."

At the gate they were stopped and questioned. They told a straightforward and truthful tale; their pass was examined and found correct; and their father's name being widely known and respected for his untiring labours in the city at this time, the boys were treated civilly enough and wished God speed and a safe return. They were the more quickly dismissed that the sound of wheels rumbling up to the gate made itself heard, and the guard darted hastily away into his shelter.

"These plague carts will be the death of us, passing

Evelyn Everett-Green

continually all the night through with their load," he said. "Best be gone before it comes through, lads. It carries death in its train."

The boys were glad enough to make off, and found themselves for the time being free of houses in the pleasant open Moor Fields, which were familiar to them as the favourite gathering place of shopmen and apprentices on all high days and holidays. The moon shone down brightly again, although near her setting now; but before long the dawn would begin to lighten in the east, and the boys cared no whit for the semi-darkness of a summer's night.

Behind them still came the rumble of wheels, and they drew aside to let the cart pass with its dreadful cargo. Behind it ran a small black object, and Benjamin exclaimed:

"It is the little dog! O brother, let us follow and see what becomes of him!"

The strange curiosity to see the burying place, which tempted only too many to their death in those perilous days, was upon Joseph at that moment. He desired greatly to see one of those plague pits, and to watch the emptying of the cart at its mouth. Forgetting their father's warnings, the brothers ran quickly after the cart, which was easily kept in view, and soon saw it halt and turn round at a spot where they could discern the outline of a great mound of earth, and the black yawning mouth of what they knew must be the pit.

Half terrified, half fascinated, they gripped each other by the hand and crept step by step nearer. They took care to keep to the windward of the pit, and were getting very near to it when the air was rent by another of the doleful cries which they had heard before, but which sounded so strange and mournful here that they stopped short in terror at the noise. It seemed even to affect the nerves of the bearers, for one of them exclaimed:

"It is that cur again, who has left the marks of his teeth in my hand. If I could but get near him with my cudgel, he should never howl again."

"I thought we had rid ourselves of the brute, but he must have followed us. A plague upon his doleful voice! They say that it bodes ill to hear a dog's howl at night. Perchance he will leap down into the pit after his master. We will take good care he comes not forth again if he does that."

With these words the rough fellows turned to the cart, which was now at the edge of the pit, and finished the rude burial which was all that could in those days be given to the dead. Every now and then one of the men would aim a heavy stone at the poor dog, who sat on the edge of the pit howling dismally. The creature, however, was never hit, for he kept a respectful distance from his enemies.

Their work done, the men got into the cart and drove away, without having noticed the two boys crouching beside the pile of soil in the shadow. The dog began running backwards and forwards along the edge of the pit, which being only lately dug was still deep, though filling up very fast in these terrible days of drought and heat.

The boys rose up and called to him kindly. He did not notice them at first, but finally came, and looked up in their faces with appealing eyes, as though he begged of them to give him back his master.

"Touch him not, Ben," said Joseph to his brother, who would have taken the dog into his embrace, "he has been in a plague stricken house. Let us coax him to yon pool, and wash him there; and then, if he will go with us, we will take him and welcome. It may be he will be a safeguard from danger; and it would be sorrowful indeed to leave him here."

The dog was divided in mind between watching the pit's mouth and going with the kindly-spoken boys, who coaxed and called to him; but at last it seemed as though the loneliness of the place, and the natural instinct of the canine mind to follow something human, prevailed over the other instinct of watching for the return of his master from this strange resting place. Perhaps the journey in the cart and the promiscuous burial had confused the poor beast's mind as to whether indeed his master lay there at all. With many wistful glances backwards, he still followed the boys; and when they paused at length beside a spring of fresh water, he needed little urging to jump in and refresh himself with a bath, emerging thence in better spirits and ravenously hungry, as they quickly found when they opened their wallet and partook of a part of the excellent provisions packed up for them by their mother.

The young travellers were by this time both tired and sleepy, and finding near by a soft mossy bank, they lay down and were quickly asleep, whilst the dog curled himself up contentedly at their feet and slept also.

When the boys awoke the sun was up, although it was still early morning. They were bewildered for a few moments to know where they were, but memory quickly returned to them, and with it a sense of exhilaration at being no longer cooped up within the walls of a house, but out in the open country, with the world before them and the plague-stricken city behind. Even the presence of the dog, who proved to be a handsome and intelligent member of his race, black and tan in colour, with appealing eyes and a quick comprehension of what was spoken to him, added greatly to the pleasure of the lads. They gave their new companion the name of Fido, as a tribute to his affection for his dead master; but they were very well pleased that he did not carry his fidelity to the pass of remaining behind by the great pit when they started forth to pursue their way to their aunt's house beyond Islington.

Fido ran backwards and forwards for a while whining and looking pathetically sorrowful; but after the boys had coaxed and caressed him, and had explained many times over that his master could not possibly come back, he seemed to resign himself to the inevitable, and trotted at their heels with drooping tail, but with gratitude in his eyes whenever they paused to caress him or give him a kind word.

And they were glad enough of his company along the road, for from time to time they met groups of very rough-looking men prowling about as though in search of plunder. Some of these fellows eyed the wallets carried by the boys with covetous glances; but on such occasions Fido invariably placed himself in front of his young masters, and with flashing eyes and bristling back plainly intimated that he was there to protect them, whilst the gleaming rows of shining teeth which he displayed when he curled up his lips in a threatening snarl seemed to convince all parties that it was better not to provoke him to anger.

The more open parts of the region without the walls looked very strange to the boys as they journeyed onwards. Numbers of tents were to be seen dotted about Finsbury and Moor Fields and whole families were living there in the hope of escaping contagion. Country people from regions about came daily with their produce to supply the needs of these nomads; and it was curious to see the precautions taken on both sides to avoid personal contact. The villagers would deposit their goods upon large stones set up for the purpose; and after they had retired to a little distance, some persons from the tents or scattered houses would come and take the produce, depositing payment for it in a jar of vinegar set there to receive it. After it had thus lain a short time, the vendor would come and take it thence; but some were so cautious that they would not place it in purse or pocket till they had passed it through the fire of a little brazier which they had with them.

Nor was it to be wondered at that the country folks were thus cautious, for the contagion had spread throughout all the surrounding districts, and every village had its tale of woe to tell. At first the people had been kind and compassionate enough in welcoming and harbouring apparently sound persons fleeing from the city of destruction; but when again and again it happened that the wayfarer died that same night of the plague in the house which had received him, and infected many of those who had showed him kindness, so that sometimes a whole family was swept away in two or three days, it was no wonder that they were afraid of offering hospitality to wayfarers, and preferred that these persons should encamp at a distance from them, though they were willing to supply them with the necessaries of life at reasonable charges. It must be spoken to the credit of the country people at this time, that they did not raise the price of provisions, as might have been expected, seeing the risk they ran in taking them to the city. There was no scarcity and hardly any advance in price throughout the dismal time of visitation. This was doubtless due, in part, to the wise and able measures taken by the magistrates and city corporations; but it also redounds to the credit of the villagers, that they did not strive to enrich themselves through the misfortunes of their neighbours.

The boys were glad to purchase fruit and milk for a light breakfast; and their fresh open faces and tender years seemed to give them favour wherever they went. They were not shunned, as some travellers found themselves at this time, but were admitted to several farm houses on their way, and regaled plentifully, whilst they told their tale to a circle of breathless listeners.

Sometimes they were stopped upon the way by the men told off to watch the roads, and turn back any coming from the city who had not the proper pass of health. But the boys, being duly provided with this, were always suffered to proceed after some parley. They began, however, to understand how difficult a thing it had now become to escape from the infected city; and several times they saw travellers turned back because their passes were dated a few days back, and the guard declared it impossible to know what infection they had encountered since.

Very sad indeed were these poor creatures at being, as it were, sent back to their death. For it began to be rumoured all about the city that not a living creature would escape who remained there. It was said that God's judgments had gone forth, and that the whole place would be given over to destruction, even as Sodom, and that none who remained in it would be left alive.

This sort of talk made the brothers very anxious and sorrowful, but, as Joseph sought to remind his brother, the people who said these things had nothing better to go by than the prognostications of old women or quacks and astrologers, whom their father had taught them to disbelieve. He had always taught them that God alone knew the future and the thing that He would do, and that it was folly and presumption on the part of man to seek to penetrate His counsels, and venture to prophesy things which He had not revealed. So they plucked up heart, these two youthful wayfarers, firmly believing that God would take care of their father and all those who were working in the cause of mercy and charity in the great city, and that they could leave the issues of these things in His hands.

Since the day was very hot, and they were somewhat weary with their long walk and short night, they lay down at noontide in a little wood, not more than three miles from their aunt's house in Islington, and there they slept again, with Fido at their feet, until the sun was far in the west, and they were ready to finish their journey in the cool freshness of the evening.

They had come by no means the nearest way, but had fetched a wide circuit, so as to avoid, as far as possible, all regions of outlying houses. Time was no particular object to them, so that they reached their destination by nightfall; and now they were quite in the open country, and delighting in the pure air and the rural sights and sounds.

Yet even here all was not so happy and smiling as appeared from the face of nature. The corn was standing ripe for the sickle, but in too many districts there were not hands enough to reap it. One beautiful field of wheat which the brothers passed was shedding the golden grain from the ripened ears, and flocks of birds were gathering it up. When they passed the farmstead they saw the reason for this. Not a sign of life was there about the place. No cattle lowed, no dog barked; and an old crone who sat by the wayside with a bundle of ripe ears in her lap shook her head as she saw the wondering faces of the boys, and said:

"All dead and gone! all dead and gone! Alive one day—dead the next! The plague carried them off, every one of them, harvest hands and all. They say it was the men who came to cut the corn that brought it. But who can tell? They got yon field in"—pointing to one where the golden stubble was to be seen short and compact—"but half were dead ere ever it was down; and then the sickness fell upon the house, and of those who did not fly not one remains. Lord have mercy upon us! We be all dead men if He come not to our aid. Who knows whose turn may come next?"

Truly the shadow of death seemed everywhere. But the boys were so used to dismal tales of wholesale devastation that one more or less did not seem greatly to matter. Perhaps the contrast was the more sharp out here between the smiling landscape and the silent, shut-up house; but the chief fear which beset them was lest their kind aunt should have been taken by death, in which case they scarcely knew what would become of themselves.

They hastened their steps as they entered the familiar lane where nestled the thatched cottage in which their aunt had her abode. Mary Harmer was their father's youngest and favourite sister. Once she had made one of the home party on the bridge; but that was long before the boys could remember. That was in the lifetime of their grandparents, and before the old people resigned their business to the able hands of their son James, and came into the country to live.

The grandfather of Joseph and Benjamin had built this cottage, and he and his wife had lived in it from that time till the day of their death. Their daughter Mary remained still in the pretty, commodious place—if indeed she had not died during the time of the visitation. The children all loved their Aunt Mary, and esteemed a visit to her house as one of the greatest of privileges.

Benjamin, who was rather delicate, had once passed six months together here, and was called by Mary Harmer "her boy." He grew excited as he marked every familiar turn in the shady lane; and when at last the thatched roof of the rose-covered cottage came in sight, he uttered a shout of excitement and ran hastily forward.

The diamond lattice panes were shining with their accustomed cleanliness. There was no sign of neglect about the bright little house. The door stood open to the sunshine and the breeze; and at the sound of Benjamin's cry, a figure in a neat cotton gown and large apron appeared suddenly in the doorway, whilst a familiar voice exclaimed: "Now God be praised! it is my own boy. Two of them! Thank Heaven for so much as this!" and running down the garden path, Mary Harmer folded both the lads in her arms, tears coursing down her cheeks the while.

"God bless them! God bless them! How I have longed for news of you all! What news from home bring you, dear lads? I tremble almost to ask, but be it what it may, two of you are alive and well; and in times like these we must needs learn to say, 'Thy will be done!'"

"We are all alive, we are all well!" cried Joseph, hastening to relieve the worst of his aunt's fears. "Some say ours is almost the only house in London where there be not one dead. I scarce know if that be true. One or two of us have been sick, and some say that Janet and Dan have both had a touch of the distemper; but they soon were sound again. They all go about amongst the sick. Father has been one of the examiners all the time through; and though they only appoint them for a month, he will not give up his office. He says that so long as he and his family are preserved, so long will he strive to do his duty towards his fellow men. There be many like him— our good Lord Mayor for one; and my Lord Craven, who will not fly, as almost all the great ones have done, but stays to help to govern the city wisely, and to see that the alms are distributed aright to the poor at this season.

"But there was naught for us to do. We were too young to be

bearers or searchers, and boys cannot tend the sick. So we grew weary past bearing of the shut-up house, and yestereve our father gave us leave to sally forth and seek news of thee, good aunt. And oh, we are right glad to find ourselves out of the city and safe with thee!"

Joseph spoke on, because Mary Harmer was weeping so plenteously with joy and gratitude that she had no words in which to answer him. She had not dared to hope that she should see again any of the dear faces of her kinsfolk. True, the distemper was yet raging fiercely, and none could say when the end would come; but it was much to know that they had lived in safety through these many weeks. It seemed to the pious woman as though God had given her a sort of pledge of His special mercy to her and hers, and that He would not now fail them.

She led the boys into her pretty, cheerful cottage, and set them down to the table, where she quickly had a plentiful meal set before them. Fido's pathetic story was told, and he was caressed and fed in a fashion that altogether won his heart. He made them all laugh at his method of showing gratitude; for he walked up to the fire before which a bit of meat was cooking, and plainly intimated his desire to be allowed to turn the spit if they would give him the needful convenience. This being done by the handy Benjamin, he set to his task with the greatest readiness, and the boys quite forgot all their sorrowful thoughts in the entertainment of watching Fido turn the spit.

Long did they sit at table, eating with the healthy appetite of growing lads, and answering their aunt's minute questions as to the welfare of every member of the household. Greatly was she interested in the home for desolate children provided by Lady Scrope, and ordered by her nieces and Gertrude. She told the boys that her house had often been used to shelter homeless and destitute persons, whom charity forbade her to send away. Just now she was alone; but even then she was not idle, for all round in the open fields and woods persons of all conditions were living encamped, and some of these had hardly the necessaries of life. Out of her own modest abundance, Mary Harmer supplied food and clothing to numbers of poor creatures, who might otherwise be in danger of perishing; and she bid the boys be ready to help her in her labour of love, because she had ofttimes more to do than one pair of hands could accomplish, and her little serving girl had run off in alarm the very first time she opened her door to a poor sick lady with an infant in her arms, who had escaped from the city only to die out in the country. It was not the plague that carried her off, but lung disease of long standing, and the infant did not survive its mother many days.

"But it frightened Sally away, poor child, just as if it had been the sickness; and I have since heard that she was taken with it a month ago in her own home, and that every one there died within three days. These be terrible times! But we know they are sent by God, and that He will help us through them; and surely, I think, it cannot be His will that we turn a deaf ear to the plaints of the afflicted, and think of naught but our own safety. I have work and enough to do, and will find you enough to fill your hands, boys. It was a happy thought indeed which sent you two hither to me."

CHAPTER XI

LOVE IN DIFFICULTIES

"It means that I am a ruined man, my poor girl!"

"Ruined! O father, how can that be? Methought you were a man of much substance. Mother always said so."

Gertrude looked anxiously into the careworn face of her father, which had greatly changed during the past weeks. He paid her occasional visits in her self-chosen home, being one of those who had ceased to fear contagion, and went about almost without precaution, from sheer indifference to the long-continued peril. He had been a changed man ever since the melancholy deaths of his son and his wife; but today a darker cloud than any she had seen there before rested upon his brow, and the daughter was anxious to learn the reason of it. This it was which had wrung from the Master Builder the foregoing confession.

"Your poor mother was partly right, and partly wrong. I might have been a rich man, I might be a rich man even now—terrible as is the state of trade in this stricken city— had it not been that she would have me adventure beyond my means in her haste to see me wealthy before my fellows. And the end of it is that I stand here today a ruined man!"

Gertrude held in her arms a little child, over whom she bent from time to time to assure herself that it slept. Her face had grown pale and thin during her long confinement between the walls of this house; yet it was a happier and more contented face than it had been wont to be in the days when she lived in luxurious idleness at her mother's side. She looked many years older than she had done then, but there was a beauty and sweet serenity about her appearance now which had not been visible in the days of old.

"What has happened during this sad time to ruin you, dear father?" asked Gertrude gently, guessing that it would ease his heart to talk of his troubles. "Is it the sudden stoppage of all trade?"

"That has been serious enough. It would have done much harm had that been the only thing, but there be many, many other causes. Thou art too young and unversed in the ways of business to understand all; but I was not content to grow rich in the course of business alone. I had ventures of all sorts afloat—on sea and on land; and through the death of patrons, through the sudden stoppage of all trade, numbers and numbers of these have come to no good. My money is lost; my loans cannot be recovered. Men are dead or fled to whom I looked for payment. Half-finished houses are thrown back on my hands, since half London is empty. And poor Frederick's debts are like the sands upon the seashore. I cannot meet them, but I cannot let others suffer for his imprudence and folly. The old house on the bridge will have to go. I must needs sell it so soon as a purchaser can be found. It may be I shall have to hand it over to one of Frederick's creditors bodily. I had thought to end my days there in peace, with my children's children round me. But the Almighty is dealing very bitterly with me. Wife and son are taken away, and now the old home must follow!"

Gertrude, who knew his great love for the house in which he had been born, well understood what a fearful wrench this would be, and her heart overflowed with compassion.

"O father! must it be so? Is there no way else? Methought you had stores of costly goods laid by in your warehouses. Surely the sale of those things would save you from this last step!"

The Master Builder smiled a little bitterly.

"Truly is it said that wealth takes to itself wings in days of adversity. I myself thought as you do, child—at least in part; and today I visited my warehouses, to look over my goods and see what there were to fetch when men will dare to buy things which have lain within the walls of this doomed city all these months. I had the keys of the place. I myself locked them up when the plague forced me to close my warehouse and dismiss my men. I saw all made sure, as I thought, with my own eyes. But what think you I found there today?"

"O father! what?" asked Gertrude, and yet she divined the answer all too well; for she had heard stories of robbery and daring wickedness even during this season of judgment and punishment which prepared her for the worst.

"That the whole place had been plundered; that there was nothing left of any price whatever. Thieves have broken in during this time of panic, and have despoiled me of the value of thousands of pounds. Whilst my mind has been full of other matters, my worldly wealth has been swept away. I stand here before you a ruined man. And like enough the very miscreants who have used this time of public calamity for plunder and lawlessness may be lying by this time in the common grave. But that will not give my property back to me."

"Alas, father, these are indeed evil days! But has no watch been kept upon the streets that such acts can be done by the evil disposed? Is all property in the city at the mercy of the violent and wicked?"

"Only too much has vanished that same way, as I have heard from many. Some owners are themselves gone where they will need their valuables no more, and others were careful to remove all they had to their own houses, or they themselves lived over their goods and could guard them by their presence. That is where my error lay. I gave your mother her will in this. She liked not the shop beneath, and I stored my goods elsewhere. Poor woman, she is dead and gone; we will speak no hard things of her weaknesses and follies. But had she lived to see this day, she had grievously lamented her resolve to have naught about her to remind her of buying and selling."

"Ah, poor mother! I often think it was the happiest thing for her to be taken ere these fearful things came to pass. The terror would well nigh have driven her distracted. Methinks she would have died of sheer fright. But, father, is all lost past recovery? Can none of the watch or of the constables tell you aught, or help you to recover aught?"

"Ah, child, in these days of death, who is to know so much as where to carry one's questions? Watchmen and constables have died and changed a score of times in the past two months. The magistrates do their best to keep order in the city, but who can fight against the odds of such a time as this? The very men employed as watchmen may be the thieves themselves. They have to take the services of almost any who offer. It is no time to pick and choose. I carried my story to the Lord Mayor himself, and he gave me sympathy and pity; but to look for the robbers is a hopeless task. It is most like that the plague pits have received them ere now.

The mortality in the lower parts of the city is more fearful than it has ever been, and it seems as though the summer heats would never end. Belike I shall be taken next, and then it will matter little that my fortune has taken unto itself wings."

Gertrude came and bent over him with a soft caress.

"Say not so, dear father. God has preserved us all this while. Let us not distrust His love and goodness now."

"It might be the greater mercy," answered the Master Builder in a depressed voice. "I am too old to start life again with nothing but my broken credit for capital. As for you, child, your future is assured. I could leave you happy in that thought. You would want for nothing."

Gertrude raised her eyes wonderingly to her father's face. She had laid the sleeping child in its cot, and had taken a place at her father's feet.

"What mean you, father?" she asked. "I have only you in the wide world now. If you were to die, I should be both orphaned and destitute. What mean you by speaking of my future thus? Whom have I in the wide world besides yourself?"

The father passed his hand over her curly hair, and answered with a sigh and a smile:

"Surely, child, thou dost know by this time that the heart of Reuben Harmer is all thine own. He worships the very ground on which thou dost tread. His father and I have spoken of it. Fortune has dealt more kindly with our neighbours than with me. Good James Harmer has laid by money, while I have adventured it rashly in the hope of large returns. This calamity has but checked his work for these months; when the scourge is past, he will reopen business once more, and will find himself but little the poorer. He is a wiser man than I have been; and his wife and sons have all been helpful to him. The love of Reuben Harmer is my assurance for thy future welfare. Thou wilt never want so long as they have a roof over their heads.

"Nay, now what ails thee, child? Why dost thou spring up and look at me like that?"

For Gertrude's usually tranquil face was ablaze now with all manner of conflicting emotions. She seemed for a moment almost too agitated to speak, and when she could command herself there were traces of great emotion in her voice.

"Father, father!" she cried, "how can you thus shame me? You must know with what unmerited scorn and contumely Reuben was treated by poor mother when it was we who were rich and they who were (in her belief, at least) poor. She would scarce let him cross the threshold of our house. I have tingled with shame at the way in which she spoke of and to him. Frederick openly insulted him at pleasure. Every slight was heaped upon him; and he was once told to his very face that he might look elsewhere for a wife, for that my fortune was to win me the hand of some needy Court gallant. Yes, father, I heard with my own ears those very words spoken—save that the term 'needy' was added in mine own heart. Oh, I could have shrunk into the earth with shame. And after all this, after all these insults and aspersions heaped upon him in the day of our prosperity—am I to be made over to him penniless and needy, without a shilling of dowry? Am I to be thrown upon his generosity in my hour of poverty, when I was denied to him in my day of supposed wealth?

"Father, father! I cannot, I will not permit it. I can work for my own bread if needs must be. But I will not owe it to the generosity of Reuben Harmer, after all that has passed. I should be humbled to the very dust!"

The Master Builder looked at his daughter in amaze. He had never seen Gertrude quite so moved before.

"Why, child," he exclaimed in astonishment. "I always thought that thou hadst a liking for the youth!"

Then at that word Gertrude burst suddenly into tears and cried:

"I love him as mine own soul, and I am not ashamed to own it. But that is the very reason why I will have none of him now. I will not be thrown upon his generosity like a bundle of damaged goods. Let him seek a wife who can bring him a modest fortune with her, and who has never been scornfully denied to him before. O father! can you not see that I can never consent to be his now?

"O mother, mother! why did you do me this ill?"

The father felt that the situation had got beyond him. Never much versed in the ways of women, he was fairly puzzled by his daughter's strange method of taking his confidence. He knew, of course, of the tactics of his wife, which he had deplored at the time, though he had been unable to bring her to a better frame of mind; but since the young people liked each other, and since madam was in her grave, it seemed absurd to let a shadow stand between them and their happiness. Perhaps if left to herself Gertrude would reach that conclusion of her own accord, and the Master Builder rose to go without pressing the matter further.

Evelyn Everett-Green

Gertrude, left alone, was weeping silently and bitterly beside the child's cot, when she was aware of a little short laugh almost at her elbow, and a familiar voice said in sharp accents:

"Good child! I like a woman with a spirit of her own. Go on as you have begun, and don't let him think he is to have it all his own way. Lovers are all very well, but husbands soon show their wives how cheap they hold them when they have won them all too cheap. Throw him aside in scorn! Let him not think or see that you care a snap of the fingers for him. That will rivet the fetters all the faster; and when you have got him like a tame bear at the end of a chain—why then you can make up your mind at leisure what you will end by doing."

Gertrude sprang up suddenly, and faced Lady Scrope with flushed cheeks and glowing eyes.

The little witch-like woman with her black-handled stick and her mobcap was no unfrequent visitor to this shut-up house. There was a communication between the two dwellings by means of a door in the cellars, and all this while curiosity, or some better motive, had prompted the eccentric old woman to come to and fro between her own luxurious house and this, paying visits to the devoted girls, and by turns terrifying and charming the children. Gertrude had been interested from the first by the piquant individuality of the old aristocrat, and was a decided favourite with her. It was plain now that she had been listening to the conversation between father and daughter, a thing so characteristic of her curiosity and even of her benevolence that Gertrude hardly so much as resented it. Nevertheless, having a spirit of her own, and being by no means prepared to be dictated to in these matters, some hot words escaped her lips almost before she knew, and were answered by Lady Scrope by an amused peal of her witch-like laughter.

"Tut! tut! tut! Hoity toity! but she is in a temper, is she, my lady? Well a good thing too. Your saints are insipid unless they can call up a spice of the devil on occasion! Oh, don't you be afraid of me, child. I've known all about you and young Harmer this long time. I agree with your late mother, that you could do better; but with all the world topsy turvy as it is now, we must take what we can get; and that young man is estimable without doubt, and a bit of a hero in his way. I don't blame you for loving him. It's the way with maids, and will be to the end of time, I take it. All I say is, don't throw yourself away too fast. Show a proper pride. Keep him dangling and fearing, rather than hoping too much. Show him that he can't have you just for the asking. Why, child, I have kept a dozen fools hanging round me for a twelvemonth together sometimes; but I only married when I was tired of the game, and when I knew I had made sure of a captive who would not rebel. I swore in church to obey poor Scrope; but, bless you, he obeyed me like a lamb to the last day of his life—and was all the better for it."

Lady Scrope's reminiscences and bits of worldly wisdom were not much more to Gertrude's taste than her father's had been. It was not pride, but a sense of humiliation and shame, which kept her from facing the thought of marriage with Reuben now that she was poor, when she had been scornfully denied to him when she was thought to be a well-dowered maiden. The idea of keeping him dangling after her in suspense was about the last that would ever have entered her head. Her feeling was one of profound humiliation and unworthiness. Her mother's bitter words could never be forgotten by her; and after what her father had told her of his ruined state, it appeared to her simply impossible that she should let Reuben take possession of her and her future when she could bring nothing in return.

But she could not speak of these things to Lady Scrope; and finding her favourite irresponsive and reserved, the dame shrugged her shoulders and passed on to another room, where the children were soon heard to utter shrieks and gasps of mingled delight and terror at the stories she told them, which stories invariably fascinated them to an extra-ordinary degree, yet left them with a sense of undefined horror that was half delightful, half terrible.

They all thought that she was a witch, and that she could spirit any of them away to fairy land. But since she brought sweetmeats in her capacious pockets, and had an endless fund of stories at her disposal, her visits were always welcomed, and she had certainly shown herself capable of a most unsuspected benevolence at this crisis, in presenting this house to the authorities for such a purpose, and in contributing considerably to the maintenance of the desolate little inmates.

She liked to hear their dismal stories almost as well as they liked to hear hers. She made a point of visiting every fresh batch of children, after they had been duly fumigated and disinfected, and she seemed to take a horrible and unnatural delight in the ghastly details of desolation and death which were revealed in the artless narratives of the children.

She was one of those who, knowing much of the fearful corruption of the times, were fond of prognosticating this judgment as a sweeping away of the dregs of the earth; although she still maintained that had the water supply been purer and differently arranged, the judgment of Heaven would have had to seek another medium.

For three or four days Gertrude lived in a state of feverish expectancy and subdued excitement. She had fancied from her father's tone in speaking that there had been some talk of a betrothal between him and his neighbour, and that Reuben might take her consent for granted. The idea made her restless and unhappy. She wished the ordeal of refusing him over. She believed she was right in taking this step; but it was a hard one, and she was sometimes afraid of her own courage. The more she thought of the matter the more she convinced herself that Reuben's love was one of compassion rather than true affection. He had almost ceased his attentions in her mother's lifetime, and had been very reserved in his intercourse of late. Doubtless if he heard of her father's ruin, generosity would make him strive to do all that he could for her in her changed circumstances. It would be like him then to step forward and avow himself ready to marry her. But it was out of the question for her to consent. She wished the matter settled and done with; she wished the irrevocable words spoken.

And yet when at dusk one evening Reuben suddenly stood before her, she felt her heart beating to suffocation, and wished that she had any reasonable excuse for fleeing from him.

His visits to the house were not frequent; he was too busy to make them so. But from time to time he brought orphaned children to the home of shelter, or took away from it some of those for whom other homes had been found with their kinsfolk in other places. Tonight he had brought in three little destitute orphans; but having given them over into the care of his sisters, he went in search of Gertrude, who was with the youngest of the children in a separate room, and, having sung them all to sleep, was sitting in the window thinking her own thoughts.

She knew what was coming when she saw Reuben's face, and braced herself to meet it. Reuben was very quiet and self-restrained—so self-restrained that she thought she read in his manner an indication that her suspicion was correct, and that it was pity rather than love which prompted his proposal of marriage.

As a matter of fact Reuben was more in love with Gertrude now than he had ever been in his life before; but he had come to look upon her as a being so far above him in every respect that he sometimes marvelled at himself for ever hoping to win her. The fact that her father was just now a ruined man seemed to him as nothing. At a time like this the presence or absence of this world's goods appeared absolutely trivial. Reuben believed that the Master Builder would retrieve his fortune in better times without difficulty, and regarded this temporary reverse as absolutely insignificant. Therefore he had no clue to Gertrude's motive in her rejection of him, and accepted it almost in silence, feeling that it was what he always ought to have looked for, and marvelling at his temerity in seeking the hand of one who was to him more angel than woman.

He said very little; he took it very quietly. It seemed to him as though all the life went out of him, and as though hope died within him for ever. But he scarcely showed any outward emotion as he rose and said farewell; and little did he guess how, when he had gone, Gertrude flung herself on the floor in a passion of tears and sobbed till the fountain of her weeping was exhausted.

"I was right! I was right! It was not love; it was only pity! But ah, how terrible it is to put aside all the happiness of one's life! Oh I wonder if I have done wrong! I wonder if I could better have borne it if I had humbled myself to take what he had to offer, without thinking of anything but myself!"

Would he come again? Would he try to see her any more?

Would this be the end of everything between them? Gertrude asked herself these questions a thousand times a day; but a week flew by and he had not come. She had not seen a sign of him, nor had any word concerning him reached her from without. There was nothing very unusual in this, certainly; and yet as day after day passed by without bringing him, the girl felt her heart sinking within her, and would have given worlds for the chance of reconsidering her well-considered judgment.

How the days went by she scarcely knew, but the next event in her dream-like life was the sudden bursting into the room of Dorcas, her face flushed, and her eyelids swollen and red with weeping.

Dorcas was a member of Lady Scrope's household, but paid visits from time to time to the other house. Also, as Lady Scrope's house was not shut up, she could go thence to pay a visit home at any time, and she had just come from one such visit now.

Gertrude sprang up at sight of her, asking anxiously:

"Dorcas! Dorcas! what is wrong?"

"Reuben!" cried Dorcas, with a great catch in her breath, and then she fell sobbing again as though her heart would break.

Gertrude stood like one turned to stone, her face growing as white as her kerchief.

"What of Reuben?" she asked, in a voice that she hardly knew for her own. "He is not—dead?"

"Pray Heaven he be not," cried Dorcas through her sobs; and then, with a great effort controlling herself, she told her brief tale.

"I went home at noon today and found them all in sore trouble. Reuben has not been seen or heard of for three days. Mother says she had a fear for several days before that that something was amiss; he looked so wan, and ate so little, and seemed like one out of whom all heart is gone. He would go forth daily to his work, but he came home harassed and tired, and on the last morning she thought him sick; but he said he was well, and promised to come home early. Then she let him go, and no one has seen him since.

"Oh, what can have befallen him? There seems but one thing to believe. They say the sickness is worse now than ever it was. People drop down dead in street and market, and soon there will be none left to bury them. That must have been Reuben's fate. He has dropped down with the infection upon him, and if he be not lying in some pest house—which they say it is death now to enter—he must be lying in one of those awful graves.

"O Reuben! Reuben! we shall never see you again!"

CHAPTER XII

EXCITING DISCOVERIES

Joseph and Benjamin found themselves exceedingly happy and exceedingly well occupied in their aunt's pleasant cottage. They rose every morning with the lark, and spent an hour in setting everything to rights in the house, and sweeping out every room with scrupulous care, as their mother had taught them to do at home, believing that perfect cleanliness was one of the greatest safeguards against infection. Hot and close though the weather remained, the air out in these open country places seemed delicious to the boys, and the freedom to run out every moment into the open fields was in itself a privilege which could only be appreciated by those who had been long confined within walls.

Sometimes they were alone in the house with their aunt. Sometimes the cottage harboured guests of various degrees—travellers fleeing from the doomed city in terror of the fearful mortality there, or poor unfortunates turned away from their own abodes because they were suspected of having been in contact with the sick, and were refused admittance again. Servant maids were often put in this melancholy plight. They would be sent upon errands by their employers to the bake house or some other place; and perhaps ere they were admitted again they would be closely

Evelyn Everett-Green

questioned as to what they had seen or heard. Sometimes having terrible and doleful tales to tell of having seen persons fall down in the agonies of death almost at their feet, terror would seize hold upon the inmates of the house, who would refuse to open the door to one who might by this time be herself infected. And when this was the case, the forlorn creature was forced to wander away, and generally tried to find her way out of the city and into the country beyond. Many such unlucky wights, having no passes, were turned back by the guardians of the road; but some succeeded in evading these men, or else in persuading them, and many such unfortunates had found rest and help and shelter beneath Mary Harmer's charitable roof.

September was now come, but as yet there was no abatement of the pestilence raging in the city. Indeed the accounts coming in of the virulence of the plague seemed worse than ever. Ten thousand deaths were returned in the weekly bill for the first week alone, and those who knew the state of the city were of opinion that not more than two-thirds of the deaths were ever really reported to the authorities. Hitherto the carts had never gone about save by night, and for all that was rumoured by those who loved to make the worst of so terrible a calamity, it was seldom that a corpse lay about in the streets for above a short while, just until notice of its presence there was given to the authorities.

But now it seemed as though nothing could cope with the fearful increase of the mortality. The carts were forced to work by day as well as by night; and so virulent was now the pestilence that the bearers and buriers who had hitherto escaped, or had recovered of the malady and thought themselves safe, died in great numbers. So that there were tales of carts overthrown in the streets by reason of the drivers of them falling dead upon their load, or of driverless horses going of their own accord to the pits with their load.

These terrible tales were reported to Mary Harmer and her nephews by the fugitives who sought refuge with her at this time. And very thankful did the lads feel to be free of the city and its terrors, albeit they never forgot to offer up earnest prayer for their father and mother and all their dear ones who were dwelling in the midst of so much peril. There was no hope of hearing news of them, save by hazard, whilst things were like this; but they trusted that the precautions taken, and hitherto successfully, would avert the pestilence from their dwelling, and for the rest the boys were too well employed to have time for brooding.

When their daily work at home was done, there were always errands of mercy to be performed to neighbours who had had sickness at home, or to the persons encamped in the fields, who were very thankful of any little presents of vegetables or eggs or other necessaries; whilst others of larger means were glad to buy from those who came to sell, and gave good money for the accommodation.

Mary Harmer had a large and productive garden and a large stock of poultry, so that she was able both to sell and to give largely; and the boys thought that working in the garden and looking after the fowls was the best sort of fun possible. They were exceedingly useful to her, and she kept them out of danger without fretting or curbing their eager spirit of usefulness. Of course, no person in those days could act with unselfish charity and not adventure something; but she took all reasonable precautions, and, like her brother, trusted the rest to Providence. And she believed that the boys were safer with her, even though not so closely restrained, than they would have been had they remained in the infected city, where the people now seemed to be dying like stricken sheep.

But the spirit of curiosity and love of adventure were not dead within the hearts of the boys; and although for some weeks they were fully contented in performing the duties set them by their aunt, there were moments when a strong curiosity would come over them for some greater sensation, and this it was which led them to an act of disobedience destined to be fraught with important consequences, as will soon be seen.

Mary Harmer's house was empty again, and she had promised to sit up for a night with a sick woman who lived some two miles off, and who had entreated her to come and see her. This was no case of plague, but fear of the infection had become so strong by this time that the sick were often rather harshly treated, and sometimes almost entirely neglected, by those about them. Mary Harmer had heard that this poor creature had been left alone by her son's wife, who had taken away her children and refused to go near her. Mary knew that her presence there for a while, and her assurances as to the nature of the malady, would be most likely to bring the woman to reason, so she decided to go and remain for one whole night, and she left her own cottage in the charge of the boys, bidding them take care of everything, and expect her back again on the following afternoon.

They were quite happy all that evening, seeing to the poultry, and running races with Fido in the leafy lane. They liked the importance of the charge of the house, although they missed the gentle presence of their aunt. They shut up the house at dark, and prepared their simple supper, and whilst they were eating it, Benjamin said:

"What shall we do tomorrow when we have finished our work?"

"I know what I should like to do," said Joseph promptly.

"What, brother?" asked Benjamin eagerly.

"Marry, what I want to do is to go and see that farm house hard by Clerkenwell which they have turned into a pest house, and where they say they have dozens of plague-stricken people brought in daily. I have never seen a pest house. I would fain know what it looks like. And we might get more news there of the truth of those things that they say about the plague in the city. Ben, what sayest thou?"

Ben's eyes were round with wonder and excitement. The boys had all the careless daring and eager curiosity which belong to boy nature. They were by this time so much habituated to living under conditions of risk and a certain amount of peril, that a little more or a little less did not now seem greatly to matter.

"Would our good aunt approve?" asked the younger boy.

"I trow not," answered Joseph frankly; "women are always timid, and she would say, perchance, that unless duty called us it were foolish to adventure ourselves into danger. But I would fain see this place, Ben, boy. If in time to come we live to be men, and folks ask us of these days of peril and sickness, I should like to have seen all that may be seen of these great things. Our father went many times to the pest houses within the city and came away no worse. Why should thou or I suffer? We have our vinegar bottles and our decoctions, and methinks we know enough now not to run needless risks."

Benjamin was almost as eager and curious as his brother. The spirit of adventure soon gets into the hearts of boys and runs riot there. Before they went to bed they had fully decided to make the excursion; and they rose earlier next morning so as to get all their work done while it was yet scarce light, so that they might start for their destination before the heat of the day came on.

It was pleasant walking through the dewy fields, and hard indeed was it to imagine that death and misery lurked anywhere in the neighbourhood of what was so smiling and gay. The boys knew what paths to take, nor was the distance very great. Benjamin on his former visit to his aunt had spent a day with the good people at this very farm house. Now, alas, all had been swept away, and the place had been taken possession of for the time being by the authorities, to be used as a supplementary pest house, where the homeless sick could be temporarily housed. Generally it was but for a few hours or a couple of days that such shelter was needed. The great common grave, barely a quarter of a mile away, received day by day the great majority of the unfortunate ones who were brought in.

In all London proper there were only two pest houses used at this time, one on some fields beyond Old Street, and the other in Westminster; but as the virulence of the distemper increased, and the suburbs became so terribly infected, and such numbers of persons fleeing this way and that would fall stricken by the wayside, it became necessary to find places of some sort where they could be received, and the authorities began to take possession of empty houses—generally farmsteads standing in a convenient but isolated position—and to use them for this melancholy purpose. It could not be expected that even the most charitable would receive plague-stricken wayfarers into their own families, nor would such a thing be right. Yet they could not remain by the wayside to die and infect the air. So they were removed by the bearers appointed to that gruesome work to these smaller pest houses, and only too often from thence to the pit in the course of a few hours.

"How pretty it all looks!" said Benjamin, as they approached the place. "See, Joseph, those are the great elm trees where the rooks build, and which I used to climb. When they cut the hay, I came often and rolled about in it and played with the boys from the farm. To think that they should all be dead and gone! Alack! what strange times these be! It seems sometimes as though it were all a dream!"

"I would it were!" said Joseph, sobered by the thought of their near approach to the habitation of death. "Ben, wouldst thou rather turn back and see no more? We have at least seen the outside of a pest house. Shall that suffice us?"

"Nay, if we have come so far, let us go further," answered Benjamin. "We have seen naught but the tiled roof and the green garden. Come this way. There is a little gate by which we may gain entrance to a side door. Perchance they will turn us back if we seek to enter at the front."

The farm house looked peaceful enough nestling beneath its sheltering row of tall elms, in the midst of its wild garden, now a mass of autumnal bloom. But as they neared the house the boys heard dismal sounds issuing thence—the groans of sufferers beneath the hands of the physicians, who were often driven to use what seemed cruel measures to cause the tumours to break—the only chance of recovery for the patient—the shriek of some maddened or delirious patient, or the unintelligible murmur and babble from a multitude of sick. Moreover, they inhaled the pungent fumes of the burning drugs and vinegar which alone made it possible to breathe the atmosphere tainted by so much pestilential sickness. The boys held their own bottles of vinegar to their noses as they stole towards the house, feeling a mingling of strong repulsion and strong curiosity as they approached the dismal stronghold of disease.

Although men were in these days becoming almost reckless, and those who actually nursed and tended the sick were naturally less cautious and less particular than others, yet it is

Evelyn Everett-Green

probable that the daring boys might have been turned back had they approached the house by the ordinary entrance, for they certainly could not profess to have business there. As it was, however, thanks to Benjamin's knowledge of the place, not a creature observed their quiet approach through the orchard and along a tangled garden path. This path brought them to a door, which stood wide open in this sultry weather, in order to let a free current of air pass through the house, and they inhaled more strongly still the aromatic perfumes, which were not yet strong enough entirely to overcome that other noisome odour which was one of the most fatal means of spreading infection from plague-stricken patients.

"We can get into the great kitchen by this door," whispered Benjamin. "I trow they will use it for the sick; it is the biggest room in all the house. Yonder is the door. Shall I open it?"

Joseph gave a sign of assent, but bid his brother not speak needlessly, and keep his handkerchief to his mouth and nose. They had both steeped their handkerchiefs in vinegar, and could inhale nothing save that pungent scent.

Burning with curiosity, yet half afraid of their own temerity, the boys stole through a half-open door into a great room lined with beds. The sound of moans, groans, shrieks, and prayers drowned all the noise their own entry might have made, and they stood in the shadow looking round them, quite unnoticed in the general confusion of that busy home of death.

There were perhaps a score or more of sufferers in the great room, and two nurses moving about amongst them, quickly and in none too tender a fashion. A doctor was also there with a young man, his assistant; and at some bedsides he paused, whilst at others he gave a shake of the head, and went by without a word. Indeed it seemed to the boys as though almost a quarter of the patients were dead men, they lay so still and rigid, and the purple patches upon the white skin stood out with such terrible distinctness.

A man suddenly put in his head from the open door at the other end and asked of anybody who could answer him:

"Room for any more here?"

And the doctor's assistant, looking round, replied:

"Room for four, if you will send and have these taken away."

Almost immediately there came in two men, who bore away four corpses from the place, and in five minutes more the beds were full again, and the nurses were calculating how soon it would be possible to receive more, some now here being obviously in a dying state. The bearers reported that the outer barn was full as well as all the house; but those without invariably died, whilst a portion of those brought in recovered.

Joseph and Benjamin had seen enough for their own curiosity. It was a more terrible sight than they had anticipated, and they felt a great longing to get out of this stricken den into the purer air without. Joseph had laid a hand on his brother's arm to draw him away, when he was alarmed by seeing his brother's eyes fixed upon the far corner of the room with such an extraordinary expression of amaze and horror, that for a moment he feared he must have been suddenly stricken by the plague and was going off into the awful delirium he had heard described.

A poignant fear and remorse seized him, lest he had been the means of bringing his brother into this peril and having

Evelyn Everett-Green

caused his attack, if indeed it were one, and he pulled him harder by the arm to get him away. But with a strange choked cry Benjamin broke from him, and running across the room he flung himself upon his knees by the side of a bed, crying in a lamentable voice:

"Reuben—Reuben—Reuben!"

It was Joseph's turn now to gaze in horror and dismay. Could that be Reuben—that cadaverous, death-like creature, with the livid look of a plague patient, lying like one in a trance which can only end in the awakening of death? Was Benjamin dreaming? or was it really their brother? But how could he by any possibility be here, so far away from home, so utterly beyond the limits of his own district?

The doctor had approached Benjamin and had pulled him back from the bedside quickly, though not unkindly.

"What are you doing here, child?" he said. "Have we not enough upon our hands without having sound persons mad enough to seek to add to the numbers of the sick? Is he a relation of yours?

"Well, well, well, he will be looked after here better than you can do it. Your brother? Well, he has been four days here, and is one of those I have hope for. The tumours have discharged. He is suffering now from weakness and fever; but he might get well, especially if we could move him out of this pestilential air. Go home, children, and tell your friends that if they have a place to take him to he will not infect them now, and will have a better chance. But you must not linger here. It may be death to you; though it is true enough that many come seeking their friends who go away and take no hurt. No one can say who is safe and who is not. But get you gone, get you gone. Your brother shall be well looked to, I say. We have none so many who recover that we can afford to let those slip back for whom there is a chance!"

He had pushed the boys by this time into the garden, and was speaking to them there. He was a kind man, if blunt, and habit had not bred indifference in him to the sufferings of those about him. He told the boys that one of the strangest features about the plague patients was the rapid recovery they often made when once the poison was discharged by the breaking of the swellings, and the rapidity with which the infection ceased when these broken tumours had healed. Reuben's case had seemed desperate enough when he was brought in, but now he was in a fair way of recovery. If he could be taken to better air, he would probably be a sound man quickly. Even as he was, he might well recover.

The boys looked at each other and said with one voice that they thought they knew of a house where he would be received, and got leave to remove him in a cart at any time. The doctor then hurried back to his work, whilst the brothers looked each other in the face, and Benjamin said gravely:

"Methinks it must have been put into our hearts to go. Aunt Mary will forgive the temerity when she hears of the special Providence."

Their aunt was at no great distance off, as Benjamin knew. Instead of going home, they found their way to a brook. Pulling off their clothes, they proceeded to drag them over the sweet-scented meadow grass. Then they plunged into the brook, and enjoyed a delightful paddle and bath in the clear cool water. After rolling themselves in the hot grass, and having a fine romp there with Fido, they donned their garments, and felt indeed as though they had got rid of all germs of infection and disease.

Evelyn Everett-Green

After this they made their way towards the cottage where their aunt had been staying, and met her just sallying forth to return home.

Without any hesitation or delay Joseph told the tale of their hardihood and disobedience, and the strange discovery to which it had led them; and although their aunt trembled and looked pale with terror at the thought of how they had exposed themselves, she did not stop to chide them, but was full of anxiety for the immediate release of Reuben from his pestilential prison, and eager to have him to nurse in her own house, if she could do this without risk to the younger boys.

They were to the full as eager as she, and promised in everything to obey her—even to the sleeping and living in an outhouse for a few days, if only she would save Reuben from that horrible pest house. None knew better than Mary Harmer, who was a notable nurse herself, how much might now depend upon pure air, nourishing food, and quiet; and how could her nephew receive much individual care when cooped up amongst scores, if not hundreds, of desperate cases?

Mary was so much beloved by all around, that she quickly found a farmer willing to lend a cart even for the purpose of removing a sick person from the pest house, if he bore the honoured name of Harmer. She would not permit any person to accompany the cart, but drove it herself, and sent the boys home to prepare the airiest chamber and make all such preparations as they could think of beforehand; and to remove their own bedding into the outhouse, till she was assured that they were in no peril from the presence of their brother indoors.

Eagerly the boys worked at these tasks, and everything was in beautiful order when the cart drove up. One of the attendants from the pest house had come with it, and he carried Reuben up to the bed made ready for him, and drove the cart away, promising to disinfect it thoroughly, and return it to the owner ere nightfall.

It was little the eager boys saw of their aunt that day. She was engrossed by Reuben the whole time. She said he was terribly weak, and that he had not yet got back the use of his faculties. He lay in a sort of trance or stupor, and did not know where he was or what was happening. It came from weakness, and would pass away as he got back his strength. The doctor had assured her that the plague symptoms had spent themselves, and that he was free from the contagion.

The boys slept in the shed that night tranquilly enough, and in the morning their aunt came to them with a grave and sorrowful face.

"Is he worse?" asked Benjamin starting up.

"Not worse, I hope, yet not better. He has some trouble on his mind, and I fear that if we cannot ease him of that he will die," and her tears ran over, for Reuben was dear to her as a nephew, and she knew what store her brother set by his eldest son.

"Trouble! what trouble? Are any dead at home?" cried the boys anxiously. "Can he speak? has he talked to you? Tell us all!"

"He has not talked with his senses awake, but he has spoken words which have told me much. Death is not the trouble. He has not said one word to make me fear that our loved ones have been taken. The trouble is his own. It is a trouble of the heart. It concerns one whose name is Gertrude. Is not that the name of Master Mason's daughter?"

Evelyn Everett-Green

"Why, yes, to be sure. She has joined with the rest—with Janet and Rebecca—to care for the orphan children whom none know what to do with, there are such numbers of them. Reuben always thought a great deal of Mistress Gertrude— and she of him. What of that?"

"Does she think much of him?" asked Mary eagerly. "I feared she had flouted his love!"

"Nay, she worships the ground he treads on!" cried Joseph, who had a very sharp pair of eyes of his own, and a great liking for sweet-spoken Gertrude himself. "It was madam, her mother, who flouted Reuben. Gertrude is of different stuff. Why, whenever she was with us she would get me in a corner and talk of nothing but him. I thought they would but wait for the plague to be overpast to wed each other!"

Mary stood with her hands locked together, thinking deeply.

"Joseph," she said, "if it were a matter of saving Reuben's life, think you that Mistress Gertrude would come hither to my house and help me to nurse him back to health?"

Joseph's eyes flashed with eager excitement.

"I am certain sure she would!" he answered.

"Ah, but how to let her know!" cried Mary, pressing her hands together in perplexity. "Alas for days like these! How shall any one get a letter safely delivered to her in time? It may be that if we tarry the fever will have swept him off. It is fever of the mind rather than the body, and it is hard to minister to the mind diseased, without the one healing medicine."

"Hold! I have a plan," cried Joseph, whose wits were

sharpened by the pressing nature of the business in hand; "listen, and I will expound it. Tomorrow morning I will sally forth with a barrow laden with eggs, vegetables, and fruit; and I will enter the city as one of the country folks for the market, with whom none interfere at the barriers. I will e'en sell my goods to whoever will buy them, and at the bottom of the barrow thou shalt put one of thy cotton gowns and market aprons, Aunt Mary. Then will I go to Mistress Gertrude and tell her all. I shall learn of the welfare of those at home, and will come back with her at my side. The watch will but take her for a market woman, and we shall both pass unchecked and unhindered. By noon tomorrow Gertrude shall be here!

"Nay, hinder me not, good aunt. We must all adventure ourselves somewhat in this dire distress and peril. Sure, if Providence kept me safe in yon pest house yesterday, I need not fear to return to the city upon an errand of mercy such as may save my brother's life!"

CHAPTER XIII

HAPPY MEETINGS

"Reuben found! Reuben alive! O Joseph, Joseph, Joseph!" and Dorcas burst into tears of joy and relief, and sobbed aloud upon her brother's neck.

Joseph had brought his news straight to Dorcas, knowing that she at least would be certainly found within Lady Scrope's house. He was secretly afraid to go home first, lest the fatal red cross upon the door should tell its tale of woe, or lest the whole house itself should be shut up and desolate, like the majority of the houses he had passed in the forlorn city that morning. He felt, however, an almost superstitious confidence that Lady Scrope's house would defy the infection. He was decidedly of the opinion that that redoubtable dame was a witch, and that she had charms which kept the plague at bay. He therefore first sought out the sister with whom he felt certain he could obtain speech; and she had drawn him into a little parlour hard by the street door, in great astonishment at seeing him there, and fearful at first (as folks had grown to be of late) that he was the bearer of evil tidings.

The joy and relief were therefore so great that she could not restrain her tears, and between laughing, crying, and repeating in astonished snatches the words of explanation which fell from Joseph's lips, she made such an unwonted commotion in the ordinarily silent house, that soon the tap of a stick could have been heard by ears less preoccupied coming down the stairs and along the passage, and the door was pushed open to admit the little upright figure of the mistress of the house.

"Hoity toity! art thou bereft of thy senses, child? What in fortune's name means all this?"

"Boy, who art thou? and what dost thou here? A brother, forsooth! Come with some news, perchance? Well, well, well; how goes it in the city? Are any left alive? They say at the rate we are going now, it will take but a month more to destroy the city even as Sodom was destroyed!"

"O madam," cried Dorcas dashing away her tears, and turning an eager face towards the witch-like old woman, who in her silk gown, hooped and looped up, her fine lace cap and mittens, and her ebony stick with its ivory head, looked the impersonation of a fairy godmother, "this is my brother Joseph, and he comes with welcome tidings. My brother Reuben is not dead, albeit he has in truth been smitten by the plague. Joseph found him yesterday in the pest house just beyond Clerkenwell; and he is in a fair way to recover, if his mind can but be set at rest.

"Oh what news this will be for our parents!—for the girls!— for Gertrude! Oh how we have mourned and wept together; and now we shall rejoice with full hearts!"

"Has Mistress Gertrude mourned for him too?" asked Joseph eagerly. "Marry that is good hearing, for I have wondered all this while whether I should obtain the grace from her for which I have come."

"And what is that, young man?" asked Lady Scrope, tapping her cane upon the ground as much as to say that in her own house she was not going to take a secondary place, and that conversation was to be addressed to her. Joseph turned to her at once and answered:

"Verily, good madam, my aunt has sent me hither to fetch Mistress Gertrude forthwith to his side. She says that he calls ceaselessly upon her, and that unless he can see her beside him he may yet die of the disappointment and trouble, albeit the plague is stayed in his case, and it is but the fever of weakness that is upon him. She thinks it will not hurt her to come, if so be that it is as we hope, and that she has in her heart for him the same love as he has for her."

"Oh, she has! she has!" cried Dorcas, fired with sudden illumination of mind about many things that perplexed her before. "Her heart is just breaking for him!

"Prithee, good madam, let me go and call her. They say that she is of little use in the house now, being weak and weeping, and too sad at heart to work as heretofore. They can well spare her on such an errand, and methinks it will save her life as well as his. Let me but go and tell her the news."

"Go, child, go. Lovers be the biggest fools in all this world of fools! And if the women be the bigger fools, 'tis but because they were meant to be fitting companions for the men!

"Go to, child!—bring her here, and let us see what she says to this mad errand of this mad boy."

"And you, young sir, whilst your sister is gone, tell me all you saw and heard in the pest house! Marry, I like your spirit in going thither! It is the one place I long to see myself; only

I am too old to go gadding hither and thither after fine sights!"

Joseph was quite willing to indulge the old lady's morbid curiosity as to the sights he had seen yesterday and today, as he had journeyed back into the city in the guise of a market lad. The things were terrible enough to satisfy even Lady Scrope, who seemed to rejoice in an uncanny fashion over the awful devastation going on all round.

"I'm not a saint myself," she said with unwonted gravity, "and I never set up for one, but many has been the time when I have warned those about me that God would not stand aside for ever looking on at these abominations. The means were ready to His hand, and He has taken them and used them as a scourge. And He will scourge this wicked city yet again, if men will not amend their evil practices."

Next minute Gertrude and Dorcas came running in together, and Gertrude almost flung herself into Joseph's arms in her eager gratitude to him for his news, and her desire to hear everything he could tell her.

Such a clamour of voices then arose as fairly drowned any remark that Lady Scrope tried from time to time to throw in. Her old face took a suddenly softened look as she watched the little scene, and heard the words that passed amongst the young people. Presently she went tapping away on her high-heeled shoes, and was absent for some ten or fifteen minutes. When she came back she held in her hands a small iron-bound box, which seemed to be very heavy for its size.

"Well," she asked in her clear, sharp tones, "and what is going to be done next?"

"O madam, I am going to him. I can do naught else," answered

Gertrude, whose face was like an April morning, all smiles and tears blended together. "I cannot let him lie wanting me and wearying for me."

"Humph! I thought you had shown yourself a girl of spirit, and had sent him about his business when he came a-wooing, eh?"

"O madam, I did so. I thought that duty bid me; but I have repented so bitterly since! They say that 'twas since then he fell into the melancholy which was like to make him fall ill of the distemper. Oh, if he were to die, I should feel his blood on my head. I should never hold it up again. I cannot let anything keep me from him now. I must go to him in my poverty and tell him all. He must be the judge!"

Lady Scrope uttered a little snort, although her face bore no unkindly look.

"Child, child, thou art a veritable woman! I had thought better things of thee, but thou art just like the rest. Thou wilt gladly lie down in the dust, so as the one man shall trample upon thee, whilst thou dost adore him the more for it. Go to! go to! Maids and lovers be all alike. Fools every one of them! But for all that I like thee. I have an old woman's fancy for thee. And since in these days none may reckon on seeing the face of a departing friend again, I give now into thine hands the wedding gift I have had in mine eyes for thee.

"Nay, thank me not; and open it not save at the bedside of thy betrothed husband—if thou art fool enough to betroth thyself to one who as like as not will die of the plague before the week is out.

"And now off with you both. If you tarry too long, the watch will not believe you to be honest market folks, and will hinder your flight. Good luck go with you; and when ye be come to the city again—if ever that day arrive—come hither and tell me all the tale of your folly and love. Although a wise woman myself, I have a wondrous love of hearing tales of how other folks make havoc of their lives by their folly."

Gertrude took the box, which amazed her by its weight, and suggested ideas of value quite out of keeping with what she had any reason to expect from one so little known to her as Lady Scrope. She thanked the donor with shy gratitude, and pressed the withered hand to her fresh young lips. Lady Scrope, a little moved despite her cynical fashion of talking, gave her several affectionate kisses; and then the other girls came in to see the last of their companion, and to charge her with many messages of love for Reuben.

Joseph during this interval darted round to his father's house, to exchange a kiss with his mother and tell her the good news. It was indeed a happy day for the parents to hear that the son whom they had given up for lost was living, and likely, under Gertrude's care, to do well. They had not dared to murmur or repine. It seemed to them little short of a miracle that death had spared to them all their children through this fearful season. When they believed one had at last been taken, they had learned the strength and courage to say, "God's will be done." Yet it was happiness inexpressible to know that he was not only living, but in the safe retreat of Mary Harmer's cottage, and under her tender and skilful care.

So used were they now to the thought of those they loved caring for the sick, that they had almost ceased to fear contagion so encountered. It appeared equally busy amongst those who fled from it. They did not even chide Joseph for the reckless curiosity which had led the boys to adventure themselves without cause in the fashion that had led to such notable results.

When Joseph returned to Lady Scrope's, it was to find Gertrude arrayed in the clothes provided for her, and looking, save for her dainty prettiness, quite like a country girl come in with marketable wares. Such things of her own as she needed for her sojourn, together with Lady Scrope's precious box, were put into the barrow beneath the empty basket and sacks. Then with many affectionate farewells the pair started forth, and talking eagerly all the while, took their way through the solitary grass-grown streets, away through Cripplegate, and out towards the pleasanter regions beyond the walls.

Joseph sought to engross his companion in talk, so that she might not see or heed too much the dismal aspect of all around them. He himself had seen a considerable difference in the city between the time he and Benjamin had left it and today. In places it almost seemed as though no living soul now remained; and he observed that foot passengers in the streets went about more recklessly than before, with a set and desperate expression of countenance, as though they had made up their minds to the worst, and cared little whether their fate overtook them today or a week hence.

Gertrude's thoughts, however, were so much with Reuben, that she heeded but little of what she saw around her. She spoke of him incessantly, and begged again and again to hear the story of how he had been found. Her cheek flushed a delicate rose tint each time she heard how he had called for her ceaselessly in his delirium. That showed her, if nothing else could convince her of it, how true and disinterested his love was; that it was for herself he had always wooed her, and not for any hope of the fortune she had at one time looked to receive from her father as her marriage dowry.

When they had passed the last of the houses, and stood in the sunny meadows, with the blue sky above them and the songs of birds in their ears, Gertrude heaved a great sigh of relief, and her eyes filled with tears.

"O beautiful trees and fields!" she cried; "it seems as though nothing of danger and death could overshadow the dwellers in such fair places."

"So Benjamin and I thought," said Joseph gravely; "but, alas, the plague has been busy here, too. See, there is a cluster of houses down there, and but three of them are now inhabited. The pestilence came and smote right and left, and in some houses not one was left alive. Still death seems not so terrible here amid these smiling fields as it does when men are pent together in streets and lanes. And the dead at first could be buried in their own gardens by their friends, if they could not take them to the churchyards, which soon refused to receive them. Many were thus saved from the horror of the plague pit, which they so greatly dreaded. But I know not whether it is a wise kindness so to bury them; for there were hamlets, I am told, where the plague raged fearfully, and where the living could scarce bury the dead."

Gertrude sighed; death and trouble did indeed seem everywhere. But even her sorrow for others could not mar her happiness in the prospect of seeing Reuben once again; and as they neared the place, and Joseph pointed out the twisted chimneys and thatched roof peeping through the sheltering trees and shrubs, the girl could not restrain her eager footsteps, and flew on in advance of her companion, who was retarded by his barrow.

The next minute she was eagerly kissing Benjamin (who, together with Fido, had run out at the sound of her footsteps), and shedding tears of joy at the news that Reuben was no

Evelyn Everett-Green

worse, that there were now no symptoms of the plague about him, but that he was perilously weak, and needed above all things that his mind should be set at rest.

At the sound of voices Mary Harmer came softly downstairs from the sick man's side, and divining in a moment who the stranger was, took her into a warm, motherly embrace, and thanked her again and again for coming so promptly.

"Nay, it is I must thank thee for letting me come," answered Gertrude between smiles and tears. "And now, may I not go to him? I would not lose a moment. I am hungry for the sight of his living face. Prithee, let me go!"

"So thou shalt, my child, in all good speed; but just at this moment he sleeps, and thou must refresh thyself after thy long, hot walk, that thou mayest be better able to tend him. I will not keep thee from him, be sure, when the time comes that thou mayest go to him."

Joseph at that moment came up with the barrow, and Gertrude found that it was pleasant and refreshing to let Mary Harmer bathe her face and hands and array her in her own garments. And then she sat down to a pleasant meal of fresh country provisions, which tasted so different from anything she had eaten these many long weeks.

The boys, who as a precautionary measure were keeping away from the house itself until it should be quite certain that their brother was free from infection, took their meal on the grass plot outside, and enjoyed it mightily.

The whole scene was so different from anything upon which Gertrude's eyes had rested for long, that tears would rise unbidden in them, though they were tears of happiness and gratitude. The dog Fido took to her at once, and showed her many intelligent attentions, and was so useful altogether in fetching and carrying that his cleverness and docility were a constant source of amusement and wonder to all, and gave endless delight to the boys, who spent all their spare time in training him.

Then just when the afternoon shadows were beginning to lengthen, and the light to grow golden with the mellow September glow, Gertrude was softly summoned to the pleasant upper chamber, which smelt sweetly of lavender, rose leaves, and wild thyme, where beside the open casement lay Reuben, in a snow-white bed, his face sadly wasted and white, and his eyes closed as if in the lassitude of utter weakness.

Mary gave Gertrude a smile, and motioned her to go up to him, which she did very softly and with a beating heart. He did not appear to note her footfall; but when she stood beside him, and gently spoke his name, his eyes flashed open in a moment, and fixed themselves upon her face, their expression growing each moment more clear and comprehending.

"Gertrude!" he breathed in a voice whose weakness told a tale of its own, and he moved his hand as though he would fain ascertain by the sense of touch whether or not this was a dream.

She saw the movement, and took his hand between her own, kneeling down beside the bed and covering it with kisses and tears.

That seemed to tell him all, without the medium of words. He asked no question, he only lay gazing at her with a deep contentment in his eyes. He probably knew not either where he was, or how any of these strange things came to pass. She was with him; she was his very own. Of that there could be no manner of doubt. And that being so, what did anything else matter? He lay gazing at her perfectly contented, till he fell asleep holding her hand in his.

That was the beginning of a steady if rather a slow recovery. It was only natural indeed that Reuben should be long in regaining strength. He had been through months of fatigue and arduous wearing toil, and the marvel was that when the distemper attacked him in his weakness and depression he had strength enough to throw it off. As Mary Harmer said, it seemed sometimes as though those who went fearlessly amongst the plague stricken became gradually inoculated with the poison, and were thus able to rid themselves of it when it did attack them. Reuben at least had soon thrown off his attack, and the state of weakness into which he had fallen was less the result of the plague than of his long and arduous labours before.

How he ever came to be in the pest house of Clerkenwell he never could altogether explain. He remembered that business had called him out in a northwesterly direction; and he had a dim recollection of feeling a sick longing for a sight of the country once more, and of bending his steps further than he need, whilst he fancied he had entertained some notion of paying a visit to his aunt, and making sure that his brothers had safely reached her abode. That was probably the reason why he had come so far away from home. He had been feeling miserably restless and wretched ever since Gertrude had refused him, and upon that day he had an overpowering sense of illness and weariness upon him, too. But he did not remember feeling any alarm, or any premonition of coming sickness. He had grown so used to escaping when others were stricken down all round, that the sense of uncertainty which haunted all men at the commencement of the outbreak had almost left him now. It could only be supposed that the fever of the pestilence had come upon him, and that he had dropped by the wayside, as so many did, and had been carried into the farm house by some compassionate person, or by one of the bearers whose duty it was to keep the highways clear of such objects of public peril. But he knew nothing of his own condition, and had had no real gleam of consciousness, until he opened his eyes in his aunt's house to find Gertrude bending over him.

There was no shadow between them now. Gertrude's surrender was as complete as Lady Scrope had foreseen. She used now to laugh with Reuben over the sayings of that redoubtable old dame, and wonder what she would think of them could she see them now. The box she had entrusted to Gertrude had been given into Mary Harmer's care for the present, till Reuben should be strong enough to enjoy the excitement of opening it. But upon the first day that saw him down in the little parlour, lying upon the couch that had been made ready to receive him, Joseph eagerly clamoured to have the box brought down and opened; and his wish being seconded by all, Mary Harmer quickly produced it, and it was set upon a little table at the side of the couch.

"Have you the key?" asked Reuben of Gertrude, and she produced it from her neck, round which it had been hanging all this while by a silken cord.

"It felt almost like a love token," she said with a little blush, "for she told me I was not to open it save at the side of my betrothed husband!"

Now, amid breathless silence, she fitted the key into the lock and raised the lid. That disclosed a layer of soft packing, which, when removed, left the contents exposed to view.

"Oh!" cried Joseph and Benjamin in tones of such wonder that Fido must needs rear himself upon his hind legs to get a peep, too; but he was soon satisfied, for he saw nothing very interesting in the yellow contents of the wooden box, which neither smelt nice nor were good for food. But the lovers looked across at each other in speechless amazement.

For the box was filled to the brim with neatly piled heaps of golden guineas—the first guineas ever struck in this country; so called from the fact that they were made of Guinea gold brought from Africa by one of the trading companies, and first coined in the year 1662. And a quick calculation, based upon the counting of one of these upright heaps, showed that the box contained five hundred of these golden coins, which as yet were only just coming into general circulation.

"Oh," cried Gertrude in amaze, "what can she have done it for? And they call Lady Scrope a miser!"

"Misers often have strange fancies; and Lady Scrope has always been one of the strangest and most unaccountable of her sex," said Reuben. "I cannot explain it one whit. It is of a piece with much of her inscrutable life. All we can do is to give her our gratitude for her munificence. She has neither kith nor kin to wrong by her strange liberality to thee, sweet Gertrude; nor can I marvel that she should have come to love thee so well. Sweet heart, this money will purchase the house upon the bridge which thy father tells us he is forced to sell. I had thought that I would buy it of him for our future home. But thou hast the first claim. At least, now the place is safe. What is mine is thine, and what is thine is mine, and we will together make the purchase, and give him a home with us beneath the old roof.

"Will that make you happy, dear heart? Methinks it will please Lady Scrope that her golden hoard should help in such an act of filial love!"

And Gertrude could only weep tears of pure happiness on her lover's shoulder, and marvel how it was that such untold joy had come to her in the midst of the very shadow of death.

CHAPTER XIV

BRIGHTER DAYS

"The plague is abating! the plague is abating! The bills were lower by two thousand last week! They say the city is like to go mad with joy. I would fain go and see what is happening there. Prithee, good aunt, let me e'en do so much. I shall take no hurt. Methinks, having escaped all peril heretofore, I may be accounted safe now."

This was Joseph's eager petition as he rushed homewards after a stroll in the direction of the town one evening early in October. There had been rumours of an improvement in the health of the city for perhaps ten days now, notwithstanding the fearful mortality during the greater part of September. Therefore were the weekly bills most eagerly looked for, and when it was ascertained that the mortality had diminished by two thousand (when, from the number of sick, it might well have risen by that same amount), it did indeed seem as though the worst were over; and great was the joy which Joseph's news brought to those within the walls of that cottage home.

Yet Mary Harmer was wise and cautious in the answer she gave to the eager boy.

"Wait yet one week longer, Joseph; for we may not presume upon God's goodness and mercy, and adventure ourselves without cause into danger. The city has been fearfully ravaged of late. The very air seems to have been poisoned and tainted, and there are streets and lanes which, they say, it is even now death to enter. Therefore wait yet another week, and then we will consider what is safe to be done. Right glad should I be for news of your father and mother; but we have been patient this long while, and we will be patient still."

"Our good aunt is wise," said Reuben, who looked wonderfully better for his stay in fresh country air, albeit still rather gaunt and pale. "It is like that this good news itself may lead men to be somewhat reckless in their joy and confidence. We will not move till we have another report. Perchance our father may be able to let us know ere long of his welfare and that of the rest at home."

All through the week that followed encouraging and cheering reports of the abatement of the plague were heard by those living on the outskirts of the stricken city; and when the next week's bill showed a further enormous decrease in the death rate, Mary Harmer permitted Joseph to pay a visit home, his return being eagerly waited for in the cottage. He came just as the early twilight was drawing in, and his face was bright and joyous.

"It is like another city," he cried. "I had not thought there could be so many left as I saw in the streets today. And they went about shaking each other by the hand, and smiling, and even laughing aloud in their joy. And if they saw a shut-up house, and none looking forth from the windows, some one would stand and shout aloud till those within looked out, and then he would tell them the good news that the plague was abating; and at that sound many poor creatures would fall a-weeping, and praise the Lord that He had left even a remnant."

"Poor creatures!" said Mary Harmer with commiseration; "it has been a dismal year for thousands upon thousands!"

"Ay, verily. I cannot think that London will ever be full again," said the boy. "There be whole streets with scarce an inhabitant left, and we know that multitudes of those who fled died of the pestilence on the road and in other places. But today there was no memory for the misery of the past, only joy that the scourge was abating. It is not that many do not still fall ill of the distemper, but that they recover now, where once they would have died. And whereas three weeks back they died in a day or two days, now even if so be as they do die, it takes the poison eight or ten days to kill them. The physicians say that that is because the malignity of the distemper is abating, wherefore men scarce fear it now, and come freely abroad, not in despair, as they did when it was so virulent a scourge, but because they fear it so much less than before."

"And our parents and those at home?" asked Reuben eagerly.

"All well, though something weary and worn; but it is wondrous how they have borne up all through. Father says that he will come hither to see us all the first moment he can. His duties are like to have a speedy end; and he is longing for a sight of Reuben's face, and of something better than closed houses and the wan faces of the sick or the mourners."

"Poor brother James!" said Mary softly; "I would that he and his would leave the city behind for a while, and remain under my roof to recover their strength and health. It must have been a sorely trying time. Think you that they could leave the house together? For we would make shift to receive them all, an they could come."

This was a most delightful idea to all the party. The

hospitable cottage had plenty of rooms, although many of these were but attics beneath the thatched roof, none too light or commodious. In summer they might have been too warm and stuffy to be agreeable sleeping places, but in the cooler autumn they would be good enough for hardy young folks brought up simply and plainly.

Joseph and Benjamin at once dashed all over the place, making plans for the housing of the whole party. It would be the finest end to a melancholy period, being all together here in this homelike place.

Everything was duly arranged in the hopes of winning the father's consent to the scheme. Mary Harmer hunted up stores of bedding and linen, the latter of her own weaving, and every day they waited impatiently for the appearing of James Harmer, who, however, was unaccountably long in making his appearance.

He came at last, but it was with a sorrowful face and a bowed look which told at once a story of trouble, and made the whole party stand silent, after the first eager chorus of welcome, certain that he was the bearer of bad news.

"My poor boy Dan!" he said in a choked voice, and sat himself heavily down upon the chair beside the hearth.

"Dan!" cried Reuben, and the word was echoed by all the brothers in tones of varying surprise and dismay. "You do not mean that he is dead!"

"Taken to the plague pit a week ago. Just when all the world is rejoicing in the thought that the distemper is abating. Dr. Hooker spoke truly when he said that the confidence of the people was like to be a greater peril than the disease itself. For those who are sick now come openly abroad into the streets, no longer afraid for themselves or others, and thus it has come about that no man knows whether he is safe, and my poor boy has been taken."

Sad indeed were the faces of all, and the two little boys were dissolved in tears, as their father told how poor Dan had fallen sick, and had succumbed on the fourth day to the poison.

"Dr. Hooker said that he was worn out with his unceasing labours, else he would not have died," said the sorrowful father. "He had treated many worse cases even when things were worse, and brought them round. But Dan was worn out with all he had been doing for the past months. He fell an easy prey; and he did not suffer much, thank God. He lay mostly in a torpor, much as Reuben did, as I hear, but slowly sank away. His poor mother! She had begun to think that she was to have all her children about her yet. But in truth we must not repine, having so many left to us, when they say there is scarce a family in all the town that has not lost its two, three, or four at best!"

It almost seemed a more sorrowful thing to lose Dan just when things were beginning to look brighter, than it would have done when the distemper was at its height. But as the good man said, gratitude for so many spared ought to outweigh any repining for those taken. After the first tears were shed, he gently checked in those about him the inclination to mourn, saying that God knew best, and had dealt very lovingly and bountifully with them; and that they must trust His goodness and mercy all through, and believe that He had judged mercifully and tenderly in taking their brother from them.

The sight of Reuben alive and well did much to assuage the father's grief; for there had been a time when he had not thought to look upon the face of his firstborn in this life. He was also greatly pleased to learn that he had another daughter in the person of gentle Gertrude, and he gladly undertook the negotiation of the purchase of his neighbour's house, so that he should not know who the purchaser was until the right moment came.

Mary Harmer's proposal to take in the whole family for a spell of fresh air and rest was gratefully accepted by the tired father.

"I trow it would be the greatest boon for all of us, and may likely save us from some peril," he said, "for, as I say, men seem to be gone mad with joy that the malignity of the plague is so greatly abating, and that the houses are no longer closed. For my own part, I would they were closed yet a little longer; but the impatience of the people would not now permit it, and they having shown themselves in the main docile and obedient these many months, must be considered now that the worst of the peril is past. When the plague was at its worst last month, there was of necessity some relaxation of stringent measures, because there were times when neither watchmen nor nurses could be found, and common humanity forbade us to close houses when the inhabitants could not get tendance in the prescribed way. Moreover, a sort of desperation was bred in men's minds, and the fear was the less because that every man thought his own turn would assuredly come ere long. So that when of a sudden the bills began to decrease, it seemed unreasonable to be more strict than we had been just before. Moreover, it was found harder to restrain the people in their joy than in their sorrow; and so we must hope for the best, and trust that the lessened malignity of the disease will keep down the mortality. For that there will continue to be many sick for weeks to come we cannot doubt. As for myself, knowing and fearing all I do, nothing would more please and comfort me

Evelyn Everett-Green

than to bring my wife and girls hither to this safe spot. I had not dared to think you could take such a party, Mary; but since you have already made provision for us, why, the sooner we all get forth from the city, the better will it please me."

Great was the joy in the cottage occasioned by this answer. Sorrow for the loss of poor Dan was almost forgotten in joyful preparation. Dan had not been much at home for many years, only coming and going as his ship chanced to put into port in the river or not. Therefore his loss was not felt as that of Reuben would have been. It seemed a sad and grievous thing, after having escaped so many perils, to come to his death at last; but so many families had suffered such infinitely greater loss, that repining and mourning seemed almost wrong. And the thought of seeing all the home faces once more was altogether too delightful to admit of much admixture of grief.

"I wonder if Dorcas will come," said Gertrude, as they hung about the door awaiting the arrival which was expected every minute.

Three days had now passed since James Harmer's first visit, and he was to bring his wife and daughters in the afternoon, and stay the night himself, returning on the morrow to transact some necessary business, but spending much of his time with his family in this pleasant spot.

Gertrude had offered to leave, if there were not room for her; but in truth she scarce knew where to go, since of her father she had heard very little of late, and knew not how long his house would be his own.

No one, however, would hear of such a thing as that she should leave them. She was already like a sister to the boys, and had in old days been as one to the girls. Moreover, as

Mary Harmer sometimes said, why should not she and Reuben be quietly married out here before they returned to the city, and then they could go back to their own house when all the negotiations had been completed and her father's mind relieved of its load of care?

"Why should Dorcas not come?" asked Mary quickly. "My brother spoke of bringing all."

"I was wondering if Lady Scrope would be willing to spare her," was the reply. "She is fond of Dorcas in her way, and is used to her. She might not be willing she should go, and she is very determined when her mind is made up."

"Yet I think she has a kind heart in spite of all her odd ways," said Mary Harmer; "I scarce think she would keep the girl pining there alone. But we shall see. My wonder would rather be if Janet and Rebecca could get free from the other house where the children are kept."

"Father said that that house was to be emptied soon. The Lord Mayor is making many wise regulations for the support of those left destitute by the plague. Large sums of money kept flowing in all the while the scourge lasted. The king sent large contributions, and other wealthy men followed his example. There be many widows left alone and desolate, and these are to have a sum of money and certain orphan children to care for. All that will be settled speedily; for who knows when my Lady Scrope's house may not be wanted by the tenant who ran away in such hot haste months ago? It will need purifying, too, and directions will shortly be issued, I take it, for the right purification of infected houses.

"My sisters will soon get their burdens off their hands. It is time they had a change; they were looking worn and tired even before I left the city."

"They are coming! they are coming! They are just here!" shouted Joseph and Benjamin in one breath, coming rushing down from a vantage post up to which they had climbed in one of the great elm trees. "They must all be there—every one of them! It is like a caravan along the road; but I know it is they, for we saw father leading a horse, and mother was riding it—with such a lot of bags and bundles!"

The next minute the caravan hove in sight through the windings of the lane, and three minutes later there was such a confusion of welcomes going on that nothing intelligible could be said on either side; nor was it until the whole party was assembled round the table in Mary Harmer's pleasant kitchen, ready to do justice to the good cheer provided, that any kind of conversation could be attempted.

The sisters felt like prisoners released. They laughed and cried as they danced about the garden in the twilight, stooping down to lay their faces against the cool, wet grass, and drinking in the scented air as though it were something to be tasted by palate and tongue.

"It is so beautiful! it is so wonderful!" they kept exclaiming one to the other, and the quaint, rambling cottage, with its bare floor, and simple, homely comforts, seemed every whit as charming.

Dorcas was there, as well as Janet and Rebecca; and the three sisters, together with Gertrude, were to share a pair of attics with a door of communication between them.

They were delighted with everything. They kept laughing and kissing each other for sheer joy of heart; and although a sigh, and a murmur of "Poor Dan! if only he could be here!" would break at intervals from one or another, yet in the intense joy of this meeting, and in the sense of escape from the city in which they had been so long imprisoned, all but thankfulness and delight must needs be forgotten, and it was a ring of wonderfully happy faces that shone on Mary Harmer at the supper board that night.

"This is indeed a kindly welcome, sister," said Rachel, as she sat at her husband's right hand, looking round upon the dear faces she had scarce dared hope to see thus reunited for so many weary weeks; "I could have desired nothing better for all of us. Thou canst scarcely know how it does feel to be free once more, to be able to go where one will, without vinegar cloths to one's face, and to feel that the air is a thing to breathe with healing and delight, instead of to be feared lest there be death in its kiss! Ah me! I think God does not let us know how terrible a thing is till His chastening hand is removed. We go on from day to day, and He gives us strength for each day as it comes; but had we known at the beginning what lay before us, methinks our souls would have well nigh fainted within us. And yet here we are—all but one—safe and sound at the other side!"

"I truly never thought to see such fearful sights, and to come through such a terrible time of trial," said Dinah very gravely. She was one of the party included in Mary Harmer's hospitable invitation, and looked indeed more in need of the rest and change than any of the others. Her brother had had some ado to get her to quit her duties as nurse to the sick even yet, but it was not difficult now to get tendance for them, and she felt so greatly the need of rest that she had been persuaded at last.

"Many and many are the times when I have been left the only living being in a house—once, so far as I could tell, the only living thing in a whole street! None may know, save those who have been through it, the awful loneliness of being so shut in, with nothing near but dead bodies. And yet the

Evelyn Everett-Green

Lord has brought me through, and only one of our number has been taken."

The mother's eyes filled with tears, but her heart was too thankful for those spared her to let her grief be loud. One after another those round the table spoke of the things they had seen and heard; but presently the talk drifted to brighter themes. Gertrude asked eagerly of her father, and where he was and what he was doing; and Mary Harmer asked if he would not come and join them, if her house could be made to hold another inmate.

"He is well in health, but looks aged and harassed," was the answer of the father. "He has had sad losses. Half-finished houses have been thrown back on his hands through the death of those who had commenced them; he has been robbed of his stores of costly merchandise; and poor Frederick's debts have mounted up to a great sum. Now that people are flocking back into the city, and business is reviving once more, he will have to meet his creditors, and can only do this by the sale of his house. I saw him yesterday, and told him I had heard of a purchaser already; whereat he was right glad, fearing that he might be long in selling, since men might fear to come back to the city, and whilst there were so many hundreds of houses left empty. If he can once get rid of his load of debt, he can strive to begin business again in a modest way. But, to be sure, it will be long before any houses will need to be built; the puzzle will be how to fill those that are left empty. I fear me he will find things hard for a while. But if he has a home with you, my children, and if we all give what help we can, I doubt not that little by little he may recover a part of what he has lost. He will be wise not to try so many different callings. If he had not had so many ventures afloat in these troubled times, he would not now have lost his all."

"That was poor mother's wish," said Gertrude softly; "she wanted to be rich quickly for Frederick's sake. I used to hear father tell her that the risk was too great; but she did not seem able to understand aright. I do not think it was father's own wish."

"That is what I always said," answered James Harmer heartily; "and I trow things will be greatly better now, if once trade makes a start again. As for us, we have lost a summer's trade, but, beyond that, all has been well with us. We have had the fewer outgoings, and so soon as the gentry and the Court come back again we shall be as busy as ever. The plague has done us little harm, for we had no great ventures afloat to miscarry, and had money laid by against any time of necessity."

That evening, before the party retired to rest, the father gathered his children and all the household about him, and offered a fervent thanksgiving for their preservation during this time of peril. After that they all separated to their own rooms, and the girls sat long together ere they sought their couches, talking, as girls will talk, of all that had happened to them, and of the coming marriage of Gertrude and their brother, over which they heartily rejoiced.

"I must e'en let Lady Scrope know when it is to be," said Dorcas, "if I can make shift to do so. I trow she would like to be there. She has taken a wondrous liking to thee, Gertrude, and she says she has a fine opinion of Reuben, too. I know not quite what she has heard of him, but so it is."

"I was fearful lest she should not be willing to spare thee, Dorcas," said Gertrude with a caress, "but here thou art with the rest."

"Yes, she was wondrous good to us," said Janet eagerly,

"else I scarce know how we could have come, for there were six children left in the house, and no homes yet found for them to go to. They were the sickly ones whom we feared to part with, and father said they would strive to get places for them in the country. When we heard what our kind aunt wished, we saw not how we could leave the little ones; but Lady Scrope, she up and chid us well for silly, puling fools, who thought the world could not wag without our help. And then she sent out and got two nice, comfortable, honest widow women to live in the house with the children. And one of them had a neat-fingered daughter, who had been in good service till the plague sent her family into the country and she was packed off home. Her she took for her maid, and sent Dorcas off with us. Sure, never was a sharper tongue and a kinder heart in one body together! I had never thought to like Lady Scrope one-tenth part as well as I do."

Those were happy days that followed. It was pure delight to the sisters to wander about the green fields and lanes, watching the play of light and shadow there, hearing the songs of the birds, and seeing the gorgeous pageantry of autumn clothing the trees with all manner of wondrous tints and hues. Reuben knew the neighbourhood by that time, and was their companion in their rambles; and happy were the hours thus spent, only less happy than the meetings round the glowing hearth or hospitable table later on, when the news of the day would be told and retold.

James Harmer went frequently into the city to see after certain things, and to ascertain that his own and his neighbour's houses were safe. What he saw and heard there day by day made him increasingly glad that big family had found so safe a retreat; for there was still some considerable peril to the dwellers in the city, owing, more than anything, to the utter carelessness of the people now that the immediate scare was removed.

The same men who had shrunk away from all contact with even sound persons six weeks ago, would now actually visit and hold converse with those who had the disease upon them. Persons afflicted with tumours that were still active and therefore infectious would walk openly about the streets, none seeming to object to their presence even in crowded thoroughfares. It seemed as though joy at the abatement of the pestilence had wrought a sort of madness in the brains and hearts of the people. So long as the death rate decreased, and the cases were no longer so fatal in character, there seemed no way of making the citizens observe proper precautions, and, as many averred, the malady increased and spread, although not in nearly so fatal a form, as it never need have done but for the recklessness of the multitudes.

One very sorrowful case was brought home to the Harmers, because it happened to some worthy neighbours of their own who had lived opposite to them for many a year.

When first the alarm was given that the plague had entered within the city walls, this man had hastily decided to quit London with his wife and family and seek an asylum in the country, and had earnestly urged the Harmers to do the same. For many months nothing had been heard of them; but with the first abatement of the malady the father had appeared, and had asked advice from Harmer as to how soon he might bring home his family, who were all sound and well. His friend advised him to wait another month at least; but he laughed such counsel to scorn, and just before the Harmers themselves started for Islington, their friends had settled themselves in their old house opposite.

Ten days later Harmer heard with great dismay that three of the children had taken the plague and had died. By the end of the week there was not one of the family alive save the unhappy man himself, and he went about like one distraught, so that his reason or his life seemed like to pay the forfeit.

It was no wonder, in the hearing of such stories as these—of which there were many—that Mary Harmer rejoiced to have her brother's household safely housed and out of danger, and that she earnestly begged them to remain with her at least until the merry Christmastide should be overpast.

CHAPTER XV

A CHRISTMAS WEDDING

"I never thought to see daughter of mine wedded from the house of a neighbour," said the Master Builder (whose title yet clung to him, albeit there was something of mockery in the sound), heaving a sigh as he looked into the happy face of his child. "But a homeless man must needs do the best he can; and our good friends have won the right to play the part of kinsfolk towards us both."

"Indeed—indeed they have, dear father," answered Gertrude; "thou canst not think how happy I have been here in this sweet cottage, nor what a home it has been to us all these weeks. I shall be almost loth to leave it on the morrow—at least I should be, were it not for the great happiness coming into my life. But the home to which Reuben will take me must be even dearer than this. And thou wilt come with us, sweet father, and make us happy by thy presence!"

"Ay, child, if thou wilt have the homeless old man who has managed his affairs so ill as to have to start life afresh when he should be thinking of resigning his work into other hands, and passing his old age in peace and—"

But Gertrude stopped him with a kiss.

Evelyn Everett-Green

"Thou art not old, father; and I trow before thou art, a peaceful and prosperous old age will be in store for thee. Whilst Reuben and I live, nothing shall lack to thee that filial love can bestow. O dearest father! methinks there are bright and happy days before us yet."

"I trust so—I trust so, my child, for thee especially. For thou dost deserve them. Thou hast been a good daughter, and wilt make a good wife."

"My heart misgives me sometimes that I was not always so tender a daughter to poor mother as I fain would have been. May God pardon me in whatever way I may have erred!"

"The error was more hers than thine," answered the father with a sigh; "and mine too, inasmuch as I checked her not early, as I perchance might have done. She would have wed thee with some needy and perhaps evil-living gallant, who would have taken thee for thy fortune. Thou hast done far better to choose such an honest, godly youth as Reuben. He will make thee an excellent husband."

"Ah, will he not!" said Gertrude, her face alight with tender love. "Poor mother did not understand what she was doing in striving to banish him from the house. But methinks, in the land of spirits all these things are seen aright; and that if it is permitted to the dead to know aught of what passes in the land they have left behind, she will be rejoicing with us today."

"Heaven send it may be so! My poor wife," and the father heaved a great sigh of mixed feelings, "it is well she has not lived to see this end to her schemings to be rich. At least she is spared the knowledge of her husband's ruin."

"Nay, call it not that, dear father. Master Harmer says that things are beginning to look up again after the terrible visitation, and surely your affairs will look up likewise."

"In a measure, yes," he answered. "I have at least sold the old house for a better sum than I expected; and the purchaser has bought all the rich furniture, save such things as I would not sell for the sake of your poor mother. These I shall move shortly to your home, my child. My good friend says that it is hard by his house, so the journey will not be a difficult one."

"No, father," answered Gertrude, with glowing cheeks. "And who has bought the old Bridge house?"

"Nay, I have not even had the heart to ask. My good friend has carried out the business for me from first to last. He has been the truest friend man ever had. I have had naught to do but to sign the papers and receive the purchase money. No doubt the pang of seeing others living there will pass in time, but just now I care not even to think of it."

Gertrude's face was still glowing a rosy red, but she turned the conversation at once.

"And thou art getting together a little business again, father, on the Southwark side of the river?"

"Yes; that again is by the advice of our good neighbour. He showed me that I could no longer afford the large buildings in the Chepe. He heard of these small premises going a-begging for a purchaser, all connected with them having perished in the plague. The small sum left to me of the purchase money of the house, after my debts were paid, sufficed to buy them; and now I have two steady workmen in my employ, instead of the scores I once had. But God be thanked, we have never been idle all these weeks. And it may be that by-and-by, as confidence returns, I may get something of a business together again."

"Thou hast been purifying and disinfecting houses, they say, for the wealthy ones of the city?"

"Ay; that was our good friend's thought. The Lord Mayor and authorities issued general directions for this work; and Harmer suggested to me that I should print handbills offering to undertake the purging of any house entrusted to me for a fixed fee. This I did, and have had my hands full ever since. All the fine folks are crowding back now that the cold weather has come, but no one cares to venture within his house till it has been purified by the burning of aromatic drugs and spices. The rich care not what they spend, so that they are sure they are free from danger. As for the poor, they do but burn tar or pitch or sulphur; and methinks these do just as well, save that the odour which hangs about is not so grateful to the senses. Yes, it was a happy thought of good James Harmer, and has put money in my pocket enough to enable me to undertake small building matters without borrowing. But I trow it will be long ere any building is wanted in and about the city. There are too many empty houses left there for that."

"Shall I see a wondrous change there when I go back, father?"

"A change, but a wondrous small one compared to what one would suppose," answered the father. "All men are amazed to see how quickly the streets have filled, and how little of change there is to note in the outward aspect of things. I had thought that half the houses would be left empty; but I think there be not more than one-eighth without inhabitants, and these are filling up apace. To be sure, in the once crowded lanes and alleys there are far fewer people than before; but it is wonderful to see how small the change is; and life goes on just as of old. It is as if the calamity was already half forgot!"

"Nay but, father, I trust it is not forgotten, and that men's consciences are stirred, and that they have taken to heart the warning of God's just anger."

The Master Builder slightly shook his head.

"I fear not, child, I fear not. I hear the same oaths and blasphemies, the same ribald jests and ungodly talk, as of old. They say the Court, which has lately returned to Whitehall, is as gay and wanton as ever. In face of the terror of death, men did resolve to amend their ways; but I fear me, that terror being past, they do but make a mock of it, and return, like the sow in Scripture, to their wallowing in the mire."

Gertrude looked gravely sorrowful for a moment; but, on the eve of her wedding day, she could not be sorrowful long. She and her father were enjoying a talk together before she sought her couch. He had been unable to come earlier to see her, business matters having detained him in town. For the past two months he had been at work with his task of purifying and setting in order the houses of the better-class people, for their return thither after the plague; and though he had sent many affectionate messages to his daughter, this was the first time for several weeks that they had met. It could not but rankle in the father's heart that, for the time being, he had no home to offer to his child. He had been staying with his good friend James Harmer all this while, who had left his wife and family at Islington to regain their full health and strength, while he spent his time between the Bridge house and the cottage. His business required his presence at home during a part of the week, since his shopmen and apprentices had already returned; but he would not permit his family to do so just yet, deeming it better for them to remain with his sister, and to enjoy with her a period of rest and refreshment which could never be theirs in the busy life of home.

A happy Christmas had thus been spent; and now it was the eve of Gertrude's wedding day, which was the one following Christmas Day. The Master Builder had spent the festival with his friends, and on the morrow would accompany his daughter and her husband to their home in the city, the Harmer family returning to their house at the same time, and bringing Mary with them on a visit after all her hospitality to them.

By nine o'clock the next morning, the quiet little wedding party was approaching the church, when to their surprise they beheld a fine coach, drawn by four horses, drawing up at the gate of the churchyard; and before Dorcas had more than time to exclaim, "Why, it is my Lady Scrope herself!" they saw that diminutive but remarkable old dame alighting from it, and walking nimbly up the path towards the porch.

"I never dreamed she would really come, albeit I did let her know the day according to promise—or rather to her command," said her handmaiden, hurrying after her as if by instinct. The little figure in its sables and strangely-fashioned velvet bonnet turned at the sound of the quick footfall; and there stood the old lady scanning the whole party with her bead-like eyes, and giving little nods to this one and the other in response to their respectful reverences.

"A pretty pair! a pretty pair!" was her comment upon the bridal couple, who walked together, and who certainly looked very handsome and happy. Reuben had regained strength and colour, though his face was thinner and finer in outline than it had been before his illness; and Gertrude had always been something of a beauty, and had greatly improved in looks during these weeks of happiness.

"Well, well, well! I am always sorry for folks who are tying burdens round their own necks; but some can do it with a better grace than others."

"Now, child," and she turned to Gertrude, and rapped her cane upon the ground, "don't make a fool of yourself or your husband! Don't begin by thinking him the best man in the world; else he may turn out all too soon to be the worst. Don't let him trample upon you. Hold your own with him.

"Pooh! I might as well spare my words. Poor fools, they are all alike at starting. They only learn to sing to another tune when experience has taken them in hand for a while. Well, well, well! 'tis a pretty sight after all. I'll say no more. Give me your arm, good Master Harmer, and let me have a good view of the tying of this knot, so that there shall be no slipping out of it later."

James Harmer, with a bow which he made as courtly as he knew how, offered his arm to the curious, little, old lady; and strange it was to see her small, richly-clad, upright figure amongst the simple group before the altar that day. Many there were who wondered what had brought her, and amongst the party themselves none could answer the question. It appeared to be one of those freaks for which, in old days, Lady Scrope had made herself famous throughout London, and the habit of which had not been overcome, although the opportunities were growing smaller with advancing years.

She insisted on accompanying the party back to Mary Harmer's cottage. A simple collation was awaiting them before they travelled back to the city. Lady Scrope looked with the greatest interest and curiosity at the cottage;

received the inquiring advances of Fido very graciously; made the boys tell her all the history of his attaching himself to them; and finally made herself the most entertaining and agreeable guest at the board, although the sharpness of her speech and the acid favour of some of her remarks bred a little uneasiness in some of her auditors.

Nevertheless the time passed pleasantly enough; and when the hands of the clock pointed to the hour of eleven, the lady rose to her feet and remarked incisively:

"My coach will be here immediately, if the varlets play me not false. The bride, bridegroom, and the bride's father shall drive with me. I mean to see the maiden's house before I return to mine own."

A glowing colour was in Gertrude's face. Now she began to have a clearer idea why Lady Scrope was there. Reuben had been to her once, and had asked her approval of their plan to expend the bulk of the dowry she had, with such eccentric and unaccountable generosity, bestowed upon the bride, upon the purchase of the house which had been for many generations in the family of her father, and which she loved well from old associations.

Reuben was going to set up in business for himself now. He had long been contemplating this step, since his father's trade was increasing steadily. They would now be partners, Reuben taking one branch of the industry, and leaving his father the other. With the changes in fashions, changes in the manufacture of Court luxuries became necessary. Reuben would advance with the times, his father would remain where he was before. It was a plan which had been carefully considered by both father and son for long, and would have been earlier carried out had it not been for the disastrous stoppage of all trade during the visitation of the plague.

Now, however, London seemed as gay as ever. Orders were pouring in. It was wonderful how little the gaps in the ranks seemed to be heeded. It was scarcely, even amongst the upper classes, that persons troubled to wear the deep mourning for departed friends which, under ordinary circumstances, they would have done. The great wish of all appeared to be to forget the awful visitation as fast as possible, and to drown the memory of it in feasting and revelry. And this spirit, however little to the liking of a godly man like James Harmer, was nevertheless good for his trade.

Lady Scrope being in the secret of the surprise in store for the Master Builder, was anxious to amuse herself by being witness to his enlightenment; and it certainly seemed as though she had full right thus to amuse herself, if it were her desire. Reuben had some savings of his own; but the purchase of the house, had it been made by him alone, would have seriously crippled his ability to carry out his further plans of business. Thus it was really Lady Scrope's golden guineas which had paved the way for the young people, and no one could grudge her the enjoyment of seeing them arrive at their new home.

The Master Builder had had some dealings of late with her ladyship; for on hearing what he was employed to do for so many of her friends, she summoned him to fumigate both of her houses when she had got rid of all her temporary inmates; and she followed him about, watching what he did, and amusing herself with making him relate all the gossip he had picked up relative to her acquaintances into whose houses he had been admitted: how many amongst them had had the plague, how many had died, and all the other details that her insatiable curiosity could glean from him.

And now the bridal couple, together with the bride's father, were being driven in state through the widest thoroughfares

Evelyn Everett-Green

of the city in the hired chariot of Lady Scrope, she chatting all the while, and pointing out this thing and that as they went, openly lamenting that so little remained to remind them of the plague, and prophesying that London had not done with calamity yet.

Gertrude was amazed at the small change in the familiar streets as they neared their home. True, she saw more strange faces than she had been wont to do, and read new names and new signs upon the gaily-painted boards hanging over the shop doors. Again and again she missed from some accustomed doorway the familiar face of the former owner, and saw that a stranger had taken the old business. But then, again, others were there in their old places; friendly faces beamed upon her as she looked out of the window. It was known upon the bridge itself that she was to come back today; and though the appearance of this fine coach caused a little thrill of surprise, there was a fine buzz of welcome as Reuben put out his head and stopped the postillion at the familiar door; for so many fears had been entertained of Reuben's death, that there were those who could not believe they should see him again in the flesh until he stood before them.

"What means all this? Why stop ye here?" asked the Master Builder, with a little agitation in his voice. "You have a home of your own, you told me, Reuben, to which to take your wife. Why stop you at your father's house? Let the postillion drive to your own abode."

"This is our own abode, dear father," said Gertrude softly, alighting from the coach and taking him by the hand to lead him in.

Her other hand was held by her husband; and Lady Scrope was forgotten for the moment by all, as the three passed the familiar threshold amid a chorus of good wishes from friends and neighbours, to which Reuben responded by a variety of signs, Gertrude being too much moved to notice them.

"Dear father," she said, as they stood within the lower room, which was being now fitted as of old for a shop, "forgive us if we have kept our happy secret till now. We wanted to have the home ready ere we brought you to it. This is our home. A wonderful thing befell me. A dowry was bestowed upon me by a generous patroness, from whom I looked not to receive a penny; that dowry bought the house. Reuben's business will give us an ample livelihood. Thou wilt remain always with us in the dear old house which thou hast loved. Oh how happy we shall be—how wondrously happy!

"Father dear, it was Lady Scrope who gave me the wonderful gift that has brought us all this. We must try to thank her ere we think of ourselves more."

So speaking Gertrude turned, with her eyes full of happy tears, towards Lady Scrope, who stood only a few paces off watching everything with her accustomed intense scrutiny, and held out both her hands in a sweet and simple gesture expressive of so much feeling that the old dame felt an unwonted mist rising in her eyes.

"Tut, tut, tut, child! I want no thanks. What good did the gold do me, thinkest thou, shut away in yonder box? What think you I had preserved it there for? Marry that I might fling it away at dice or cards with those who came to visit me? It was my pleasure money, as I chose to call it. And then came the plague and smote hip and thigh amongst those who called me friend. And what good did the gold do me or any person else? If it pleases me to throw it away on a pair of fools, whose business is that but mine?

"There, there, there, that will do, all of you good people. I want to see the house. I want none of your fool's talk. Going to keep a shop here?—sensible man. I'll come and buy all my finery when you start business, and sit and gossip at the counter the while. So mind you have plenty of fine folks to gossip with me. If I were young again, I vow I'd keep a shop myself."

And she made Reuben show samples of his goods, which were piled up in readiness, albeit he was not quite ready to open shop; and very excellent of their kind they were, as Lady Scrope was not slow to remark.

"I'll send the whole city to you. I'll make you the fashion yet. If I were a younger woman, and had my own old train of gallants after me, I'd have made your fortune for you before the year was out. But I'll do something yet, you shall see. And mind that you never begin to lend money, young man, to any needy young fool who may ask it of you. Those greedy court gallants would eat up all the gold of the Indies, and be no whit the richer for it. No money lending, young man, for in that way lies ruin, as too many have found."

The Master Builder winced like one touched in a tender part, whilst Reuben answered boldly:

"I have no such intentions. I hate usury, nor care I to earn money for others to filch from me. I get my wealth by honest trade; and if any man comes to me for aid, all the help I can give him is to put him in the way of doing the like."

Lady Scrope nodded her head and laughed her shrill witch-like laugh.

"He! he! he! Offer honest work to a needy gallant! May I be there to hear when thou dost. Work, forsooth!—a turn at the galleys would do most of them a power of good. Well, well, well, young man, thou speakest sound sense. Thou shouldst prosper in thy business.

"Now, girl, show me the rest of the house, for I must needs be getting home ere long. I shall weary my old bones with all this gadding to and fro."

Gertrude was willing enough to obey. The house was hardly changed from the time she had left it, save that all which was faded and worn had been replaced and furbished anew, and the whole place made sweet and wholesome, and as clean and bright as hands could make it. Gertrude would have preferred a plainer and simpler abode, more like that of her neighbours; but she had not had the heart to undo all her mother's dainty handiwork, and Reuben had thought nothing too good for his bride.

Lady Scrope gibed and jeered a little, but not unkindly. She knew all the family history by this time, and how that Gertrude was not responsible for the luxuries with which her life would be surrounded.

"Go to, child, go to; I am no judge over thee. What matters it a few years earlier or later? It began in Shakespeare's time, as you may read if you will, and it grows worse every generation. Soon the shopmen and traders will be the fine gentlemen of the land, and we may hope for the pickings and leavings of their tables. What does it matter to me? I shall not be troubled by it. And if I be not troubled thereby, what matter if all the world goes mad?

"Now fare you well, young folks; and thou, good Master Builder, thank Heaven for a good and dutiful daughter, for they grow not on every hedge in these graceless days."

Evelyn Everett-Green

"See me to my coach, young man, if thou canst leave devouring thy wife with thine eyes for so much as a minute."

"Poor fools! poor fools! both of you."

"Give me a kiss, maiden—nay, mistress I must call thee now. Be a good child, and be not too meek. Remember the fate of the hapless Griselda."

Nodding her head and shaking her finger, Lady Scrope vanished down the stairs upon Reuben's arm; and Gertrude, moved beyond her powers of self restraint by all she had gone through, flung herself into her father's arms, and the two mingled together their tears of thankfulness and joy.

CHAPTER XVI

A FLAMING CITY

Many happy months passed away, and the great city began to forget the terrible calamity through which it had passed. There was a little fear at first when the summer set in exceptionally hot and dry—very much as it had done the preceding year; but the plague seemed to have wreaked its full vengeance upon the inhabitants, and there was no fresh outbreak, although isolated cases were reported, as was usual, from time to time, and sometimes a slight passing scare would upset the minds of men in a certain locality, to be shortly laid at rest when no further ill followed.

The two houses on the bridge, standing sociably side by side, were pleasant and flourishing places of business. Benjamin was now apprenticed to his brother Reuben, his old master the carpenter having fallen a victim to the plague. Dorcas remained with Lady Scrope, who was now reckoned as a kind friend and patroness to the Harmers, father and son. Rebecca fulfilled her old functions of the useful daughter at home, though it was thought she would not long remain there, as she was being openly courted by a young mercer in Southwark, who had bought a business left without head through the ravages of the plague, and was rapidly working it up to something considerable and successful.

Evelyn Everett-Green

The Master Builder, too, was getting on, although still doing a very small trade compared to what he had done before. Many of his patrons were dead, others had been scared away altogether from London for the present, and with so many vacant houses to fill nobody cared to think of building. Still he found employment of a kind, and was never idle, although things were very different from what they had been, and he thought rather of paying his way in a quiet fashion than of building up a great fortune. He lived in the old house with his daughter and son-in-law, and was happier than in the old days, when his wife had always been trying to make him ape the ways of the gentry, and his son had been wearying his life out with ceaseless importunities for money, which would only be wasted in drunkenness and rioting.

Now the days passed happily and peacefully. Gertrude was a loving wife and a loving daughter. Her father's comfort and welfare were studied equally with that of her husband. She did her utmost not to permit him ever to feel lonely or neglected, and she considered his needs as his own fine-lady wife had never thought of doing.

He had also his friends next door to visit, where he was always welcome. There was now another door of communication opened between the two houses, and almost every evening the Master Builder would drop in for an hour to smoke a pipe with his friend and exchange the news of the day, leaving the young married couple to themselves, for a happy interchange of affection and confidences.

The Harmer household remained unchanged, save for the death of Dan and the marriage of Reuben; but the sailor had been so little at home, that there was no great blank left by his absence, and Reuben was too close at hand to be greatly missed. Janet had not returned to service. Her mother had been rather horrified at the manner in which the poor girl had been treated by her mistress when the plague had appeared in the house. She did not care to send her back to Lady Howe, and Janet had become so accomplished a nurse, and took such interest in the life, that she begged to be allowed to follow the calling of her aunt Dinah, and to spend her time amongst the sick, wherever she might be needed. So both she and Dinah Morse lived at the house on the bridge, but went about amongst the sick in the neighbourhood, generally directed by Dr. Hooker, but sometimes called specially to urgent cases by neighbours or friends. Sometimes they returned home at night to sleep, sometimes they remained for several days or weeks at a time with their patients, according to their degree and the urgency of the case. Janet found herself very well content in her new life, and her mother liked it for her, since it brought her so much more to her home.

It began to be noted that when Dinah Morse was at the house on the occasions of the visits of the Master Builder, he addressed a great part of his conversation to her, seemed never to weary hearing her talk, and would sit looking reflectively at her when other people were doing the talking. He had never forgotten how she had come to them in their hour of dire need, when poor Frederick had sickened of the fell disease which so soon carried him off. He always declared that her tenderness to his wife and daughter at that time had been beyond all price, and it seemed as though his sense of obligation and gratitude did not lessen with time.

Sometimes James Harmer would say smilingly to his wife:

"Methinks our good neighbour hath a great fancy for Dinah. I always do say that such a woman as she ought to be the wife of some good honest man. They might do worse, both of them, than think of marriage. What think you of Dinah? Tends her fancy that way at all?"

And at that question Rachel would shake her head wisely and respond:

"Dinah is not one to wear her heart upon her sleeve! A woman hides her secret in her heart till the right time comes for giving an answer. But we shall see! we shall see!"

In this manner the spring and summer passed happily and quickly away.

August had come and gone, and now the first days of September had arrived. The heat still continued very great, and a parching east wind had been blowing for many weeks, which had dried up the woodwork of the houses till it was like tinder. Sometimes the Master Builder, coming home from his work of repairing or altering some house either great or small, would say:

"I would we could get rain. This long drought is something serious. I never knew the houses so dry and parched as they are now. If a fire were to break out, it would be no small matter to extinguish it. The water supply is very low, and the whole city is like tinder."

It was Saturday night. The sun had gone down like a great ball of fire, and Gertrude had observed to her husband how it had dyed the river a peculiarly blood-red hue. One of those wandering fortune tellers, who had paraded the city so often during the early days of the plague (till the poor wretches were themselves carried off in great numbers by it), had passed down the street once or twice during the day, and had been always chanting a rude song like a dirge, in which many woes were said to be hanging over London town.

These prognostications had been frequent since the appearance in the sky of another comet, which had been seen on all clear nights of late. It had considerably alarmed the citizens, who remembered the comet of the previous year, and the terrible visitation which had followed. This one was not very like the former; it was far more bright, and burning, and red, and its motion appeared more rapid in the sky. The soothsayers and astrologers, of which there were still plenty left, all averred that it bespoke some fresh calamity hanging over the city, and for a while there was considerable alarm in many minds, and some families actually left London, fearful that the plague would again break out there; but by this time the panic had well nigh died down. The comet ceased to be seen in the sky, and even the mournful words of the fortune tellers did not attract the notice they had done at first. The summer was waning, and no sickness had appeared; and of any other kind of calamity the people did not appear to dream.

The Master Builder had gone in as usual to the next house to have a talk with his neighbour. But tonight he looked in vain for Dinah.

"She and Janet have both been summoned to a fine lady who is sick in a grand house nigh to St. Paul's. Dr. Hooker fetched them thither this morning. They will be well paid for their work, he says. The lady has sickened of a fever, and some of her household took fright lest it should be the plague, albeit the symptoms are quite different. So he must needs take both Dinah and Janet with him, that she might be rightly served and tended. Tomorrow Joseph shall go and ask news of her, and get speech with Janet if he can, and learn how it fares with her. I confess I am glad, when she goes to fine houses, that Dinah should be there also. Janet is a pretty creature, and those young gallants think of nothing but to amuse themselves by turning girls' heads, be they ever so humble.

"Ah me! ah me! there is a vast deal of wickedness in the world! I cannot wonder that men foretell some fresh calamity

Evelyn Everett-Green

upon this city. I am sure some of the things we hear and see—well, well, well, we must not judge others. It is enough that judgment and vengeance are the Lord's."

Rachel stopped short because she saw the look of pain which always came into the Master Builder's face when he thought of his profligate young son, cut off in the prime of his youthful manhood, and that without any assurance on the part of those about him that he had repented of the error of his ways. The carelessness and wickedness of the young men of the city were always a sore subject, and he still winced when the pranks of the Scourers were commented upon by his neighbours.

"It is my Lady Desborough who has fallen ill," concluded Rachel, anxious to turn the subject. "Methinks you had some dealings with her lord not such very long time since. The name fell familiarly upon my ears."

"Yes, truly, I did much to garnish their house, and I built out a private parlour for my lady, all of looking glass and gilding. Not long since I purified the house for them with the costliest of spices. Lord Desborough thinks all the world of his beauteous lady. They are devoted to each other, which is a goodly thing to see in these days. He will be greatly alarmed if she be seriously indisposed. He is a right worthy gentleman; and with thy permission I will accompany Joseph to St. Paul's tomorrow and learn the latest tidings of her."

"With all my heart," answered the mother; and soon after that the Master Builder took his departure, and both houses settled to rest for the night.

It might have been two or three o'clock in the morning, none could say exactly how time went on that memorable day, when the Master Builder was awakened by sounds in the adjoining chamber, where Reuben and his wife slept; and before he was fully awake, he heard Gertrude's voice at his door crying out:

"O father, father! there is such a dreadful fire! Reuben is going out to see where it is. Methinks it must be very nigh at hand. Prithee go with him, and see that he comes to no hurt!"

The Master Builder was awake in an instant, and although it was an hour at which the room should be dark, he found it quite sufficiently light to dress without trouble, owing to the red glare of fire somewhere in the neighbourhood.

"Pray Heaven it be not very near us!" was the cry of his heart as he hurried into his clothes, remembering his own auguries of a short time back respecting the spread of fire, if once it got a hold upon a street or building.

He was dressed in a moment, and had joined Reuben as the latter was feeling his way to the fastenings of the door. Two of the shopmen, who slept below, were already aroused and wishful to join them; and as they emerged into the street, which was quite light with the palpitating glow of fire, the door of the Harmers' house opened to admit the exit of the master of the house and his son Joseph.

"Thou hast seen it also! I fear me it is very nigh at hand. I had a good look from my topmost window, and methought it must surely be in Long Lane or in Pudding Lane; certainly it is in one of the narrow thoroughfares turning off northward from Thames Street. It must have been burning for some while. It seems to have taken firm hold. Belike the poor creatures there are all too terrified to do aught to check the spread of the flames. We must see what can be done. It will not do to let the flames get a hold. This strong dry wind will spread them west and north with terrible speed, if something

Evelyn Everett-Green

be not done to check them!"

James Harmer spoke with the air of a man who is used to offices of authority. He had exercised one so long during the crisis of the plague, that the habit of thinking for his fellow citizens still clung to him. It appeared to him to be his bounden duty to do what he could to save life and property; and all the time he spoke he was hastening along the bridge in the direction of the smoke clouds and flames.

The Master Builder hurried along at his side, and before they had reached the end of the bridge there were quite a dozen of the householders or their servants joining the procession to the scene of the conflagration. Until they reached the corner of Thames Street they saw nothing beyond the red column of flame and the showers of sparks mingling with clouds of smoke; but when once they reached the corner, a terrible sight was revealed to them, for the whole block of buildings between Pudding Lane and New Fish Street was a mass of flames, and the fire seemed to be like a living thing, driven onwards before some mighty compelling power.

"God preserve us all! it will be upon us in an hour if nothing be done to check it," cried Harmer in sudden dismay.

"What is being done? What are the people doing?" cried a score of voices.

But what indeed could the terrified people do, wakened out of their sleep in the dead of night to find their houses burning about their ears? They were running helter skelter this way and that, not knowing which way to turn, like so many frightened sheep. Not that they thought as yet that this fire was going to be so very different from other bad fires which some of them had seen; for their wooden and plaster houses burned down too readily at all times, and were built up easily enough afterwards. A little farther off the people were trying to get their goods out of the houses, that they might not lose all if the fire came their way. But those actually burned out seemed to do nothing but stand helplessly by looking on; and perhaps it was only the Master Builder himself who at this moment realized that there was a very serious peril threatening the whole quarter of the city where the fire had broken out, and had already taken such hold.

The wind being slightly north as well as east in its direction, it seemed reasonable to hope that the conflagration would not cross Thames Street in a southerly direction, in which case the bridge would be safe; and, indeed, as New Fish Street was a fairly wide thoroughfare, it was rather confidently hoped that this might prove a check to the fire. The Master Builder ran up the street crying out to the terrified inhabitants to get all the water they could and fling it upon the roofs and walls of their dwellings, to strive to keep the flames at bay; but there was scarcely one to listen or try to obey. The people were all hurrying out of their houses, bringing their families and their goods and chattels with them. The street was so blocked by hand carts and jostling crowds, that it was hopeless to attempt any plan of organization here.

Then all too soon a cry went up that the fire had leaped the street and had ignited a house on the west side. A groan and a scream of terror went up as it was seen that this was all too true, and already great waves of flame seemed to be rushing onwards as if driven from the mouth of some vast blasting furnace; and the Master Builder returned to his friends with a very grave face.

"Heaven send the whole city be not destroyed!" he exclaimed; "never have I seen fire like unto this fire!

"Reuben, lad, make thy way with all speed to the Lord Mayor, and tell him of the peril in which we stand. He is the man to find means to check this fearful conflagration. Would to Heaven it were good Sir John Lawrence who were Mayor, as he was in the days of the plague! He was a man of spirit, and courage, and resource. But I much fear me that poor Bludworth has little of any of these qualities. Nevertheless go to him, Reuben. Tell him what thou hast seen, and tell him that if he wishes not to see London burned about his ears it behoves him to do something!"

Reuben dashed off along Thames Street westward to do his errand, and then the Master Builder turned gravely to his friend and said:

"Harmer, I like not the aspect of things. I fear me that even we are likely to stand in dire peril ere long. Yet we shall have time to take steps for our salvation, seeing the wind is our friend so far, though Heaven alone knows when that may change, and drive the flames straight down upon us. Yet, methinks, we shall have time for what must be done. Wilt thou work hand in hand with me for the salvation of our goods and houses, even though it may mean present loss?"

"I will do whatever is right and prudent," answered Harmer, hurrying hack towards the bridge with his friend and with those who had followed them, and in a short while they were surrounded by a number of frightened neighbours, all asking what awful thing was happening, and what could be done to save themselves.

The Master Builder was naturally the man looked to, and he gave answer quietly and firmly. If the fire once leaped Thames Street, and attacked the south side, nothing short of a miracle could save the bridge houses, unless some drastic step were taken; and the only method which he could devise in the emergency, was that some of the houses at the northern end should be demolished by means of gunpowder, and the ruins soaked in water, so that the passage of the flames might be stayed there.

But at this suggestion the faces of those who lived in these same houses grew long and grave, as indeed the speaker had anticipated. The owners were not prepared for so great a sacrifice. They argued that with the wind where it was, the fire might in all probability not extend southward at all, in which case their loss would he useless. They talked and argued the matter out for about twenty anxious minutes, and in fine flatly refused to have their houses touched, preferring to take their chance of escaping the fire to this wholesale demolition.

This was no more than the Master Builder had foreseen, and without attempting further argument he turned to his neighbour and said:

"Then it must be your workshops and storerooms that must go. You can better spare them than the house itself; and on the opposite side there is the empty house where poor David Norris lived and died. There is none living there now to hinder us. We must take the law into our own hands and make the gap there. If the fire comes not this way, I will bear the blame with the Mayor, if we be called to account; but methinks a little promptitude now may save half the bridge, and perchance all the southern part of London likewise!"

"Do as you will, good friend, your knowledge is greater than mine," answered James Harmer with cheerful alacrity; "Heaven forbid that I should value my goods beyond the life and property and salvation of the many in this time of threatened peril."

"We shall save the goods first. It is only the sheds and workshops that must go," answered the Master Builder cheerily, and forthwith he and his men, who had come hurrying up, together with all the men and boys in the double Harmer household, commenced carrying within shop and houses all the valuables stored in the smaller buildings hard by. It was a work quickly accomplished, and whilst it was being carried out, the Master Builder himself was carefully making preparations for the demolition of the empty house opposite, which indeed was already in some danger of falling into decay, and was empty and desolate.

It had been the abode of the unfortunate man who brought his family back too soon to the city, and lost them all of the plague within a short time. He himself had lingered on for some months, and had then died of a broken heart. But nobody had cared to live in the house since. It was averred that it was haunted by the restless spirit of the poor man, and strange noises were said to issue from it at night. Others declared that the ghost of the wife was seen flitting past the windows, and that she always carried a sick moaning child in her arms. So ill a name had the house got by reason of these many stories that none would take it, and there was therefore none to interfere when, with a loud report and showers of dust and sparks, the whole place and the workshop at the side were blown up at the command of the Master Builder, and reduced to a pile of ruins.

In spite of all the excitement and fear caused by the spreading fire, the neighbours looked upon the Master Builder as an enthusiast and a madman, and upon James Harmer as a poor dupe, to allow such destruction of property. No sooner were both sets of buildings destroyed than men were set to work with buckets and chains to drench the dusty heaps of the ruins with water, nor would the Master Builder permit the workers to slacken their efforts until the whole mass of demolished ruin was reduced to the condition of a soppy pulp.

By this time the day had broken; but the sun was partially obscured by the thick pall of smoke which hung in the air, whilst the ceaseless roar of the flames was becoming terrible in its monotony. Backwards and forwards ran excited men and boys, always bringing fresh reports as to the alarming spread of the fire. Even upon the bridge the heat could plainly be felt. The workers who were called within doors to be refreshed by food and drink were almost too anxious to eat. Never had such a fire been seen before.

Whilst the Master Builder and his friend were snatching a hasty meal, Reuben came hurrying back with a smoke-blackened face. He too showed signs of grave anxiety.

"Well, lad, hast thou seen the Lord Mayor?" was the eager question.

"Ay, verily, I have seen him," answered Reuben, with a bent brow, and a look of severity on his young face, "but I might as well have spoken to Fido there for all the good I did."

"Why, how so?" asked his father quickly and sternly; "is the man lost to all sense of his duties? Where was he? what said he? Come sit thee down, lad, and eat thy fill, and tell us all the tale."

Reuben was hungry enough, and his wife hung over him supplying his needs; but he was thinking more of the perils of his fellow citizens, and of the supine conduct of the Mayor, than of anything else.

"I found the worshipful fellow in bed," he answered. "Other messengers had arrived with the news, but his servant had not ventured to disturb him. I, however, would not be denied. I went up to him in his bed chamber, and I told him what I had seen, and warned him that there was need for prompt action. But he only answered with an oath and a ribald jest, which I will not repeat in the hearing of my wife or mother; and he would have turned again to his slumbers, had I not well nigh forced him to get up, and had not some of the aldermen arrived at that minute to speak of the matter, and inquire into its magnitude. They be all of them disposed to say that it will burn itself out fast enough like other fires; but I trow some amongst them are aroused to a fear that it may spread far in this dry wind, and with the houses so parched and cracked with heat. Then I came away, having done mine errand, and went back to the fire. It had spread all too fast even in that short time, and the worst thing is that no means seem to be taken to stop it. The people run about like those distraught, crying that a second judgment has come, that it is God's doing, and that man cannot fight against it. They are all seeking to convey away their goods to some safe place; but the fire travels quicker than they, and they are forced to leave their chattels and flee for their lives. I trow such a sight has never been seen before."

"It must be like the burning of Rome in the days of the wicked emperor Nero," said Gertrude in a low, awed voice. "Pray Heaven they extinguish the flames soon! It would be fearful indeed were they to last till nightfall."

At this moment Rachel Harmer came hurrying into the room with a pale scared face.

"The child Dorcas!" she cried. "Why have we not thought of her? Is she safe? Where has the fire reached to? God forgive me! I must surely be off my head! Husband, go for the child; she must be scared to death, even if naught worse has befallen her!"

"I had not forgot the maid," answered the father; "but it is well she should be looked to now. The fire has not crossed Thames Street. Lady Scrope's house is safe yet a while; but unless things quickly improve, both she and the child should come hither.

"Make ready the best guest chamber in thy house, Gertrude, and thy husband and I will go and bring her hither."

"Come, lad, as thy mother saith, the child may be scared at the heat and the flames. And my lady has many valuables to be rescued, too. It would be shame that they should perish in the flames if these leap the street. We will take the boat and moor it at Cold Harbour, and slip up by the side street out of the way of the smoke and the heat. We can thus bring her and her goods with most safety here. Marry that is well bethought! We will lose not an hour. One cannot tell at what moment the fire may change its direction."

Reuben rose at once, and accompanied by two of the steadiest of the shopmen, they prepared to carry out their plan of seeking to rescue Lady Scrope and her valuables.

CHAPTER XVII

SCENES OF TERROR

"Father! sweet father! thank Heaven thou art come! Methought we should be burned alive in this terrible house. Methought perchance all of you had been burned. O father! tell me, what is befalling? It is like the last judgment, when all the world shall be consumed with fervent heat!"

Dorcas, with a white face and panting breath, stood clinging to her father's arm, as though she would never let it go. He soothed her tenderly, striving to pacify her terrors, but it was plain that she had been through some hours of terrible fear.

"My little bird, didst thou think we should leave thee to perish here?" asked the father, half playfully, half reproachfully; "and if so affrighted, why didst thou not fly home to thy nest? That, at least, would have been easy."

"Ah, but I could not leave my lady when all besides had fled—even the two old creatures who were never afraid of remaining when the distemper was raging all around. She stands at the window watching the flames devouring all else opposite, and it is hot enough there well nigh to singe the hair on her head; but she laughs and chuckles the while, and says the most horrible things. I cannot bear to go anigh her;

and yet I cannot leave her alone.

"O father, father! come and get her away. She seems like one made without the power of fear. The more that others are affrighted, the more she seems to rejoice!"

Dorcas and her father and brother were in the narrow entry upon which the back door of the house opened. This alley led right down to the river, where the boat was moored under the charge of the two shopmen. It would be easy to carry down any valuables and load it up, and then transport the intrepid old woman, when she had looked her fill, and when she saw her own safety threatened.

For it began to be evident that the flames would quickly overleap the gap presented by Thames Street. They were gathering so fearfully in power that great flakes of fire detached themselves from the burning buildings and leaped upon other places to right and left, as though endowed with the power of volition.

The fire was even spreading eastward in spite of the strong east wind—not, of course, with anything like the rapidity with which it made its way westward, but in a fashion which plainly showed how firm a hold it had upon the doomed houses.

There was no time to lose if Lady Scrope and her valuables were to be saved. The house seemed full of smoke as they entered it; and Dorcas led them up the stairs into the parlour, at the window of which her mistress was standing, leaning upon her stick, and uttering a succession of short, sharp exclamations, intermingled with the cackling laugh of old age.

"Ha! that is a good one! Some roof fell in then! See the

Evelyn Everett-Green

sparks rushing up like waters from a fountain! I would not have missed that! Pity it is daylight; 'twould have been twice as fine at night! Good! good! good! yes run, my man, run, or the flames will catch you. Ha! they gave him a lick, and he has dropped his bundle and fled for his very life. Ha! ha! ha! it is as good as the best play I ever saw in my life! Here comes another. Oh, he has so laden himself that he can scarcely run. There! he is down; he struggles to rise, but his pack holds him to the ground. O my good fool! you will find that your goods cost you dear today. You should have read your Bible to better purpose. Ah! there is some good-natured fool helping him up and along. It is more than he deserves. I should have liked to see what he did when the next wave of fire ran up the street.

"Dorcas, child, where art thou? Thou art losing the finest sight of thy life! If thou hast courage to stay with me, why hast thou not courage to enjoy such a sight as thou wilt not see twice in a lifetime?"

"Madam! madam!" cried the girl running forward, "here are my father and brother, come to help to save your goods and escape by the back. They have brought the boat to Cold Harbour, where it is moored; and, if it please you, they will conduct you to it, and come back and fetch such goods as you would most wish saved."

But the old woman did not even turn her head. She was eagerly scanning the street without, along which sheets of flame seemed to be driven.

"Great powers, what a noise! Methinks some church tower has collapsed. St. Lawrence, Poultney, belike. St. Mary's, Bush Lane, will be the next. Would I were there to see. I will to the roof of the house to obtain a better view. Zounds, but this is worth a hundred plagues! I had never thought to live to see London burned about my ears. What a noise the fire makes! It is like the rushing of a mighty flood. Oh, a flood of fire is a fine thing!"

The weird old woman looked like a spirit of the devouring element, as she stood at her window talking aloud in her strange excitement and enjoyment of the awful destruction about her. The heat within the room was becoming intolerable, yet she did not appear to feel it. The house being well built, with thick walls and well-fitting windows, resisted the entrance of the great volumes of smoke that roiled along laden with sparks and burning fragments of wood; but these fiery heralds were becoming so menacing and continuous, that the Harmers saw plainly how little time was to be lost if they would save either the old woman or her valuables.

"Madam," said James Harmer approaching, and forcing his presence upon the notice of the mistress of the house, "there is little time to lose if you would save yourself or your goods. We have come to give such assistance as lies in our power. Will you give me your authority to bear away hence all such things as may be most readily transported and are of most value? When we have saved these, belike you will have looked your fill on the fire. And, at least, you can see it as well from any other place in the neighbourhood without this risk. May we commence our task of rescue?"

"Oh yes, my good fellow, take what you will. Dorcas will show you what is of greatest value. Lade yourselves with spoil, and make yourselves rich for life. I drove forth the hired varlets who would fain have robbed me ere they left; but take what you will, and my blessing with it. Your daughter deserves a dowry at my hands. Take all you can lay hands upon; I shall want it no more. Ha! I must to the roof! I must to the roof! Why, if it only lasts till nightfall, what a sight it will be! Right glad am I that I have lived to see this day."

Without particularly heeding the words of the strange old woman, father and son, directed by Dorcas, set about rapidly to collect and transport to the boat the large quantities of silver plate and other valuables which, during her long life, Lady Scrope had collected about her. The rich furniture had, perforce, to be left behind, save a small piece here and there of exceptional value; but there were jewels, and golden trinkets, and strangely-carved ivories set with gems, and all manner of costly trophies from the distant lands whither vessels now went and returned laden with all manner of wonders. The Harmers were amazed at the vast amount of treasure hoarded up in that small house, and wondered that Lady Scrope had not many times had her life attempted by the servants, who must have known something of the contents of cabinet and chest.

But her reputation as a witch had been a great safeguard, and her own intrepid spirit had done even more to hold robbers at bay. All who knew her were fully aware that she was quite capable of shooting down any person found in the act of robbing her, and that she always kept loaded pistols in her room in readiness. There was a story whispered about, of her having locked up in one of her rooms a servant whom she had caught pilfering, and it was said that she had starved him to death amid the plunder he had gathered, and had afterwards had his body flung without burial into the river. Whether there was more than rumour in such a gruesome tale none could now say, but it had long become an acknowledged axiom that Lady Scrope's goods had better be let alone.

Twice had the boat been laden and returned, for all concerned worked with a will, and now all had been removed from the house which it was possible to take on such short notice and in such a fashion. The fire was surging furiously across the road, and in more than one place it had leaped the street, and the other side, the south side, was now burning as fiercely as the northern. Dorcas had been dispatched to call down Lady Scrope, for her father reckoned that in ten minutes more the house would be actually engulfed in the oncoming mass of flames. And now the girl hurried up to them, her face blanched with terror.

"She will not come, father; she will not come. She laughs to scorn all that I say. She stands upon the parapet of the roof, tossing her arms, and crying aloud as she sees building after building catch fire, and the great billows of flame rolling along. Oh, it is terrible to see and to hear her! Methinks she has gone distraught. Prithee, go fetch her down by force, dear father, for I trow that naught else will suffice."

Father and son looked at each other in consternation. They had not seriously contemplated the possibility of finding the old woman obstinate to the last. But yet, now that Dorcas spoke, it seemed to them quite in keeping with what they had heard of her, that she should decline to leave even in the face of dire peril.

"Run to the boat, child!" cried the father. "Let us know that thou art safe on board, and leave thy mistress to us. If she come not peaceably, we must needs carry her down.

"Come, Reuben, we must not tarry within these walls more than five minutes longer. The fire is approaching on all sides. I fear me, both the Allhallowes will be victims next."

Springing up the staircase, now thick with smoke, father and son emerged at last upon a little leaden platform, and saw at a short distance from them the old woman whom they sought, tossing her arms wildly up and down, and bursting into awful laughter when anything more terrible than usual made itself apparent.

They could not get quite up to her without actually crawling along an unguarded ridge of masonry, as she must have done to attain her present position; but they approached as near as was possible, and called to her urgently:

"Madam, we have saved your goods as far as it was possible; now we come to save you. Lose not a moment in escaping from the house. In a few more minutes escape will be impossible."

She turned and faced them then, dropping her mocking and excited manner, and speaking quite calmly and quietly.

"Good fellow, who told you that I should leave my house? I have no intention whatever of doing any such thing. What should I do in a strange place with strange surroundings? Here I have lived, and here I will die. You are an honest man, and you have an honest wench for your daughter. Keep all you have saved, and give her a marriage portion when she is fool enough to marry. As for me, I shall want it no more."

"But, madam, it is idle speaking thus!" cried Reuben, with the impetuosity of youth. "You must leave your house on the instant—"

"So they told me in the time of the plague," returned Lady Scrope, with a little, disdainful smile; "but I told them I should never die in my bed."

"Madam, we cannot leave you here to perish in the flames," cried the youth, with some heat and excitement of manner. "I would that you would come quietly with us, but if not I must needs—" and here he began to suit the action to the words, and to make as though he would creep along the ledge and gain the old woman's vantage ground, as, indeed, was his intention.

But he had hardly commenced this perilous transit before he felt himself pulled back by his father, who said, in a strange, muffled voice:

"It is useless, Reuben; we can do nothing. We must leave her to her fate. Either she is truly a witch, as men say, or else her brain is turned by the fearsome sight."

And Reuben, following his father's glance, saw that the redoubtable Lady Scrope had drawn forth a pistol from pocket or girdle, and was pointing it full at him, with a light in her eyes which plainly betokened her intention of using it if he dared to thwart her beyond a certain point.

When she saw the action of James Harmer, she smiled a sardonic smile.

"Farewell, gentlemen," she said, with a wave of her hand. "I thank you for your good offices, and for your kindly thought for me. But no man has ever yet moved me from my purpose, and no man has laid hands on me against my will— nor ever shall. Go! farewell! Save yourselves, and take my blessing and good wishes with you; but I move not an inch from where I stand. I defy the fire, as I defied the plague!"

It was useless to remain. Words were thrown away, and to attempt force would but bring certain death upon whoever attempted it. The fire was already almost upon them. Father and son, after one despairing look at each other, darted down the stairs again, and had but just time to make their escape ere a great wave of flame came rolling along overhead, and the house itself was wrapped in the fiery mantle.

Dorcas, waiting with the men in the boat, devoured them with her eyes as they appeared, and uttered a little cry of horror and amazement when she saw them appear, choked and blackened, but alone.

"She would not come! she would not come! Oh, I feared it from the first; but it seemed so impossible! Oh, how could she stay there alone in that sea of fire! O my mistress! my mistress! my poor mistress! She was always kind to me."

Neither father nor brother spoke as they got into the boat and pushed off into the glowing river. It was terrible to think of that intrepid old woman facing her self-chosen and fiery doom alone up there upon the roof of that blazing house.

"She must have been mad!" sobbed Dorcas; and her father answered with grave solemnity:

"Methinks that self-will, never checked, never guided, breeds in the mind a sort of madness. Let us not judge her. God is the Judge. By this time, methinks, she will have passed from time to eternity."

Dorcas shuddered and hid her face. She could not grasp the thought that her redoubtable mistress was no more; but the weird sight of the fire, as seen from the river, drew her thoughts even from the contemplation of the tragedy just enacted. The great pall of smoke seemed extending to a fearful distance, and the girl turned with a sudden terror to her father.

"Father, will our house be burned?"

"I trust not, my child, I trust not. It is of great moment that the bridge should be saved, not for its own sake only, but to keep the flames from spreading southward, as they might if they crossed that frail passage. We have done what we could; and we cannot be surrounded as are other houses. The fire can advance but by one road upon us. I trust the action we have taken will suffice to save us and others. I would fain be at home to see how matters are going there. I fear me that the pillar of fire over yonder is the blazing tower of St. Magnus. If so, the fire is fearfully near the head of the bridge. God help the poor families who would not consent to the demolition of their houses for the common weal! I fear me now they are in danger of losing both houses and goods!"

It was even so, as the Harmers found on reaching their own abode, which they did by putting across the river to the Southwark side, to avoid the peril from the burning fragments which were flying all about the north bank of the river.

The flames, having once leaped Thames Street, were devouring the houses on the southern side of the street with an astonishing rapidity; and the river was crowded with wherries, to which the affrighted people brought such goods as they could hastily lay hands upon in the terror and confusion. St. Magnus was now burning furiously, and great flakes of fire were falling pitilessly upon the houses at the northern end of the bridge. Even as the Harmers came hurrying up, a shout of fear told them that one of these had ignited, and the next minute there was no mistaking it. The houses on both sides of the northern end of the bridge were in flames; and the people who had somehow trusted that the bridge would, on account of its more isolated position, escape, were rushing terrified out of their doors, or were flinging their goods out of the windows with a recklessness that caused many of them to be broken to fragments as they reached the ground, whilst others were seized and carried off by the thieves and vagabonds who came swarming out of the dens of the low-lying parts of the city, eager to turn the public calamity into an occasion of private gain, and lost no opportunity of appropriating in the general confusion anything upon which they could lay their hands.

Evelyn Everett-Green

"Pray Heaven the means we have taken may be blessed to the city!" cried James Harmer, as he hurried along.

He found his men hard at work pumping water and drenching the ruins with it; for, as they said, the great heat dried up the moisture with inconceivable rapidity, and if once these ruins fired, nothing short of a miracle could save the remainder of the houses. Other stout fellows were upon the roofs with their buckets, emptying them as fast as they were filled upon the roofs and walls, so that when burning fragments and showers of sparks or even a leaping billow of flame smote upon them, it hissed like a live thing repulsed, and died away in smoke and blackness.

It was the same when the flames reached the gap which had been made in the buildings by the Master Builder. The angry fire leapt again and again upon the drenched ruins, but each time fell back hissing and throwing off clouds of steam.

For above two long hours that seemed like days the hand-to-hand fight continued, resolute and determined men casting water ceaselessly upon the ruins and the roofs and walls of the adjoining houses, the fire on the other side of the gap blazing furiously, and seeking to overstep it whenever a puff of wind gave it the right impetus. Had the wind shifted a point to the south, possibly nothing could have saved the bridge; but the general direction was northeast, and it was only an occasional eddy that brought a rush of flames to the southward. But there was great peril from the intense heat generated by the huge body of burning buildings close at hand, and from the flying splinters and clouds of sparks.

Fearlessly and courageously as the workers toiled on, there were moments when their hearts almost failed them, when it seemed as though nothing could stop the oncoming tyrant, which appeared more like a living monster than a mere inanimate agency. But as the daylight waned, it began to be evident that victory would be with the devoted workers. Although the ever-increasing light in the sky told them that in other directions the fire was spreading with tireless fury, in the neighbourhood of the bridge and the places where it had broken out it had almost wreaked its fury.

It had burned houses, and shops, and churches to the very ground. The lambent flames still played about the heaps of burning ruins, but the fury of the conflagration had abated through lack of material upon which to feed itself. Victory remained finally with those who had worked so well to keep the foe in check, and keep in safety the southern portion of the city. The Master Builder's scheme had been attended with marked success. The demolished buildings had arrested the progress of the flames, although not without severe labour on the part of those concerned.

When the Harmer family met together to eat and drink after the toils of the day, so wearied out that even the knowledge that the terrible fire was still devouring all before it in other quarters could not keep them from their beds that night, the master of the house said to his friend the Master Builder:

"Truly, if other means fail, we had better set about blowing up whole streets of houses in the path of the flames. We will to the Lord Mayor at daybreak, and tell him how the bridge has been saved. The people may lament at the destruction of their houses, but sure that is better than that all the city should be ravaged by fire!"

Busy indeed were the women of both those abodes upon that memorable night. From basement to attic their houses were crowded with neighbours who had been burned out, and who must either pass the night in the open air or else seek shelter from friends more fortunate than themselves.

Evelyn Everett-Green

The men, for the most part, were abroad in the streets, drawn thither by the excitement of the great fire, and by the hope of helping to save other persons and goods. But the women and children crowded together in helpless dismay, watching from the windows the increasing glow in the sky as the sun sank and night came on, and mingling tears of terror for others with their own lamentations over the loss of houses and goods.

Good Rachel Harmer and her daughters and daughter-in-law moved amongst the poor creatures like ministering angels. The children were fed and put to bed by twos and threes together. The mothers were bidden to table in relays, and everything was done to cheer and sustain them. Good James Harmer thought not of his own goods when his neighbours were in dire need, and neither he nor his son grudged the hospitality which was willingly accorded to all who asked it, even though the houses would not stretch themselves out for the accommodation of more than a certain number.

But as in times of trouble men draw very near together, so the misfortune of the citizens of London opened the hearts of their neighbours of Southwark and the surrounding villages, who themselves were now safe and in no danger from the great fire. Hospitable countrymen came with wagons and took away homeless creatures with their few poor goods, to be entertained for a while by their own wives and daughters. Others who had to encamp in the open fields were supplied with food by the surrounding inhabitants; and although there were much sorrow of heart and distress, the kindness shown to the burned out families did much to assuage their woes.

James Harmer, who had done much to see to the safe housing of multitudes of women and children, came home at last, and gathering his household about him, gave thanks for their timely preservation in another great peril; and then he dismissed them to their beds, bidding them sleep, for that none knew what the morrow might bring forth. And they went to such couches as they could find for themselves, ready to do his behest; and though London was in flames, and the house almost as light as day, there were few that did not sleep soundly on the night which followed that strange eventful Sunday.

Evelyn Everett-Green

CHAPTER XVIII

WHAT BEFELL DINAH

Dinah Morse and her niece Janet were faring sumptuously in Lord Desborough's house, hard by St. Paul's Churchyard. His young wife lay sick of a grievous fever, and he was well nigh distracted by the fear of losing her.

Nothing was too good for her, or for the gentle-faced, soft-voiced nurses who had come to tend her in her hour of need. The best of everything was at their disposal; and it was no great source of regret to them that several of the hired servants had fled before their arrival, a whisper having gone through the house that her ladyship had taken the plague.

Dinah and Janet had seen too much of the plague to be deceived by a few trifling similarities in some of the symptoms. They were able to assure the distracted husband that it was not the dreaded distemper, and then they settled to the task of nursing like those habituated to it; and so different were they in their ways from the women he had seen before in the office of sick nurse, many of whom were creatures of no good reputation, and of evil habits and life, that his mind was almost relieved of its fears and anxiety, and he began to entertain joyful hopes of the recovery of his spouse.

Upon the Sunday morning which had passed so strangely and eventfully for those in the east of the city, there was nothing to disturb the tranquillity of patient or of nurses. It had been a hot night, and Janet, when she relieved Dinah towards morning, said she had seen a red light in the sky towards the east, and feared there had been a bad fire. But neither of them thought much of this; and when the bell of St. Paul's rang for morning service, Dinah bade Janet put on her hood and go, for Lady Desborough was sleeping quietly, and would only need quiet watching for the next few hours.

When Janet entered the great building she was aware that a certain excitement and commotion seemed to prevail in some of the groups gathered together in Paul's Walk, as the long nave of the old building was called. Paul's Walk was a place of no very good repute, and any modest girl was wont to hurry through it with her hood drawn and her eyes bent upon the ground. Disgraceful as such desecration must be accounted, there can be no doubt that Paul's walk was a regular lounge for the dissipated and licentious young gallants of the day, a place where barter and traffic were shamelessly carried on, and where all sorts of evil practices prevailed.

The sacredness of a building solemnly consecrated to God by their pious forefathers seemed to mean nothing to the reckless roisterers of that shameless age. The Puritans during the late civil war had set the example of desecrating churches, by using them as stables and hospitals, and for other secular purposes. It was a natural outcome of such practices that the succeeding generation should go a step further and do infinitely worse. If God-fearing men did not scruple to desecrate consecrated churches, was it likely that their godless successors would have greater misgivings?

Janet therefore hurried along without seeking to know what men were talking of, and during the time that the service

Evelyn Everett-Green

went on she almost forgot the impression she had taken in on her first entrance.

As she came out she joined the old door porter of Lord Desborough's house, and was glad to walk with him through the crowded nave and into the bright, sunny air without.

Although the sun was shining, she was aware of a certain murkiness in the air, but did not specially heed it until some loudly-spoken words fell upon her ears.

"But forty hours, and this whole city shall be consumed by fire!" shouted a strange-looking man, who, in very scanty attire, was stationed upon the top of the steps, and was declaiming and gesticulating as he addressed a rather frightened-looking crowd beneath him. "Within forty hours there shall not be left standing one stone upon another in all this mighty edifice. The hand of the Lord is stretched forth against this evil city, and judgment shall begin at His sanctuary. Beware, and bewail, and repent in dust and ashes, for the Lord will do a thing this day which will cause the ears of every one who hears it to tingle. He is coming! He is coming! He is coming in clouds and majesty in a flaming fire, even as He appeared on the mount of Sinai! Be ready to meet Him. He comes to smite and not to spare! His chariots of fire are over us already. They travel apace upon the wings of the wind. I see them! I hear them! They come! they come! they come!"

The fanatic waved his hands in the air with frantic gestures, and pointed eastward. Certainly there did appear to be a strange murkiness and haze in the air; and was there not a smell as of burning? or was it but the idea suggested by the man's words? Janet trembled as she slipped her arm within that of the old porter.

"What does he mean?" she asked nervously. "The people seem very attentive to hear. They look affrighted, and some of them seem to tremble. What does it all mean?"

"I scarce know myself. I heard men speak of a terrible fire right away in the east that has been burning many hours now. But sure they cannot fear that it will come nigh to St. Paul's. That were madness indeed! Why, each dry summer, as it comes, brings us plenty of bad fires. The fellow is but one of those mad fools who love to scare honest folks out of their senses. Heed him not, mistress. Belike he knows no more than thou and I. It is his trade to set men trembling. Let us go home; there is no danger for us."

Rather consoled by these words, and certainly without any real apprehensions for their personal safety, Janet returned to the house, where she and Dinah passed a quiet day. Neither of them went out again; and though they spoke sometimes of the fire, and wondered if it had been extinguished, they did not suffer any real anxiety of mind.

"I trust it went not nigh to our homes," said Janet once or twice. "I would that one of the boys might come and give us news of them. But if folks are in trouble over yonder, father is certain to have his hands full. He will never stand by idle whilst other folks are suffering danger and loss."

"He is a good man," answered Dinah, and with her these words stood for much.

Towards nightfall Lord Desborough came in with rather an anxious look upon his face. His eyes first sought the face of his wife; but seeing her lie in the tranquil sleep which was her best medicine, he was satisfied of her well being, and without putting his usual string of questions he began abruptly to ask of Dinah:

"Have you heard news of this terrible fire?"

Both nurses looked earnestly at him.

"Is it not yet extinguished, my lord?"

"Extinguished? no, nor likely to be, if all we hear be true. I have not seen it with mine own eyes. I was at Whitehall all the day, and heard no more than that some houses and churches in the east had been burned. But they say now that the flames are spreading this way with all the violence of a tempest at sea, and those who have been to see say that it is like a great sea of fire, rushing over everything so that nothing can hinder it. The Lord Mayor and his aldermen have been down since the morning, striving to do what they can; but, so far as report says, the flames are yet unchecked. It seems impossible that they should ever reach even to us here; but I am somewhat full of fear. What would befall my poor young wife if the fire were to threaten this house?"

Dinah looked grave and anxious. Lady Desborough's condition was critical, and she could only be moved at considerable risk. But it seemed impossible that the fire could travel all this distance. Only the troubled look on the husband's face would have convinced her that such a thing could be contemplated for a moment even by the faintest-hearted.

"You would not have us move her now, ere the danger approaches?" asked the husband anxiously.

"No, my lord. To move her tonight would be, I think, certain death," answered Dinah gravely. "She has but passed the crisis of a very serious fever, and is weak as a newborn babe. We will strive all we can to get up her strength, that she may be able for what may come. But I trust and hope the fire will be extinguished long ere it reaches us. Oh, surely never was there fire that burned for days and destroyed whole streets and parishes!"

"And oh, my lord, can you tell us if the bridge is safe?" asked Janet clasping her hands together in an agony of uncertainty and fear. "Have you heard news of the bridge? Oh, say it is not burned! They all talk of the east, but what does that mean? Who can tell me if my father's house has escaped?"

Lord Desborough was a very kindly man, and the distress of the girl touched him.

"I will go forth and ask news of all who have been thither to see," he answered. "Many have gone both by land and water to see the great sight. I would go likewise, save that I fear to leave my wife. But, at least, I will seek all the news I can get, and come again to you."

The master of the house went forth, and the two anxious watchers, after a long look at their patient to satisfy themselves that she was sleeping peacefully, and not likely to wake suddenly, crept silently into an adjoining room, where a large window looking eastward enabled them to see in the sky that strange and terrible glow, which was so bright and fierce as darkness fell that they were appalled in beholding it spreading and brightening in the sky.

"Good lack, what a terrible fire it must be!" cried Janet, wringing her hands together. "O good aunt, what can resist the oncoming fury of such a fearful conflagration? Would that I knew my father's house was safe. But, at least, those within must have had warning, and they could with ease escape by water if even the streets were in flames. Alack, this poor city! It does indeed seem as though the vials of

Evelyn Everett-Green

God's wrath were being poured out upon it! Will His hand be stayed till all is destroyed? Surely the hearts of men must turn back to Him in these days of dire calamity!"

Dinah gravely shook her head, her face lighted up by the ever-increasing light in the eastern sky, which grew brighter and brighter with the gathering shades of night.

"Methought in those terrible days of the plague that surely men's hearts would, for the future, be set upon higher things, seeing how they had learned by fearful experience that man's life is but a vapour that the wind carrieth away. But as soon as the pressing peril abated, they hardened their hearts, and turned hack to their evil ways. It may be that even this warning will be lost upon them. God alone knows how many will see His hand in this great judgment, and will turn to Him in fear if not in love!"

Before many minutes had passed affrighted servants began peeping and then crowding into the room, as though they felt more assurance in presence of Dinah's quiet steadfastness and courage. The faces of the maids were pale with apprehension. It was difficult to believe, in the midst of this ruddy glare which actually palpitated as the lights and shadows danced upon the wall, that the fire was yet as distant as was reported. All the menservants had run out into the streets after news of the progress of the fire, and the women were scared by their absence. Dinah did what she could to calm them, pointing out that since they could as yet neither hear nor feel anything of so great a fire, it must still be a great way off. It was hardly possible to believe that it would be permitted to sweep onwards much longer unchecked. By this time men's minds must be fully alive to the great peril in which all London stood, and she doubted not that some wise measures would soon be taken to stay the spread of the flames. She advised the maidens to go to bed and not think any more about it. Let them commend themselves to God and seek to sleep. She would undertake to watch, and to rouse them up should there be any need during the night.

Somewhat appeased and comforted by these words, the maids withdrew and sought their needed rest. But Janet and Dinah returned to the sickroom, resolved to keep vigil there, and only to sleep by turns upon the couch, ready dressed in case of emergency.

It was nigh upon midnight before Lord Desborough returned, and he was so blackened and begrimed that they scarcely knew him.

His wife was still sleeping the sleep of exhausted nature, and, after one glance at her, the young nobleman turned towards Janet, who was quivering all over in her anxiety to hear the news.

"Well, maiden, thy father's house is safe, and half the bridge is safe; and the thanks of that are due to him and to a worthy neighbour, who by their wise exertions stayed the fire, which might else have spread even to the other side of the river."

Janet and Dinah exchanged looks of unspeakable relief, and Lord Desborough continued in the same cautious undertone:

"Once out of doors, the fire fever quickly got its hold on me, even as it has gotten hold upon almost every person in the city. I had not meant to go far but I took a wherry, and, the tide serving well, I was swiftly borne along towards the bridge, and from the river I saw the raging of such a fire as, methinks, the world has never seen before. No words of mine can paint the awful grandeur of the sight I saw. It was as light as day upon the water, and there were times when the river itself seemed ablaze. For, as the flames wrought havoc amongst the warehouses and stores along the wharfs, burning masses of oil and tar would pour out upon the bosom of the water, blazing terribly, and the boatmen had to keep a sharp watch sometimes lest they and their craft should be engulfed in the fiery stream. To the ignorant, who knew not what caused the water to wear this aspect of burning, it appeared as though even the river had ignited. This increased their terrors tenfold, and they say that some poor distraught creatures actually flung themselves into the fire or the water, convinced that the end of the world had come, and careless as to whether they perished soon or late."

"But my father—my father!" cried Janet earnestly.

"Ah, true, thy father. I heard of him from the watermen in the wherries, who told me the tale of how he had saved the bridge by pulling down his workshops and drenching the ruins with water. It seemeth to me that unless some prompt and resolute course of a similar kind is taken tomorrow or tonight, infinite loss must ensue. No ordinary means can now check this great fire. But surely the Lord Mayor and his advisers will have by now a plan on foot. Were I not so weary, and anxious about my wife, I would go forth once more to see what was doing. But I must wait now for the morrow, and then, pray Heaven all danger may be at an end. Fear not, good friends, if you hear terrible sounds as of an earthquake shaking the house this night. Men say that if the city is to be saved it must be by the blowing up of whole streets of small houses somewhere in the path of the flames, so that they shall have nothing whereon to feed. Others say that nothing will stop them, and that none will be found ready to make sacrifice of their dwellings for the public good, preferring to risk the chance of the flames reaching them. I know not the truth of all the rumours flying about; but the thing might be, and might be wisely done. So fear not if you should hear some sounds that will make you think of an earthquake. And call me if aught alarms you, or if my wife should change either for the better or the worse."

So saying, Lord Desborough took himself off to his well-earned repose; and the two nurses passed the night, sometimes waking and sometimes sleeping, but not disturbed by any strange sounds of explosion, and hopeful, as the night passed without special event, that the fire had been extinguished.

But .morning brought appalling accounts of its spread. Nothing had been done, it seemed, to stay its course. It had reached Cheapside, and was rushing a headlong course down it, and even the Guildhall, men said, would not escape. North and west the great, rolling body of the flames was spreading; churches were going down before it, one after the other, as helplessly as the timber and plaster houses, which burned like so much tinder. Hour after hour as that day passed by fresh and terrible items of news were brought in. Would anything ever stop the oncoming sea of fire? Surely—surely something would be done to save St. Paul's. Surely that magnificent and time-honoured structure would not be permitted to perish without some attempt to save it!

Dinah went out at midday for a mouthful of air, leaving Janet in charge of the sick lady. She turned her steps towards the great edifice towering up in all its grandeur towards the sunny sky. It was hard indeed to believe that it could succumb to the devouring element, so solid and unconsumable it looked. Yet, although all men were asserting vehemently that "Paul's could never burn," all faces were looking anxious, and all ears were eagerly attuned to catch any new item of news which a messenger or passerby might bring.

The murkiness in the air, faintly discernible even yesterday, had become very marked by this time. The smell of fire was in the air, although as yet the terrible roaring of the flames, of which all men who had been near it were speaking, had not yet become audible in the Babel of talk going on in the streets and about the great church. The dean and canons were grouped about the precincts, looking anxiously into each other's faces, as though to seek to read encouragement from one another. Nothing was talked of but the fire, the incapacity shown by the civic authorities in dealing with it, and lamentations that good Sir John Lawrence, who had coped so ably with the pestilence last year, should be no longer in office at this second great crisis.

Still it was averred on all hands that something was about to be done; that it was too scandalous to stand by panic stricken whilst the whole city perished. Every one seemed to have heard talk respecting the demolition or blowing up of houses in the path of the flames; but none could say actually that it had been done, or was about to be done, in any given locality.

Burned out households were pouring continually along the choked thoroughfares, striving to find safe places where they might bestow such goods as they had succeeded in saving. Charitable persons were occupied in housing and feeding those who had nothing of their own; whilst others, whose fears were on a larger scale, were fleeing altogether away from the city to friends in the country beyond, desiring only to escape the coming judgment, which seemed like that poured out on Sodom.

Dinah went back with a very grave face to her charge. The poor lady had now recovered her senses, and though as weak as a newborn babe, was able to smile from time to time upon her husband, who sat beside her holding her hand between his. He was so overjoyed at this happy change in his wife's condition that he had no thought to spare at this moment for the peril of the city. He asked for no news as Dinah appeared; and indeed it was very necessary that the patient should not be in any wise alarmed or excited.

Dinah, however, was becoming very uneasy as time went on; and she was certain that the air grew darker than could be accounted for by the falling dusk, and upon going to the east window as the twilight fell, she was appalled by the awful glare in the sky, and was certain that now, indeed, she did begin to distinguish the roaring of the flames as the wind drifted them ever onwards and onwards.

Had it not been for the exceedingly critical state in which the patient lay, she would have suggested her removal before things grew worse. As it was, it might be death to move her; and perhaps the flames would be stayed ere they reached the noble cathedral pile. Surely every effort would be made for that end. It was difficult to imagine that the citizens would not combine together in some great and mighty effort to save their homes and their sanctuary before it should be too late.

"What an awful sight!" exclaimed a soft voice behind her. "Heaven grant the peril be not so nigh as it looks!"

It was Lord Desborough, who had come in and was looking with anxious eyes at the flaming sky, over which great clouds of sparks and flaming splinters could be seen drifting. It might only be fancy, but the room seemed to be growing hot with the breath of the fire. The young nobleman's face was very grave and disturbed.

"What must we do?" he asked of Dinah. "Can she be moved? Ought we to take her elsewhere?"

Evelyn Everett-Green

"I would we could," answered Dinah, "but she is so weak that it may be death to carry her hence, and if we spoke to her of this terrible thing that is happening, the shock might bring back the fever, and then, indeed, all would be lost."

The husband wrung his hands together in the utmost anxiety. Dinah stood thinking deeply.

"My lord," she presently said, "it may come to this, that she will have to be moved, risk or no risk. Should we not think about whither to take her if it be needful?"

"Ay, verily; but where may that be? Who can know what place is safe? And to transport her far would be certain death. She would die on the road thither."

"That is very true, my lord," answered Dinah; "but it has come into my mind that, perchance, my sister's house could receive her—that house upon the bridge, which is now safe, and which can be in no danger again, since all the city about it lies in ashes. By boat we could transport her most gently of all; and tonight, upon the rising tide, it might well be done, if the need should become more pressing."

"A good thought! a happy thought indeed!" cried Lord Desborough. "But art thou sure that thy good kinsmen will have room within their walls? They may have befriended so many."

"That is like enow," answered Dinah; "I have thought of that myself. My lord, methinks it would be a good plan for you to take boat now, at once, taking the maid Janet with you as a guide and spokeswoman. She will take you to her father's house and explain all; and then her father and brothers will come back with you, if need presses more sorely, and help us to transport thither the poor lady. I will sit by her the while, and by plying her with cordials and such food as she can swallow, strive to feed her feeble strength; and if the flames seem coming nearer and nearer, I will make shift to dress her in such warm and easy garments as are best suited to the journey she may have to take. And I will trust to you to be back to save us ere the danger be over great."

"That I will! that I will!" cried the eager husband. "The plan is an excellent one! I will lose not a moment in acting upon it. I like not the look of yon sky. I fear me there will be no staying the raging of the flames. I will lose not a minute. Bid the girl be ready, and we will forth at once. We will take boat at Baynard's Castle, and be back again ere two hours have passed!"

Janet was delighted with the plan. She was restless and nervous here, and anxiously eager to know what had befallen her own people. She would gladly have had Dinah to go also, but saw that the sick lady could not be left, and that it would not be right to move her save on urgent necessity; but to go and get a band of eager helpers to come to the rescue if need be satisfied her entirely, and she said a joyful farewell to her aunt, promising to send help right speedily.

Left alone with her patient, Dinah commenced her task of feeding the lamp of life, and seeking by every means in her power to prepare the patient for the possible transit. Once she was called from the room by some commotion without, and found the frightened servants all huddled together outside the door, uncertain whether to fly the place altogether or to wait till some one came with definite news as to the magnitude of the peril. The light in the sky was terrible. The showers of sparks were falling all round the houses and the cathedral. The roar of the approaching fire began to be clearly distinguished above every other sound.

Dinah, who knew that tumult and affright were the worst things possible for her patient, counselled the cowering maids to make good their escape at once, since there was nothing to be done in the house that night, and they were far too frightened to sleep. All had friends who would give them shelter. And soon the house was silent and empty, for the men had gone off either to the fire or out of sheer fright, and Dinah was left quite alone with her patient.

"What is that noise I hear all the time?" asked Lady Desborough presently, in a feeble voice. "I feel as though there was something burning in the room. The air seems thick and heavy. Is it my fantasy, or do I smell burning? Where is my husband? Is there something the matter going on?"

"There is a bad fire not very far from here, my lady," answered Dinah quietly. "My lord has gone to see if it be like to spread, that he may take such steps as are needful. Be not anxious; we are safe beneath his care. He will let no hurt come nigh us before he is back to tell us what we shall do."

A tranquil smile lighted the lady's face at these words. She was in that state of weakness when the mind is not easily ruffled, and Dinah's calm face and steady voice were very tranquillizing.

"Ah yes, my good lord will not let hurt come nigh us. We will await his good pleasure. I trust no poor creatures are in peril? There will be many to help them I trow?"

"Yes, my lady. I have not heard of lives lost; and many say that it is good for some of the old houses to burn, that they may build better ones little by little. Now take this cordial, and sleep once more. I will awaken you when my lord returns."

The lady obeyed, and soon slept again, her pulse stronger and firmer and her mind at rest.

But Dinah was growing very uneasy. Far though she was above the street, she heard shouts and cries—muffled and distant truly, but very apparent to her strained faculties—all indicative of alarm and the presence of peril. She dared not leave her post at the bedside, but the air was becoming so thick with smoke that the patient coughed from time to time, and the nurse was not certain how much longer it would be possible to breathe in it. She was certain, too, that the place was becoming hot, increasingly hot, each minute.

Oh, where was Lord Desborough? why did he not come? At last she stole from the room and into the adjoining chamber, and then indeed an awful sight met her shrinking gaze.

A pillar of lambent flame, which seemed to her to be close at hand, was rising up in the air as though it reached the very heavens. It swayed slowly this way and that, surrounded by clouds of crimson smoke and a veritable furnace of sparks. Then, as she watched with awed and fascinated gaze, it suddenly seemed to make a bound towards the tower of St. Paul's standing up majestic and beautiful against the fiery sky. It fastened upon it like a living monster greedy of prey. Tongues of flame seemed to be licking it on all sides, and a mass of fire encircled it.

With a gasp of fear and horror Dinah turned away.

"St. Paul's on fire!" she exclaimed beneath her breath; "God in His mercy have pity upon us! Can any one save us now?"

CHAPTER XIX

JUST IN TIME

Lady Desborough sat up in bed propped up with pillows, dressed in such flowing garments as Dinah had been able to array her in, her eyes shining in anxious expectation, her panting breath showing the oppression caused by the murkiness of the atmosphere. But in spite of the peril of the situation, to which she had now awakened with full comprehension; in spite of the fatigue of being partially dressed, with a view to sudden flight; in spite of the horror of knowing herself to be alone with Dinah in this flame-encircled house, her spirit rose to the occasion, triumphing over the weakness of the flesh. Dinah had feared that the knowledge of the peril would extinguish the faint flame of life; but it seemed rather to cause it to burn more strongly. The fragile creature looked full of courage, and the fears she experienced at this moment were less for herself than for others.

"My dear lord! my dear lord!" she kept repeating. "Dinah, if he were living nothing would keep him from me. Where is he gone? Dost thou think he will return in time?"

"I think so, my dear lady," answered Dinah in her full, quiet voice; "I pray he may come soon!"

"Yes, pray for him, pray for him!" cried the lady clasping her hands, "I have not prayed for him enough. Pray that his precious life may be preserved!"

Dinah clasped her hands and bent her head. Her whole faculties seemed merged in one great stress of urgent prayer. The lady looked at her and touched her hand gently.

"You are a good woman, Dinah Morse. I am glad to have you with me; but if my good lord come not soon, you must save yourself and fly. I will not have you lose your life for me. You have not strength to bear me hence, and I cannot walk. You must fly and save yourself. For me, if my dear lord be dead, life has nothing for me to desire it."

"Madam," answered Dinah, in her calm, resolute way, "your good lord, my master, entrusted you to my care, and that charge I cannot and will not quit whatever may betide. God is with us in the midst of the fire as truly as He was in the raging of the plague. He brought me safe through the one peril, and I can trust Him for this second one. Our lives we may not recklessly cast away, neither may we fly from our post of duty lightly, and without due warrant."

Lady Desborough's thin white fingers closed over Dinah's steady hand with a grateful pressure.

"Thou art a good woman, Dinah," she said. "Thy presence beside me gives me strength and hope. Truly I should dread to be left alone, and yet I would not have thee stay if the peril becomes great."

"We will trust that help may reach us shortly," answered Dinah, who realized the magnitude of the peril far more clearly than did the sick lady, who had no idea of the awful extent of the fire.

Evelyn Everett-Green

That it was a bad one she was well aware, and in perilous proximity to their dwelling; but Dinah had not told her, nor had she for a moment guessed, that half the city of London was already destroyed.

"Go and look from the windows," she said a few minutes later, when the two had sat in silent prayer and meditation for that brief interval. "Go see what is happening in the street below. I marvel that I hear so little stir of voices. But the walls are thick, and we are high up. Go and see what is passing below, and bring me word again."

Dinah was not loth to obey this behest, being terribly anxious to know what was happening around them. Neither by word nor by sign would she add to the anxieties of Lady Desborough, knowing how much might depend upon her calmness if the chance of rescue offered itself; but she herself began to entertain grave fears for the safety of this house, wedged in, as it appeared to her to be, between masses of blazing buildings.

Running up to the top attics of the house, which commanded views almost every way, the sight which greeted her eyes was indeed appalling. The whole mass of St. Paul's grand edifice was alight, and the flames were rushing up the walls like fiery serpents whilst the dull roar of the conflagration was like the booming of the breakers on an iron-bound coast. Grand and terrible was the sight presented by that vast sea of flame, which extended eastward as far as the eyes could see. It was more brilliantly light now, in the middle of the night, than in the brightest summer noontide, although the blood-red glare was terrible in its intensity, and brought to Dinah's spirit, with a shudder of horror, a vision of the bottomless pit with its eternal fires.

But without pausing to linger to watch the awful grandeur of the burning cathedral, she hastily passed from attic to attic to see how matters were going in other quarters, and she soon discovered, to her dismay and anxiety, that the flames had crept around the little wedge-like block of buildings in which this mansion stood, and that they were literally ringed round by fire. By some caprice, or perhaps owing to its solidity of structure, this small three-cornered block, containing about three good houses, had not yet ignited; but the hungry flames were creeping on apace, and, as it seemed to Dinah, from all sides. As she took in this fact, it seemed to her that help could never reach them now, and that all they could do was to strive to meet death with as calm and bold a spirit as they could, commending their souls to God, and trusting that He would raise up their bodies at the last day, even though they might be consumed to ashes in the midst of this burning fire.

What was that noise? Surely a shout from below. Dinah started, and fled hastily down the staircase. In another moment she heard more plainly.

"Sweet heart, sweet heart, where art thou—oh where art thou?"

It was Lord Desborough's voice; she recognized it with a thrill of gladness. But there was another voice mingling with it which she also knew, and she heard her own name called with equal urgency.

"Dinah! Mistress Dinah! Ah, pray God we have not come too late! Dinah, we are here to save you both! Show yourself, if you be still there. Pray Heaven they have not rushed forth in their fears and perished in the flames!"

In another instant Dinah had rushed to a window, which seemed to be on the same side of the house as the voices— namely, at the back; and, in the narrow court below, she saw

Lord Desborough, the Master Builder, her brother, and Reuben, all clustered together, with ladders and ropes, and all calling aloud to those within to show themselves.

"We are here! we are safe! but the fire is well nigh upon us," answered Dinah, who had just been convinced by the rolling of the smoke up the staircase that the lower part of the house was in flames.

"Thank God! thank God! they are still there!" cried Lord Desborough at sight of her; whilst the Master Builder, who was getting a ladder into position in order to run it up to the window where she stood, spoke rapidly and commandingly:

"There is no time to lose. The house is ringed by fire. It will be all we can do to make good our escape. The front of the place is in flames already; we cannot approach that way, and the street is full of waves of fire. Can you make shift to bring out the sick lady to this window? or—"

Dinah vanished the moment she understood what was to be done; but quick as were her movements, Lord Desborough was in the room almost as soon as she was. He must have darted up the ladder almost ere it was in position, and the next moment he had his wife in his arms, straining her passionately to his breast, as she cried in joyful accents:

"O my love, my dear, dear love! methought thou hadst perished in yon fearful fire!"

"It is more fearful than thou dost know, sweet heart, but with Heaven's help we will bear thee safe through it. Shut thine eyes, dear heart, and trust to me. We have won our way thus far in the teeth of many a peril. Pray Heaven we make good our escape in like fashion. We have taken every measure of precaution."

In her great delight at having her husband back safe and sound, and in her state of exceeding weakness, Lady Desborough understood little of the terrible nature of what was happening. She felt her husband's arms round her; she knew he had come to save her from danger; and her trust was so perfect and implicit that it left no room in her heart for anxious fears. She closed her eyes like a tired child, and laid her head upon his shoulder.

He was a strong man, and she had wasted in the fever to a mere shadow, and was always small and slight. He carried her as easily as though she had been an infant; and making straight for the open window, he climbed out upon the ladder and went slowly and steadily down it, whilst those below held it for him.

Dinah watched the descent with eager eyes, unheeding all else. She never thought to look behind her. She had no idea that a mass of flames had suddenly come rushing up the stairway behind her. She was conscious of an overpowering heat and a rush of blinding smoke that caused her to stagger back gasping for breath; but it was only as she actually felt the hot breath of the flames upon her cheek, and saw that the whole house had suddenly become involved in the universal destruction, that she knew what had befallen her, and that death was striving hard to clutch her and make her its prey.

With a short, sharp cry, she staggered towards the open window, but the heat and the smoke made her dizzy. She fell against the frame, and uttered a faint cry for help; and then it seemed to her that the body of flame behind leaped upon her like a live thing. She was conscious for a moment of making a fierce and desperate struggle, and then she knew no more, for black darkness swallowed her up, and her last moment of consciousness was spent in a prayer that the Lord would be with her in death and receive her spirit into His hands.

Evelyn Everett-Green

When next Dinah opened her eyes it was to find a cool wind blowing on her face, and to feel an unwonted motion of the bed (as she supposed it for a moment) on which she was lying. Everything was bright as day about her, but everything seemed to be dyed the hue of blood. The next moment sense and memory returned. She realized that she was lying in the bottom of a boat, which men were rowing with steady strokes. She saw Lord Desborough sitting in the stern, only a few feet away, still clasping his wife in his arms. She knew that her head was lying in somebody's lap, and the next moment she heard a familiar voice saying:

"Ah! she is better now. She has opened her eyes!"

"Rachel!" exclaimed Dinah sitting suddenly up, in spite of a sensation of giddiness which made everything swim before her eyes for a few moments; and Rachel Harmer looked down into her face and smiled.

"Dear Dinah, thank Heaven thou art safe! I hear that thou wert in fearful peril in this burning city; but our good neighbour brought thee forth from the blazing house just as the boards on which thou wert standing gave way beneath thy feet. Oh, how thankful must we be that our home and our dear ones have all been preserved to us, when half the city is lying in ruins!"

Dinah raised herself up still more at these words, and turned her eyes in the direction of the raging flames on the north side of the river; and only then was she able to realize something of the terrible magnitude of that great conflagration.

The boat was hugging the Southwark shore, for indeed it was scarce safe to approach the other, save from motives of dire necessity, and so thickly did sparks and fragments of blazing matter fall hissing into the river for quite half its width, that boats were chary of adventuring themselves much beyond the Southwark bank, save those conveying persons or goods from some of the many wharfs; and these made straight across with their cargoes as soon as they could quit the shore.

"It is terrible! terrible!" gasped Dinah. "It is like the mouth of a volcano! And to think that but a short hour since I was in the midst of it. O sister, tell me how thou comest to be here. Tell me how I was snatched from the flames, for, verily, I thought I was their prey."

Rachel put a trembling arm about her sister's shoulders as she made reply.

"Truly there were those standing by who thought the same. But for the brave expedition of our neighbour there, methinks thou wouldst have perished; but let me tell the tale from the beginning.

"It was some time after dark—I scarce know how the hours have sped through these two strange nights and days, when the day seems almost dimmer than the night. But suddenly there was Janet with us—Janet and my Lord Desborough, come with news that the fire had threatened even St. Paul's, and that he desired help to save his sick wife and thee, Dinah, ere the flames should have reached his abode. Janet told us much of the poor lady's state, and we made all fitting preparation to receive her. But none were at home save the boys, and they had to go forth and find their father and brother, to return with Lord Desborough to help him in his work of rescue. He would fain have got others and not have tarried so long. But all men seem distraught by fear, and would not listen to his promises of reward, nor face the perils either of the journey by water or of an approach to the flaming city."

"Indeed it hath a fearful aspect!" said Dinah thoughtfully, as she turned her eyes upon the blazing mass that had been teeming with life but a few short hours ago. "Hast heard, sister, whether many poor creatures have perished in the flames? Oh, my heart has been sad for them, thinking of all the homeless and all the dead!"

"They say that wondrous few have fallen victims to the fire," said Rachel, "and those that have perished are, for the most part, poor, distraught creatures, whom terror caused to fling away their lives, or like my Lady Scrope, who would not leave her home and preferred to perish with it. It is sad enough to think of the thousands who have lost home and goods in the fire. But had it come before the plague had ravaged the city so fearfully, it must have been tenfold worse. Methinks if the lanes and courts of the city had been crowded as they were then, the loss of life must needs have been far greater."

"But to proceed with thy tale," said Dinah after a pause. "How was it that thou didst adventure thyself with the rescuing party in the boat?"

"Methought that, as there were helpless women to be saved, a woman might find work to do suited more to her than to the men folks. Moreover, I may not deny that I felt a great and mighty desire to see this wonderful fire more nigh. Custom has used us to so much since it commenced that the terror of it has somewhat faded. They were saying that St. Paul's was blazing or like to blaze. I desired to see that awful sight; and see it I did right well, as we pushed the boat into mid-water after landing Lord Desborough and his assistants at Baynard's Castle. They were some half hour gone, and we sat and watched the fire, in some fear truly for them, for the flames seemed devouring everything, but with confidence that they would act with all prudence, and in the full belief that the fire had not yet attacked my lord's house."

"Ah, but it had!" said Dinah with a little shiver. "I would not have believed that flames could sweep on at such a fearful pace. One minute we seemed safe, the next it was seething round us!"

"That is what they all say of this fire. It travels with such an awful rapidity, and will suddenly pounce like a live thing upon some building hitherto unharmed, and in an incredibly short time will have licked it up, if one may so speak, leaving nothing but a mass of smouldering ashes behind."

"I know how it leaps," spoke Dinah, with a little shiver. "I cannot think even now how I came to be saved."

"It was our good neighbour, the Master Builder, who saved thee at risk of his life," answered Rachel with a little sob in her voice. "It was a terrible thing to see, Reuben tells me. He and his father were holding the ladder, and Lord Desborough was bringing down his wife, when all in a moment the house seemed engulfed in one of those great flame waves of which all men are speaking, and they saw you totter and fall, as if it had engulfed thee in its deadly embrace. Lord Desborough was not yet down the ladder, and knew nothing of thy peril, being engrossed in tender care for his wife. Nobody could pass him, nor would the ladder bear a greater weight; but the next moment they saw that our good neighbour had somehow got another ladder against the wall and was rushing up it at a pace that seemed impossible. Reuben ran to steady this ladder, for it was like to fall with the quaking and shaking. And then, just before they heard the fall of the burning floors, he saw the Master Builder coming down bearing his burden safely; and once having both of you safe, there was not a moment to lose in making for the boat. Already the alley was full of blinding flame and choking smoke, and it was all the men could do to carry the pair of you safe to Baynard's Castle, where we took you all on board, but only two minutes before the fire began to blaze there also. See, by looking back thou canst see how fiercely it is burning!

"God alone knows how and where it will be stayed. They say it is spreading northward as furiously as it flies westward. If the city walls stay not its course, all London will surely perish."

Dinah was silent a while, looking seriously before her. Then she lifted her face nearer to her sister's and said:

"Prithee, tell me, has our good friend and neighbour suffered hurt in thus adventuring his life for me?"

"He has not spoken of it, if so be that he has," was the answer; "but the haste and peril and confusion were too great for many words. We shall soon be at home now, and all who need it will receive tendance. I fear me, dear sister, that thou canst not altogether have escaped the cruel embrace of the fire. Thy garments were singed and charred: but this cloak covers thee well and protects thee from the night air."

Dinah moved herself, and felt no hurt. She looked anxiously towards Lord Desborough, as though to ask how it went with his lady. Fortunately the night was warm and calm, save for the light breeze that was enough to fan the fierce flames onward and onward. By day the wind blew hard from the east; but it dropped at night, and this was no small boon to the many homeless creatures who had no roofs to shelter their heads.

Once landed at the Southwark wharf, the party was soon within the sheltering doors of the twin houses. Gertrude came forth to meet them, anxious solicitude written on every line of her face.

The first care was for the poor lady, for whom they had made ready a pleasant and airy room. She was carried thither, and Dinah followed to see what was her condition; and although she was exceedingly weak, she was not unconscious, and so long as she had her husband beside her holding her hand, she seemed to care nothing for the strangeness of her surroundings, or for the perils through which she had passed.

"Verily, I think she will live," said Dinah, when Janet had fed her with some of the strong broth which had been made in readiness. "She looks not greatly worse than when she started up in bed in her own house with the consciousness that there was fire near. I had not thought so tender a frame could go through so much of peril and hardship; but methinks her lord's return was the charm that worked so marvellously for her; for, truly, she had begun to fear him dead."

Satisfied as to her patient, Dinah allowed herself to be taken care of by Gertrude, who insisted on removing her burned garments, and assuring herself that no other hurt had been done. It was wonderful what an escape Dinah's had been, for there was scarcely any mark of fire upon her, only a little redness here and there, but nothing approaching to a severe burn. She declared that she could not go to bed in the midst of so much excitement; and after telling Gertrude of the wonderful nature of her own escape, she added, with a slightly heightened colour:

"I would fain assure myself of the welfare of thy brave father, for it may be that he may have sustained some hurt; and if that be so, we must minister to his needs right speedily. Much depends in burns upon the promptness with which they are dressed."

Gertrude's filial anxiety was at once aroused, as well as her warm admiration for her father's courage and devotion. Together they sought him out and found him in one of the lower rooms, a plate of food before him, which, however, he had hardly touched.

The moment he saw his daughter, who entered a little in advance, he rose hastily and exclaimed:

"Tell me how she does. Has she received any hurt?"

"Lady Desborough?" asked Gertrude; "they all say she—"

"Nay, nay, child, not Lady Desborough! What is Lady Desborough to me? I mean Dinah, that noble, devoted woman, who would not leave her mistress even in the face of deadly peril. Tell me of her! Tell me—"

And here the Master Builder came to a dead stop, and paused for a moment in bashful shamefacedness most unwonted with him, for there was Dinah entering behind his daughter, and surely she must have heard every word.

"Dinah is not hurt, father," said Gertrude, covering the awkward pause with ready tact; "her escape has been truly wonderful. She wishes to know whether you also have escaped; for she tells me that you must have faced a sea of flame in order to get to her."

"Your arm is hurt—is burned!" said Dinah coming forward quickly, her eye detecting that much in a moment. "Gertrude, bring me the oil and the linen. I will bind it up before I do aught else. When the air is kept away the smart is wonderfully allayed."

The burn was rather a severe one, but the Master Builder seemed to feel no pain under the dexterous manipulation of Dinah's gentle, capable hands. When he would have thanked her she gave him a quick look, and made a low-toned answer.

"Nay, nay, I can hear no thanks from thee. Do I not owe thee my life? But for thee I should not be here now. It is I who must thank thee—only I have no words in which to do it."

"Then let us do without words between us for the future, Dinah," said the Master Builder, possessing himself of one of her hands, which was not withdrawn. "If thou hadst perished in the fire, life had had nothing left for me. Does not that show that we belong to each other? I have not much to give, but all I have is thine; and I think thou mightest go the world over and not find a more loving heart!"

Evelyn Everett-Green

CHAPTER XX

THE FLAMES STAYED

"Something must be done! The whole city must not perish! It is a shame that so much destruction has already taken place. What are the city magnates about that they stand idle, wringing their hands, whilst all London burns about their ears?"

Young Lord Desborough was the speaker. He had risen in some excitement from the table where he had been seated at breakfast, for James Harmer had just come in with the news that the fire was still burning with the same fierceness as of old; that it had spread beyond the city walls, Ludgate and Newgate having both been reduced to a heap of smoking ruins; that it was spreading northward and westward as fiercely as ever; whilst even in an easterly direction it was creeping slowly and insidiously along, so that men began to whisper that the Tower itself would eventually fall a prey.

"Nay, now, but that must not, that shall not be!" cried Lord Desborough in great excitement. "Shame enough for London that St. Paul's is gone! Are we to lose every ancient building of historic fame? What would his Majesty say were that to perish also? Zounds! methinks my Lord Mayor must surely be sleeping. In good King Henry the Eighth's reign his head would have been struck off ere now.

"Thou hast seen him, thou sayest, good Master Harmer. What does he purpose to do? Surely he cannot desire all the city to perish. Yet, methinks, that will be what will happen, if indeed it be not already accomplished."

"He is like one distraught," answered Harmer. "I went to him yesterday, and I have been again at break of day this morn. I have told him how we saved the bridge, and have begged powers of him to effect great breaches at various points to stay the ravages of the flames; but he will do naught but say he must consider, he must consider."

"And whilst he considers, London burns to ashes!" cried the young nobleman in impetuous scorn. "A plague upon his consideration and his reflections! We want a man who can act in times like these. Beshrew me if I go not to his Majesty myself and tell him the whole truth. Methinks if he but knew the dire need for bold measures, London might even now be saved—so much of it as yet remains. If the Lord Mayor is worse than a child at such a crisis, let us to his Majesty and see what he will say!"

"A good thought, in truth," answered Harmer thoughtfully. "But surely his Majesty knows?"

"Ay, after a fashion doubtless; but it takes some little time to rouse the lion spirit in him. He is wont to laugh and jest somewhat too much, and dally with news, whilst he throws the dice with his courtiers, or passes a compliment to some fair lady. He takes life somewhat too lightly does my lord the King, until he be thoroughly roused. But the blood of kings runs in his veins; and let him but be awakened to the need for action, then he can act as a sovereign, indeed."

Evelyn Everett-Green

"Then, good my lord, in the name of all those poor townsfolk whose houses are standing yet, let the King be roused to a full sense of the dire peril!" cried Harmer, in almost passionate tones; "for if some one come not to their help, I trow there will not be a house within or without the city that will not be reduced to ashes ere two more days have passed."

"It is terrible to think of," said the Master Builder, who was taking his meal with the young lord, by his special desire, both having slept late into the morning after the exertions of the previous night. "If you, my lord, can get speech of the King, and show him the things you have seen and suffered, methinks that that should be enough to rouse him. And doubtless you could get speech of his Majesty without trouble, whereas a humble citizen might sue for hours in vain."

"Yes, I trow that I could obtain an audience without much ado," answered Lord Desborough, though he gave rather a doubtful glance at his soiled and fire-blackened garments, which were all he had in the world since the burning of his house. "But I would have you go with me also, good Masters Harmer and Mason; for it was your prompt methods that saved the bridge, and perchance all Southwark too. I would have you with me to add your testimony to mine.

"Master Harmer, your name was spoken often in the time of the raging of the plague, as that of a brave and loyal citizen. It is likely his Majesty may bear it still in mind, and it will give weight to any testimony you have to offer."

Harmer and the Master Builder exchanged glances. They had not thought to appear before royalty, but they were willing to do anything that might be for the good of the town; and whilst the one hurried away to procure a wherry to take them as near as might be to Whitehall, the other supplied, from the stores in the shop, a new court suit to young Lord Desborough befitting his rank and station.

Lady Desborough was going on better than any had dared to hope. Her husband stole in to look at her before his departure, and was rewarded by a sweet and tranquil smile. He stole towards the bedside and kissed her, telling her he was going to see the King; and she, knowing that his duties called him often to Court, asked no question, and seemed to remember nothing of the fire, but only bade him return anon to her when he could.

Reuben was going also in the boat, and some of the men as rowers. Gertrude had donned her best cloak and holiday gown, and asked wistfully of her husband:

"Prithee take me also; I will not be in your way. But I would fain see something of this great sight of which all men talk, and they say it may best be seen from the river."

"Come then, sweet heart, so as thou dost not ask to run into peril," said Reuben; and by noon the party were well on their way, their progress being somewhat slow, as the tide was running out, and there was a considerable press of craft on the river, which was the only safe roadway now from one part of the burned city to the other.

As boats passed each other, items of news were exchanged between the occupants, and every tale added some detail of horror to the last. Bridewell was in flames now, and many said Newgate also. Some averred that the prisoners had been left locked up in their cells to perish miserably, others that they had all been released, and that London would be swarming with felons and criminals, who would lead the van in the many acts of plunder which were already being perpetrated. What might be the truth of all these rumours none could say; but one thing could at least be gathered, which was that the fire was still raging unchecked, and that nothing had as yet been done to stay its progress.

When the boat had reached its destination, Lord Desborough courteously invited Gertrude and her husband to accompany the deputation. They had not anticipated any such thing; but curiosity overcame every other feeling, and before another half hour had passed they found themselves absolutely within the precincts of Whitehall, passing along corridors where fine-feathered gallants and royal lackeys and pages walked hither and thither, and where their appearance excited some mirthful curiosity, although nobody spoke openly to them.

Lord Desborough was challenged on all hands, but gave only brief replies. He would tell no word of his mission; and presently he led his companions into a small anteroom, which was quite empty, and charged the servant, who had accompanied them thus far, not to permit any one to enter so long as they were there. Then he hurried away to seek audience of the King, but promised to join his companions again in as brief a time as possible.

"Belike it will be long enough ere we see him again," said Harmer, who almost regretted having come when there might be work to do elsewhere. "The ear of royalty is often besieged in vain, or at least it is a case of hours before an audience can be obtained. Yon pleasure-loving monarch will care but little if all London burn, so as he has his ladies and his courtiers about him to make merry by day and by night!"

By which sentiment it may be gathered that a good deal of the Puritan sternness of character and distrust of royalty lingered in the mind of James Harmer, although in this case he was not destined to be a true prophet.

Half an hour may have passed, certainly not more, before a sound of approaching voices from the inner room, to which this one was but the antechamber, announced the approach of some persons. The listeners within thought they distinguished the tones of Lord Desborough's voice; nor were they mistaken, for next moment, when the doors were flung wide open, and the party instinctively rose to their feet, it was to see the young noble approaching in earnest talk with a very dark, sallow man in an immense black periwig, whom in a moment they knew to be the King himself. He was followed by a still darker man, less richly dressed than himself, but still very fine and gay, who was so like the King as to be recognized instantly for the Duke of York.

The little group made deep obeisance as the royal party came forward, and received in return a carelessly gracious nod from the King, who flung himself into a seat, and looked at Lord Desborough.

"His Majesty would know from you, good Masters Harmer and Mason, what you have seen with your own eyes of this fire, and in particular how the flames were stayed upon the bridge by your efforts. He has heard so many contradictory stories from those who are less well informed, that he will have the tale from first to last by worthy citizens who are to be trusted to speak truth."

There was no mistaking the ring of truth in the narratives which were told by the Master Builder and his neighbour.

The King listened almost in silence, but when he did ask a question it was shrewd and pertinent in its import. The dark face was lacking neither in force nor in power; and if the eyes of royalty did, from time to time, stray towards the fair face of Gertrude, who followed her father's tale with breathless interest, his talk was all of the means which must

Evelyn Everett-Green

forthwith be taken for the arrest of the fire, and from the sparkle in his eyes it was plain that he was aroused at last to some purpose.

"Good citizens," he said at length, "since our worthy Mayor has proved himself a fool and a poltroon, I must needs use such tools as I have under my hand.

"Bring me pen and paper, knave!" he cried to a servant who was in attendance; and when the man returned, the King hastily scrawled a few lines upon the paper, and gave it into the hands of the citizens.

"My good fellows," he said, in his easy and familiar way, "take there your authority under my hand, and go and save the Tower. The Tower must not and shall not perish. Pull down, blow up, sacrifice as you will, but save you the Tower. As for me, I will forth instantly and see what may be done in this quarter. The people shall not say that their King cared no whit whilst the whole city was burned to ashes. Would I had known more before, but each messenger brought news that something was about to be done.

"About to be done, forsooth! that is ever the way. Zounds! I would like to pitch yon cowardly Mayor and his whole corporation into the heart of the flames! And if something be not done to save what remains of the city, I will make good my word!"

Then, with a complete change of manner, he rose and came forward to the corner where Gertrude stood shrinking and quivering, half frightened by this strange man, yet impressed by some indescribably kingly quality in him that fascinated her imagination in spite of all she had heard of him.

"Fair mistress," he said gallantly, "hast thou nothing to ask?

These good citizens have all had their word to say. Am I not to hear the music of thy voice also?"

Gertrude, startled and abashed, dropped her eyes, and knew not what to say; but something in the King's glance compelled an answer of some kind, and a sudden inspiration flashed upon her.

"Sire," she said, in a sweet tremulous voice, her colour coming and going in her cheek in a most becoming fashion, "may I ask a boon of your gracious Majesty?"

"A hundred if thou wilt, fair mistress; there is nothing so sweet to me as obeying the behests of beauty."

She shrank a little from his glance, and her grasp tightened upon her husband's arm; but she took courage, and went on bravely:

"I have but one boon to crave, gracious Sire. For myself I have all that heart of woman could crave; but there is still one small trouble in my life. My dear father, who stands before you now, was well-nigh ruined a year ago in that fearful visitation of the plague. By trade he is a builder, and right well does he know his business. After this terrible fire there must needs be much building to do ere the city can be dwelt in. May it please your gracious Majesty to grant to him a portion of the work, that he may retrieve his lost fortune, and regain the place which he once held amongst his fellow citizens!"

"It shall be done, mistress, it shall be done!" answered the King, with a smile at the girl and a friendly look towards the Master Builder. "Marry, it is a good thought too; for we shall want honest and skilful men to rebuild us our city.

"Thy prayer is heard and granted, fair lady. I will not forget thy petition. I will see to it myself. Farewell, sweet heart! think always kindly of your King," and he saluted her upon the cheek, after the fashion of the day.

Then turning briskly to the men he said, in a very different tone, "Now to our respective tasks, good sirs. We have our work cut out before us this day. Let it not be our fault if, ere the night fall upon us, the spreading flames, which are devastating this city, are stopped, and further destruction arrested."

With a friendly nod, and with a smile to Gertrude, the King went as suddenly as he came. Lord Desborough lingered only a few moments to say, in hurried tones:

"Thank Heaven his Majesty is roused at last! Now, indeed, something will be accomplished. I must remain with him. I shall have my work, doubtless, somewhere, as you have yours in the east. Fare you well. We shall meet again at nightfall; and pray Heaven the fire may by that time be stayed in its ravages!"

Need it be told here how that fire was stayed? how the King and the Duke, his brother, rode in person at the head of a gallant band of men-at-arms and soldiers, and directed those measures—long urged upon the Mayor, but never efficiently carried out—of blowing up and pulling down large blocks of houses in the path of the flames, so that their ravages were stayed? It was the King himself who saved Temple Bar and a part of Fleet Street, the fire being checked close to St. Dunstan's in the west. Lord Desborough superintended like operations at Pye corner, hard by Smithfield; whilst the good citizens, Harmer and Mason, took boat to the Tower as fast as possible, and with the assistance of the governor, and by the mandate of the King, checked the slowly advancing flames just as they had reached the very walls of the fortress itself.

The great and terrible fire was stayed ere nightfall. True, the flames smouldered and even raged in the burning area for another day and night, but the spread of them was checked. The citizens, recovering from their apathetic despair, and encouraged by the example of their King, no longer stood trembling by, but joined together to imitate his actions and sacrifice a little property to save much.

"Thank God, thank God, the peril is at an end! The very flames have glutted themselves, and are sinking down into the smouldering heaps of the ruins they have wrought!" said Reuben, coming back on the Thursday evening from an expedition of inquiry and discovery. "Terrible indeed is the sight, but the worst is now known. Four hundred streets, ninety churches—if what I heard be true—and thirteen thousand houses—fifteen wards destroyed, and eight more half burned! Was ever such a fire known before? Yet can we say, Heaven be praised that it has spread no further. Verily, it seemed once as though nothing would escape!"

Gertrude, too, was full of excitement.

"Father has had a summons from the Lord Mayor. He was urgently sent for soon after thou hadst gone. O Reuben, dost think the King has remembered my words to him? dost think he has put in a plea for my father when the city is rebuilt?"

"It is like enough," answered Reuben; "they say his Majesty does not forget when his word is plighted. He will be a rich man if he be employed by the corporation. And how goes the sick lady?"

"So well that my lord has taken her away by boat to a villa hard by Lambeth, where she will be quieter and more at rest than she could be here. Janet and Dorcas have gone with her as her maids, her own servants having fled hither and thither. She would fain have had Dinah, too, but Dinah was not willing."

Husband and wife smiled a little at each other, and then Reuben said:

"Thou, wilt have a stepmother soon, little wife. How wilt thou like that?"

"Well enow, so it be Dinah," answered Gertrude, smiling; "but there is the father coming in. Prithee, let me run to him and hear his news!"

Others had seen the approach of the familiar figure, and there was quite a little group around the door of the two houses to ask news of the Master Builder as he approached. His face wore a beaming look, and in reply to the many questions showered upon him he answered gaily:

"In truth, good friends, if the plague ruined me, it seems as though the fire was to set me up again. Here is my Lord Mayor, prompted thereto by his gracious Majesty the King, giving into my hands the task of seeing to the rebuilding of Bridge Ward, Within, Billingsgate Ward, Dowgate Ward, and Candlewick Ward. Four wards to build! why, my fortune is made!"

He gave one quick look at Dinah, and then took her hand in his, all looking smilingly on the while.

"Thou didst not repulse me when I was but a poor and broken man," he said; "but, please Heaven, before many months have passed over my head it will be no mockery to speak of me as Master Builder once again!"

Choose from Thousands of 1stWorldLibrary Classics By

A. M. Barnard
Ada Leverson
Adolphus William Ward
Aesop
Agatha Christie
Alexander Aaronsohn
Alexander Kielland
Alexandre Dumas
Alfred Gatty
Alfred Ollivant
Alice Duer Miller
Alice Turner Curtis
Alice Dunbar
Allen Chapman
Alleyne Ireland
Ambrose Bierce
Amelia E. Barr
Amory H. Bradford
Andrew Lang
Andrew McFarland Davis
Andy Adams
Angela Brazil
Anna Alice Chapin
Anna Sewell
Annie Besant
Annie Hamilton Donnell
Annie Payson Call
Annie Roe Carr
Annonaymous
Anton Chekhov
Archibald Lee Fletcher
Arnold Bennett
Arthur C. Benson
Arthur Conan Doyle
Arthur M. Winfield
Arthur Ransome
Arthur Schnitzler
Arthur Train
Atticus
B.H. Baden-Powell
B. M. Bower
B. C. Chatterjee
Baroness Emmuska Orczy
Baroness Orczy
Basil King
Bayard Taylor
Ben Macomber
Bertha Muzzy Bower
Bjornstjerne Bjornson

Booth Tarkington
Boyd Cable
Bram Stoker
C. Collodi
C. E. Orr
C. M. Ingleby
Carolyn Wells
Catherine Parr Traill
Charles A. Eastman
Charles Amory Beach
Charles Dickens
Charles Dudley Warner
Charles Farrar Browne
Charles Ives
Charles Kingsley
Charles Klein
Charles Hanson Towne
Charles Lathrop Pack
Charles Romyn Dake
Charles Whibley
Charles Willing Beale
Charlotte M. Braeme
Charlotte M. Yonge
Charlotte Perkins Stetson
Clair W. Hayes
Clarence Day Jr.
Clarence E. Mulford
Clemence Housman
Confucius
Coningsby Dawson
Cornelis DeWitt Wilcox
Cyril Burleigh
D. H. Lawrence
Daniel Defoe
David Garnett
Dinah Craik
Don Carlos Janes
Donald Keyhoe
Dorothy Kilner
Dougan Clark
Douglas Fairbanks
E. Nesbit
E. P. Roe
E. Phillips Oppenheim
E. S. Brooks
Earl Barnes
Edgar Rice Burroughs
Edith Van Dyne
Edith Wharton

Edward Everett Hale
Edward J. O'Biren
Edward S. Ellis
Edwin L. Arnold
Eleanor Atkins
Eleanor Hallowell Abbott
Eliot Gregory
Elizabeth Gaskell
Elizabeth McCracken
Elizabeth Von Arnim
Ellem Key
Emerson Hough
Emilie F. Carlen
Emily Bronte
Emily Dickinson
Enid Bagnold
Enilor Macartney Lane
Erasmus W. Jones
Ernie Howard Pie
Ethel May Dell
Ethel Turner
Ethel Watts Mumford
Eugene Sue
Eugenie Foa
Eugene Wood
Eustace Hale Ball
Evelyn Everett-green
Everard Cotes
F. H. Cheley
F. J. Cross
F. Marion Crawford
Fannie E. Newberry
Federick Austin Ogg
Ferdinand Ossendowski
Fergus Hume
Florence A. Kilpatrick
Fremont B. Deering
Francis Bacon
Francis Darwin
Frances Hodgson Burnett
Frances Parkinson Keyes
Frank Gee Patchin
Frank Harris
Frank Jewett Mather
Frank L. Packard
Frank V. Webster
Frederic Stewart Isham
Frederick Trevor Hill
Frederick Winslow Taylor

Friedrich Kerst
Friedrich Nietzsche
Fyodor Dostoyevsky
G.A. Henty
G.K. Chesterton
Gabrielle E. Jackson
Garrett P. Serviss
Gaston Leroux
George A. Warren
George Ade
Geroge Bernard Shaw
George Cary Eggleston
George Durston
George Ebers
George Eliot
George Gissing
George MacDonald
George Meredith
George Orwell
George Sylvester Viereck
George Tucker
George W. Cable
George Wharton James
Gertrude Atherton
Gordon Casserly
Grace E. King
Grace Gallatin
Grace Greenwood
Grant Allen
Guillermo A. Sherwell
Gulielma Zollinger
Gustav Flaubert
H. A. Cody
H. B. Irving
H.C. Bailey
H. G. Wells
H. H. Munro
H. Irving Hancock
H. R. Naylor
H. Rider Haggard
H. W. C. Davis
Haldeman Julius
Hall Caine
Hamilton Wright Mabie
Hans Christian Andersen
Harold Avery
Harold McGrath
Harriet Beecher Stowe
Harry Castlemon
Harry Coghill
Harry Houidini

Hayden Carruth
Helent Hunt Jackson
Helen Nicolay
Hendrik Conscience
Hendy David Thoreau
Henri Barbusse
Henrik Ibsen
Henry Adams
Henry Ford
Henry Frost
Henry James
Henry Jones Ford
Henry Seton Merriman
Henry W Longfellow
Herbert A. Giles
Herbert Carter
Herbert N. Casson
Herman Hesse
Hildegard G. Frey
Homer
Honore De Balzac
Horace B. Day
Horace Walpole
Horatio Alger Jr.
Howard Pyle
Howard R. Garis
Hugh Lofting
Hugh Walpole
Humphry Ward
Ian Maclaren
Inez Haynes Gillmore
Irving Bacheller
Isabel Cecilia Williams
Isabel Hornibrook
Israel Abrahams
Ivan Turgenev
J.G.Austin
J. Henri Fabre
J. M. Barrie
J. M. Walsh
J. Macdonald Oxley
J. R. Miller
J. S. Fletcher
J. S. Knowles
J. Storer Clouston
J. W. Duffield
Jack London
Jacob Abbott
James Allen
James Andrews
James Baldwin

James Branch Cabell
James DeMille
James Joyce
James Lane Allen
James Lane Allen
James Oliver Curwood
James Oppenheim
James Otis
James R. Driscoll
Jane Abbott
Jane Austen
Jane L. Stewart
Janet Aldridge
Jens Peter Jacobsen
Jerome K. Jerome
Jessie Graham Flower
John Buchan
John Burroughs
John Cournos
John F. Kennedy
John Gay
John Glasworthy
John Habberton
John Joy Bell
John Kendrick Bangs
John Milton
John Philip Sousa
John Taintor Foote
Jonas Lauritz Idemil Lie
Jonathan Swift
Joseph A. Altsheler
Joseph Carey
Joseph Conrad
Joseph E. Badger Jr
Joseph Hergesheimer
Joseph Jacobs
Jules Vernes
Julian Hawthrone
Julie A Lippmann
Justin Huntly McCarthy
Kakuzo Okakura
Karle Wilson Baker
Kate Chopin
Kenneth Grahame
Kenneth McGaffey
Kate Langley Bosher
Kate Langley Bosher
Katherine Cecil Thurston
Katherine Stokes
L. A. Abbot
L. T. Meade

L. Frank Baum
Latta Griswold
Laura Dent Crane
Laura Lee Hope
Laurence Housman
Lawrence Beasley
Leo Tolstoy
Leonid Andreyev
Lewis Carroll
Lewis Sperry Chafer
Lilian Bell
Lloyd Osbourne
Louis Hughes
Louis Joseph Vance
Louis Tracy
Louisa May Alcott
Lucy Fitch Perkins
Lucy Maud Montgomery
Luther Benson
Lydia Miller Middleton
Lyndon Orr
M. Corvus
M. H. Adams
Margaret E. Sangster
Margret Howth
Margaret Vandercook
Margaret W. Hungerford
Margret Penrose
Maria Edgeworth
Maria Thompson Daviess
Mariano Azuela
Marion Polk Angellotti
Mark Overton
Mark Twain
Mary Austin
Mary Catherine Crowley
Mary Cole
Mary Hastings Bradley
Mary Roberts Rinehart
Mary Rowlandson
M. Wollstonecraft Shelley
Maud Lindsay
Max Beerbohm
Myra Kelly
Nathaniel Hawthrone
Nicolo Machiavelli
O. F. Walton
Oscar Wilde

Owen Johnson
P.G. Wodehouse
Paul and Mabel Thorne
Paul G. Tomlinson
Paul Severing
Percy Brebner
Percy Keese Fitzhugh
Peter B. Kyne
Plato
Quincy Allen
R. Derby Holmes
R. L. Stevenson
R. S. Ball
Rabindranath Tagore
Rahul Alvares
Ralph Bonehill
Ralph Henry Barbour
Ralph Victor
Ralph Waldo Emmerson
Rene Descartes
Ray Cummings
Rex Beach
Rex E. Beach
Richard Harding Davis
Richard Jefferies
Richard Le Gallienne
Robert Barr
Robert Frost
Robert Gordon Anderson
Robert L. Drake
Robert Lansing
Robert Lynd
Robert Michael Ballantyne
Robert W. Chambers
Rosa Nouchette Carey
Rudyard Kipling
Saint Augustine
Samuel B. Allison
Samuel Hopkins Adams
Sarah Bernhardt
Sarah C. Hallowell
Selma Lagerlof
Sherwood Anderson
Sigmund Freud
Standish O'Grady
Stanley Weyman
Stella Benson
Stella M. Francis

Stephen Crane
Stewart Edward White
Stijn Streuvels
Swami Abhedananda
Swami Parmananda
T. S. Ackland
T. S. Arthur
The Princess Der Ling
Thomas A. Janvier
Thomas A Kempis
Thomas Anderton
Thomas Bailey Aldrich
Thomas Bulfinch
Thomas De Quincey
Thomas Dixon
Thomas H. Huxley
Thomas Hardy
Thomas More
Thornton W. Burgess
U. S. Grant
Upton Sinclair
Valentine Williams
Various Authors
Vaughan Kester
Victor Appleton
Victor G. Durham
Victoria Cross
Virginia Woolf
Wadsworth Camp
Walter Camp
Walter Scott
Washington Irving
Wilbur Lawton
Wilkie Collins
Willa Cather
Willard F. Baker
William Dean Howells
William le Queux
W. Makepeace Thackeray
William W. Walter
William Shakespeare
Winston Churchill
Yei Theodora Ozaki
Yogi Ramacharaka
Young E. Allison
Zane Grey